Cracking the GRE® Literature in English Subject Test

Douglas McMullen, Jr.

Sixth Edition

Random House, Inc.
New York

PrincetonReview.com

The Princeton Review®

The Princeton Review, Inc.
2315 Broadway
New York, NY 10024
E-mail: editorialsupport@review.com

Excerpt from "Junk" in ADVICE TO A PROPHET AND OTHER POEMS by Richard Wilbur. Copyright © 1961 and renewed in 1989, reprinted by permission of Harcourt Brace & Company.

Excerpt from HOUSE OF MIRTH by Edith Wharton courtesy of Penguin USA.

Excerpt from THE AWAKENING by Kate Chopin courtesy of Penguin USA.

Excerpt from ASPECTS OF THE NOVEL by Edward M. Forster. Copyright © 1927 by Harcourt Brace & Company and renewed 1954 by Edward M. Forster, reprinted by permission of the publisher. Canadian rights granted by King's College, Cambridge, and the Society of Authors as the literary representatives of the E. M. Forster Estate.

Excerpt from A ROOM OF ONE'S OWN by Virginia Woolf. Copyright © 1929 by Harcourt Brace & Company and renewed 1957 by Leonard Woolf, reprinted by permission of the publisher.

"Leda and the Swan" excerpted with the permission of Simon & Schuster from THE POEMS OF W. B. YEATS: A NEW EDITION, edited by Richard J. Finneran. Copyright © 1928 by Macmillan Publishing Company, and renewed 1956 by George Yeats.

Stanza II from "A Prayer For My Daughter" reprinted with the permission of Simon & Schuster from THE POEMS OF W. B. YEATS: A NEW EDITION, edited by Richard J. Finneran. Copyright © 1928 by Macmillan Publishing Company and renewed 1956 by George Yeats.

Excerpt from NATIVE SONS: A CRITICAL STUDY, by Edward Margolies, reprinted by permission of Edward Margolies.

"Fern Hill" by Dylan Thomas, from THE POEMS OF DYLAN THOMAS. Copyright © 1952 by The Trustees for the Copyrights of Dylan Thomas. Reprinted by permission of New Directions Publishing Corp.

"Dream Deferred" ("Harlem"), from THE PANTHER AND THE LASH by Langston Hughes. Copyright © 1951 by Langston Hughes, reprinted by permission of Alfred A. Knopf, Inc.

Selected excerpt from UNDER THE VOLCANO by Malcolm Lowry. Copyright © 1947 by Malcolm Lowry and renewed 1975 by Margerie Lowry. Reprinted by permission of Harper Collins Publishers, Inc.

Selected excerpt from THE LITERARY HISTORY OF THE UNITED STATES, Revised edition, edited by Robert E. Spiller, Willard Thorp, Thomas H. Johnson, Henry Seidel, and Robert M. Ludwig. Copyright © 1953 by Macmillan Publishing Company, and renewed in 1981 by Robert E. Spiller and Willard Thorp. Reprinted with the permission of Simon & Schuster.

Excerpt from EQUUS by Sir Peter Shaffer. Copyright © 1973 by Sir Peter Shaffer. Reprinted with the permission of the author.

Excerpt from THE DRAMATIC WORKS OF EDWARD BULWER LYTTON: RICHELIEU & MONEY! by Edward Bulwer Lytton courtesy of Kessenger Publishing, LLC.

Excerpt from ESSAY ON CRITICISM by Alexander Pope courtesy of Kessinger Publishing.

Excerpts from JOHN MILTON: THE COMPLETE POEMS by John Milton courtesy of Penguin Classic.

Excerpts from THE OXFORD SHAKESPEARE: THE COMPLETE WORKS, 2nd EDITION by William Shakespeare courtesy of Oxford University Press.

Excerpt from THE COMPLETE WORKS OF EMILY DICKINSON by Emily Dickinson courtesy of Little, Brown, and Company.

Excerpts from THE BIBLE AUTHORIZED KING JAMES VERSION WITH APOCRYPHA courtesy of Oxford University Press.

Excerpt from GERARD MANLEY HOPKINS: POEMS AND PROSE by Gerard Manley Hopkins courtesy of Penguin Classics.

Excerpts from EDMUND SPENSER'S POETRY by Edmund Spenser, Hugh Maclean, and Anne Lake Prescott courtesy of Norton Critical Anthologies.

Excerpts from WHITMAN: POETRY AND PROSE by Walt Whitman courtesy of Library of America.

Excerpts from MOBY DICK by Herman Melville courtesy of Oxford University Press.

Excerpts from Kipling: Poems by Rudyard Kipling courtesy of Knopf Doubleday Publishing Group.

Excerpts from THE WASTELAND AND OTHER POEMS by T.S. Eliot courtesy of The Penguin Group.

Excerpt from JOHN SKELTON: THE COMPLETE ENGLISH POEMS by John Skelton courtesy of The Penguin Group.

Excerpts from FIFTEEN POETS: CHAUCER, SPENSER, SHAKESPEARE, MILTON, DRYDEN, POPE, COWPER, COLERIDGE, WORDSWORTH, SHELLEY, BYRON, KEATS, BROWNING, TENNYSON, ARNOLD courtesy of Oxford University Press.

Excerpt from JOHN DONNE: THE COMPLETE ENGLISH POEMS by John Donne courtesy of Penguin Classics.

Excerpt from EMERSON'S PROSE AND POETRY by Ralph Waldo Emerson courtesy of Norton Critical Anthologies.

ISBN: 978-0-375-42971-2
ISSN: 1541-3500

Edited by: Keely Robinson
Production Coordinator: Ryan Tozzi
Production Editor: Emma Parker

Printed in the United States of America on partially recycled paper.

10 9 8 7 6 5 4 3 2

6th Edition

Editorial

Rob Franek, VP Test Prep Books, Publisher
Seamus Mullarkey, Associate Publisher
Rebecca Lessem, Senior Editor
Laura Braswell, Senior Editor
Selena Coppock, Editor
Heather Brady, Editor

Production Services

Scott Harris, Executive Director, Production Services
Kim Howie, Senior Graphic Designer
Ryan Tozzi, Production Manager

Production Editorial

Meave Shelton, Production Editor
Jennifer Graham, Production Editor
Kristen O'Toole, Production Editor

Random House Publishing Team

Tom Russell, Publisher
Nicole Benhabib, Publishing Manager
Ellen L. Reed, Production Manager
Alison Stoltzfus, Associate Managing Editor
Elham Shabahat, Publishing Assistant

ACKNOWLEDGMENTS

The author would like to thank Celeste Sollod for her superb editorial work, her courage in the face of adversity, and her stern "No"; Illeny Maaza for combining hard work with art and making it look easy; Jeannie Yoon for her support, direction, and even sterner "No"; Tucker Zinke for his knowledge, insight, advice, wonderful laugh, and *hideous* puns; B. Young for his rare expertise; P. J. Waters for his advice, his library, and his friendship; and Corinna, for more reasons than space allows.

Thanks also to Dr. James Murphy for his extremely thorough expert review and excellent suggestions for this book, Brian Becker for his stellar writing skills and sense of humor, and Dr. William Slayton, the greatest teacher ever, for sharing his infinite knowledge of the literary realm.

A special thanks to Adam Robinson, who conceived of and perfected the Joe Bloggs approach to standardized tests and many of the other successful techniques used by The Princeton Review.

CONTENTS

Foreword

WHAT IS THE PRINCETON REVIEW?

The Princeton Review is an international test-preparation company with branches in all major U.S. cities and several branches abroad. In 1981, John Katzman started teaching an SAT prep course in his parents' living room. Within five years, The Princeton Review had become the largest SAT coaching program in the country.

Our phenomenal success improving students' scores on standardized tests is due to a simple, innovative, and radically effective philosophy: Study the test, not what the test claims to test. This approach has led to the development of techniques for taking standardized tests, techniques based on the principles the test writers themselves use to write the tests.

We here at The Princeton Review have found that our philosophy works not just for cracking the SAT, but for any standardized test. We've already successfully applied our system to the GMAT, LSAT, and MCAT, to name just a few. Although in many ways the GRE Literature in English Subject Test is very different from those just mentioned, in the end, a standardized test is a standardized test. This book on the GRE Literature in English Subject Test uses our time-tested principle: Crack the system based on how the test is written.

The book you hold in your hands has been designed for one purpose: to improve your score on the GRE Literature in English Subject Test. In order to accomplish this, we take an irreverent approach to the test, but not to English literature, and certainly not to your score. We know how much can be riding on these scores. We know the gut-lurching sensation of taking a standardized test upon which one's very future seems to hang. We take these concerns seriously.

We cannot emphasize enough that this book is not a review of all major works of literature in English. We will give you what you need to excel on the GRE Literature in English Subject Test and not much more, which brings up a touchy point. Our process leads us to do things like summing up Dante's *Divine Comedy* in a single page, and then writing simply, "That's all you need to know." Of course, we don't actually mean that's all you, as a literary scholar, need to know. All we mean to convey is that, for the purposes of the GRE Literature in English Subject Test, Dante is an author whose work can be summed up in one page worth of material. Ridiculous? Oh yes, absolutely! Keep this in mind as we proceed. Remember that this book is not about deepening your knowledge of all literature in English (a profoundly silly idea), but about focusing this knowledge to key points so that you can crack the GRE Literature in English Subject Test.

Good Luck!
Douglas McMullen, Jr.

PART ◆ I

The Big Picture

1
Orientation

WHAT IS THE GRE LITERATURE IN ENGLISH SUBJECT TEST?

The GRE Literature in English Subject Test is a supplementary test to the GRE (Graduate Record Examination) General Test. Both tests are written by the folks at ETS (Educational Testing Service).

Almost everyone applying to grad school takes the GRE General Test. The subject tests cover specialty areas broadly corresponding to undergraduate majors, and they are taken by those students who intend to apply to graduate programs which request subject test scores. You may find you do not have to take the GRE Literature in English Subject Test at all. Some English programs do not require a subject test. But, as you are no doubt aware, many do.

> The GRE Literature in English Subject Test measures only your proficiency on the GRE Literature in English Subject Test—*not* your knowledge of English literature.

WHY A GENERAL TEST AND A SUBJECT TEST?

According to ETS, the general test "measures analytical writing, verbal, and quantitative skills that have been acquired over a long period of time and that are not related to any specific field of study." The subject tests, again according to ETS, "are intended to indicate students' knowledge of the subject matter emphasized in many undergraduate programs as preparation for graduate study."

Well, that's all very nice, but it's just a lot of ETS hooey. According to us, the general test (like all standardized color-in-the-dots tests) is designed to measure your standardized test-taking skills. As for the GRE Literature in English Subject Test, it's a hopeless attempt at quantifying a subject that cannot be quantified. It ends up testing one thing: your ability to take the GRE Literature in English Subject Test. Just what that means for you is the subject of this book.

WHAT IS ON THE GRE LITERATURE IN ENGLISH SUBJECT TEST?

The GRE Literature in English Subject Test asks questions concerning every period of British and American literature, from *Beowulf* to contemporary works. It tests reading comprehension of difficult texts, basic concepts of critical literary theory, terms relevant to the study of literature in English, and knowledge of well-known works and authors from around the world.

Sound terrifying? Relax. When we get to the Cracking the System part of this book, you'll find that the monster has a lot fewer teeth than might appear.

HOW IS THE GRE LITERATURE IN ENGLISH SUBJECT TEST STRUCTURED?

- The test is 2 hours and 50 minutes long.

- The test contains 230 questions. (ETS says that this number might vary slightly, but we've only seen tests of exactly 230 questions.)

That sums up the structure of the test, but what is really notable is how little structure there is. Unlike many other tests written by ETS (including the GRE General Test), the Literature in English Test lacks a couple of important features. First, there are no sections that focus on a particular topic or skill. Second, the questions come in no particular order of difficulty—that is, the hardest question on the test might be followed by the easiest. We'll address how to get a handle on this unwieldy 230-question sprawl in Chapter 3, in a section called "The Two-Pass System."

Who Writes the Test?

ETS hires academics of various stripes, on the advice of the Modern Language Association of America, to write the GRE Literature in English Subject Test. Using ETS guidelines, the assembled scholars conjure up questions, which ETS then grinds through a statistical mill to ensure that the proper proportions of topics are tested and that the overall question difficulty is appropriate. If all goes well, out comes a subject test. The test-creation process for a subject test is unpleasant and expensive. The first administration of a new version can reveal that the questions are too difficult, or too easy, causing ETS to perform statistical somersaults and backflips in order to make the results comparable with previous versions. Because of these difficulties, ETS hoards its subject test material fanatically. When they find something that works, they like to stick with it. What this means for you is that there is a dearth of practice tests out there. ETS makes only one available, and, at the time of this revision, that test is ten years old.

The GRE Literature in English Subject Test is written by people like your college professors.

Contact Information

Official ETS information about the GRE Literature in English Subject Test can be found online at www.gre.org. Here's additional contact information for ETS:

Address: GRE-ETS
             PO Box 6000
             Princeton, NJ 08541

Phone: 1-866-473-4373 (Toll Free)
             1-609-771-7670
             Monday–Friday, 8:00 A.M.–7:45 P.M. EST
             (Except for U.S. holidays)

Fax: 1-610-290-8975

E-mail: gretests@ets.org

Test Dates

Currently, the GRE Literature in English Subject Test is offered on just three Saturdays throughout the year, in April, October, and November. It is important to plan to take the test well in advance of any graduate school application to allow yourself the option, if necessary, of retaking the exam.

Note that students claiming special circumstances may request to take the test on the Mondays following each of the Saturday testing dates. Monday testers always receive a different exam, because ETS is concerned about minimizing any chance of cheating.

TESTING FEE

As of press time, the fee is $130 if you are taking the exam in the U.S., and $150 everywhere else in the world, but don't be surprised if it goes up $5 or $10 in the next year or so.

TEST FORMAT

Answering 230 questions in 170 minutes is an average of about 40 seconds per question.

The GRE Literature in English Subject Test is a conventional paper-and-pencil exam. Each of its 230 multiple-choice questions has five answer choices, (A) through (E), which you select by bubbling in the proper oval on the answer sheet. The testing time is 2 hours and 50 minutes. There is no break. We repeat: There is no bathroom break. If you finish more than 30 minutes early (neither likely nor a good idea), you can leave. Otherwise, you must stay until the test is over.

ON THE DAY OF THE TEST

According to ETS, you should be at the testing center no later than 8:30 A.M. or else you risk being turned away. Plan on being at the testing center for a total of 3-plus hours because of the extra time required for administrative paperwork associated with the exam.

Required/Restricted Items on Test Day

You need a bunch of no. 2 pencils and a big eraser. As far as documentation goes, once you register for the exam, ETS will remind you of the required documentation that you need on test day. Basically, you'll need the registration card that they send you in advance as well as a photo ID with your signature on it, such as a Passport, Driver's License, Military ID, or National ID. If you don't have one of these, pay extra attention to ETS's fine print when you register for the exam to see what you will need to bring instead; otherwise, they will delay you outside the testing center.

The list of forbidden items is long and glorious and can be found in the GRE registration materials or on the GRE website, but the most important items to mention at this point are: *no calculators, no timers that make noise, and no headsets!*

SENDING YOUR SCORES

When you register for the GRE Literature in English Test (and again on the day of the exam), you can list up to 4 schools that you want ETS to send your scores to for free. Having your scores sent to additional schools will cost you $13 per school. Test takers receive their scores by mail 6 weeks after the test date. Note that GRE scores are good for 5 years.

CANCELING SCORES

You can void the exam at any point during the morning of the test. Voiding essentially results in your answer key getting tossed in the trash, and no record of that day ever appears on any future GRE report. You should only consider doing this if you're convinced that things have gone seriously wrong (for example, if you have a 104°F fever and are hallucinating).

TAKING THE TEST MORE THAN ONCE

ETS will let you take the GRE Literature in English Subject Test or other subject tests as many times as you want—after all, they make at least $130 a pop. However, because all previous scores show up on the report sent to schools (only voided tests are left off), make every attempt to take the GRE just once. Don't take the test without preparing and consider it just a practice run. Each additional GRE score on your report makes you look more like a professional test-taker and less like a potential graduate student.

WHAT ABOUT THE COMPUTERIZED ADMINISTRATION OF THE GRE?

ETS now offers computerized testing for the GRE General Test. As of yet, there are no computerized versions of the subject tests.

HOW IS THE TEST SCORED?

ETS will send you not one, but *three* scores for your subject test. There will be a raw score, a scaled score, and a percentile ranking.

- **Scaled score:** The scaled score is derived from your **raw score**, which is calculated as follows:
  - You are given 1 point for each correct answer.
  - You are given 0 points for a question left blank.
  - One-fourth of a point is deducted from your score for an incorrect answer. We'll discuss that –1/4 point "guessing penalty" and what to do about it in Chapter 3.

Next, ETS takes your raw score and calculates it in a method known only to them. The scaled score will be a number from 200 to 990. On any given test, the actual scores reported will fall within a narrower range, typically between 250 and 800. If this three-digit score looks suspiciously like the 200 to 800 range of the math and verbal parts of the SAT, it's because that's exactly what ETS intends. What other purpose the scaled score serves is difficult to fathom.

There is no practical reason to concern yourself with the details of the scaled score. For your purposes, the score that matters on the GRE Literature in English Subject Test is the percentile score.

Your percentile ranking is the score that matters.

- **Percentile ranking:** This is a number from 0 to 99 that indicates the percent of examinees who scored lower than you. In other words, if your percentile ranking is 50, then out of 100 test takers, 50 scored less than you. Note: Your percentile is determined by your performance against past and present takers of that edition of the test, not just the examinees who took the test on the same date that you did.

The relationship between scaled score and percentile ranking varies greatly between disciplines. On recent administrations of GRE subject tests, identical scaled scores of 500 were worth: 6th percentile (Computer Science), 22nd percentile (Geology), 41st percentile (Literature in English), and 80th percentile (Sociology).

ETS strives for consistency within each discipline. On your Literature in English Subject Test, a 50th percentile score will be around 530, a 99th percentile score around 750, and a first percentile score around 310. How the raw scores fit in and what it all means for you in terms of study are topics we'll cover in the Cracking the System section.

By the way, when ETS sends you your scores, they will send along a six-page brochure of statistical gibberish called "Interpreting your GRE Scores."

How Important Are My Scores?

It depends. A score's importance is entirely up to the graduate department to which you are applying. As we mentioned earlier, there are good programs that don't want a subject test score; some don't even ask for a general test score (and we say good for them). Even ETS goes out of its way to say that the GRE Literature in English Subject Test should not be used "as the sole arbiter in the selection process or in decisions relating to scholarship assistance." At almost all schools, the subject test is less significant than your grade point average or your letters of recommendation. However, a lackluster grade point average might be bolstered (or your excuses for it taken more seriously) with an outstanding subject-test score. For many schools, the GRE tests (both general and subject) are used as tie breakers. When candidates are otherwise equivalent, the test scores can make the difference. One thing is certain: A poor score cannot help and might hurt you. A good score can only help.

Can I Use Techniques in This Book as a Study Aid for the GRE General Test?

Not really. Only a tiny portion of this book applies to the general test, and there is a great deal to learn about the general test. In other words, if you're thinking of saving a few bucks and buying just one book to study for both tests, sorry. The General Test and the Literature in English Subject Test are very different, and each should be approached with techniques designed specifically for them.

HOW TO USE THIS BOOK

The material in this book has been designed based on a thorough study of the available ETS material and long-term study of standardized tests in general. The book has been written to address preparing for the GRE Literature Test in as efficient a way as possible. Other than our occasional lame jokes, there is no fluff here. Everything is important. To best use this book:

- Read through the information and the study materials.

- Make flash cards of all necessary terms, works, and authors. See our section on flash cards as study materials, page 42.

- Take the practice test. Read the explanations to *all* the questions.

- Based on what you've learned, identify where you've made errors and glance over our study materials again. By this time, you should have a very good idea of where your weaknesses lie and what further study you might need. Be sure to familiarize yourself with works and authors you don't know.

- Go online to www.gre.org and download the free practice GRE Literature in English Subject Test (you'll also receive a copy of this practice test when you register). If you've already taken that test, don't despair; we'd just *prefer* you take the ETS-published version after you've finished our program, because you'll see the results of our methods and be pumped for the real thing.

ABOUT THE PRACTICE TEST AND THE EXPLANATIONS

If you've used books to prepare for standardized tests before, you may think of a practice test (sometimes called a diagnostic) as the place where you put into practice what you've learned earlier in the book. You may be accustomed to consulting the explanations only on questions you've gotten wrong in order to see what you forgot to do. *You must not use our practice test and explanations that way.*

Although our test does let you put into practice the instruction you've received earlier in the book, the practice test and explanations are a continuation of the learning process. *In many of the explanations, there is new information found nowhere else in the book.* Literature in English, unlike mathematics, is a subject composed almost entirely of details: titles, authors, characters, settings, terms, and so on. . . . The explanations are the best place to show you how the details you already know can be pieced together to answer a question, or to give you the details you need. You will learn as much from the practice test and explanations as you do from the rest of this book. Keep in mind that our explanations go into detail not only about the correct answers, but also about important incorrect answers.

The explanations on pages 197–239 contain important information—make sure to read them thoroughly.

2

What's on the Test

WHAT ETS SAYS IS ON THE LITERATURE IN ENGLISH SUBJECT TEST

ETS's Literature In English Test Practice provides a breakdown of the material on the test. The test is available for free download online. It isn't a valuable breakdown for you as a student; the ETS categories are structured so as to make the test look good. For the sake of completeness, here are ETS's numbers:

- Literary analysis: 40–55 percent

- Identification: 15–20 percent

- Cultural and historical contexts: 20–25 percent

- History and theory of literary criticism: 10–15 percent

ETS also gives a breakdown of the literary historical scope, which is as follows:

- Continental, Classical, and Comparative literature through 1925: 5–10 percent

- British Literature to 1660 (including Milton): 25–30 percent

- British Literature 1660–1925: 30–35 percent

- American Literature through 1925: 15–25 percent

- American, British, and World Literatures after 1925: 20–30 percent

WHAT WE HAVE TO SAY ABOUT THE ETS NUMBERS

We don't think the ETS numbers or categories are worth a second look. These numbers better reflect the test ETS wishes it could write than what's on the actual test.

What ETS calls literary analysis includes recognizing allusions and references. For example, we think recognizing something like, "It wasn't the best of times; it wasn't the worst of times. It was medium times," as a parodic allusion to the opening of Dickens's *Tale of Two Cities* has much more to do with identification than with literary analysis. Likewise, ETS considers identifying a synopsis of "The Merchant's Tale" (from Chaucer's *The Canterbury Tales*) factual information. How is that factual? It's *identification*. In short, a huge portion of the test is identification, despite ETS's protest that identification makes up only 15–20 percent of the test.

There are similarly ridiculous problems with the literary–historical breakdown. For example, ETS offers a question that requires you to recognize a twentieth-century poet's reworking of lines from Shakespeare's *The Tempest*. You might have read the poem a hundred times but never caught the Shakespeare reference. You'd miss the question. Conversely, if you were familiar with *The Tempest*, you'd get the question right. They never ask who actually wrote the poem. Get this—ETS puts that question in its "British and American Literature after 1925" category!

We've included this information so that, should you see it in ETS's book, you won't wonder, "Hey, how come The Princeton Review didn't tell me this stuff?" Well, we told you, and we also told you it's useless and misleading—ignore it.

CATEGORY BREAKDOWNS YOU CAN USE

- **Reading comprehension: 25 percent**—Our reading comprehension category refers to questions that involve understanding a text that ETS provides.

- **Identification: 65 percent**—Our identification category refers to questions that require you to choose the correct name from among the answer choices. The name might be an author, a literary work, a character, a setting, or some other closely associated person or thing.

- **Grammar, terms, literary criticism: 10 percent**—That percentage may not seem like much, but on a 230-question test, that's 23 questions. However, terms and literary criticism (as tested on the GRE Literature in English Subject Test) are fairly easy to study for.

WHAT ABOUT LITERARY HISTORICAL SCOPE?

If we told you there are a lot of nineteenth-century British authors tested, say 15 percent of the identification questions, what could you possibly do with that information? It doesn't mean anything.

> Student (to librarian): I'd like some books by nineteenth-century British authors.
>
> Librarian: Which authors?
>
> Student: You know, nineteenth-century ones, from Britain.
>
> Librarian: You'll have to be more specific.
>
> Student: Well, *specifically*, I need 15 percent of the nineteenth-century British authors, and uh, I'll need 10 percent of the American authors from the twentieth century and about 5 percent of the world authors from all time, and I'll need . . .

The test covers English and American literature from *Beowulf* to today.

The student needs serious help, but not from a librarian.

You need to know what to study in far more detail than "15 percent of the nineteenth-century British authors." Well, that's why we're here. We can't tell you everything that will be on the test, but we can point you toward the key works to which the test writers love to refer.

We've structured our study material for the identification portion of the test according to individual authors and titles. In the most general terms (and we get much more specific later), the test covers English and American literature from *Beowulf* to today, making an attempt to give roughly equal weight to each period. (Colonial-American writing is an exception in that it is almost entirely absent from the test.) What this means for you and what you need to concentrate on when studying is covered in detail in Part III of this book.

THE FORM OF QUESTIONS ON THE GRE LITERATURE IN ENGLISH SUBJECT TEST

The content of a question isn't the only thing that matters to you as a test taker; the form a question takes can make a difference in your approach to it, or even whether you choose to answer the question at all. For your purposes, the Literature in English Subject Test has two types of questions.

THE STANDARD FORM

Typically, a Literature in English question has a passage:

> 11. It was a dark and clichéd night. Authoress Ima Hack shook her raven tresses in frustration and glared moodily over her typewriter at the gusting drops of rain lashing in rhythmic waves at the panes of the broad black window across from her oaken desk. "Why? Why does everything I write seem both leaden and overwrought?" she pondered.

Then a question:

> Which of the following terms can be appropriately applied both to the use of the word "clichéd" in line one, and to the passage as a whole?

And then five answer choices:

> (A) Self-referential
> (B) Onomatopoeic
> (C) Hyperbolic
> (D) Gothic
> (E) Arabesque

The answer, by the way, is (A), self-referential.

VARIATIONS ON THE STANDARD FORM

There are a few common variations to the standard form:

- **Multiple questions asked about one passage.** With some literary selections, especially longer ones, ETS will ask more than one question.

List these authors in order of the dates they were active, from past to present:
Charles Lamb
Elizabeth Gaskell
Sherwood Anderson
Andrew Marvell
Ernest Hemingway

- **There is no passage, only a question and five (long) answer choices.** Questions structured this way can be time consuming. In effect, a question of this type requires reading five passages instead of one. For example:

> Which of the following choices is excerpted from Milton's *Paradise Lost*?

Five answer choices would follow, each one several lines long. Try to scan when possible, since that's a lot of reading for one point.

- **Stand-alone questions.** These are direct questions, without a passage, followed by five short answers. For example:

> 131. Of the following works, which was written by Miguel Cervantes?

The titles of five works would then follow, like this:

(A) *The Rape of the Lock*
(B) *Don Quixote*
(C) *Cyrano de Bergerac*
(D) *Love in the Time of Cholera*
(E) *Candide*

Stand-alone questions take very little time. Unfortunately, they are quite rare. (The answer is (B).)

Super POE Questions

POE stands for Process of Elimination. Although you are probably already somewhat familiar with this technique, we cover it in detail in Chapter 3. Right now, we want you to know that we call a common type of question on the test a "super POE question." These are questions (actually *sets* of questions) formatted in a way that makes POE especially effective. Here's an example:

> 17. Which of the following is a title by the author of *Tess of the D'Urbervilles?*
>
> 18. Which of the following is a title by the author of *For Whom the Bell Tolls*?
>
> 19. Which of the following is a title by the author of *Orlando*?
>
> (A) *Jane Eyre*
> (B) *The Awakening*
> (C) *The Waves*
> (D) *The Sun Also Rises*
> (E) *Far From the Madding Crowd*

By stacking questions, ETS has given you the opportunity to answer questions which have fewer than five answer choices. It is an opportunity you should take advantage of. If you knew that Charlotte Brontë is the author of *Jane Eyre*, but none of her other works are mentioned in the questions, you would suddenly be faced with three questions, each having, in effect, four answer choices. If you

Andrew Marvell
1621–1678
Charles Lamb
1775–1834
Elizabeth Gaskell
1810–1865
Sherwood Anderson
1876–1941
Ernest Hemingway
1899–1961

then knew that Hemingway wrote both *For Whom the Bell Tolls* and *The Sun Also Rises*, the remaining two questions would each have only three answers apiece. Even if you knew absolutely nothing more, guessing would make sense and be likely to improve your score. (Of course we're hoping you know Virginia Woolf wrote both *Orlando* and *The Waves*, and that Thomas Hardy wrote both *Far from the Madding Crowd* and *Tess of the D'Urbervilles*, and that Kate Chopin wrote *The Awakening*—the answer to question 19 is (C).)

TEST-TAKING TECHNIQUES

You may have noticed that in our discussion of categories and forms we've mentioned studying effectively, managing time, and guessing. These are topics of crucial importance to your performance on the Literature in English Subject Test. Keep reading, and we'll cover them in detail.

PART II

Cracking the System

3

Basic Principles

WHAT ARE THE BASIC PRINCIPLES OF CRACKING THE SYSTEM?

There will come a time when the studying is over and you are as prepared as you are going to be. You will be sitting in the test center with a sealed exam booklet and an answer sheet in front of you. The proctor, droning on at the front of the room, will finally finish reading all those instructions no one needs to hear, and say, "You may break the seal and begin the test."

At that moment, what you know isn't going to change. Your head will be crammed with literary knowledge, but now your score depends on getting what you know onto that answer sheet.

Imagine your exact double sitting over at the next desk. In terms of literature in English, your double knows just what you know, neither more nor less. Will your and your double's scores be the same? *Not if you know how to take a standardized test and your double doesn't.* You will squeeze every possible drop of what you know onto that answer sheet. Your double will let half of his or her knowledge go unused. The scores will reflect the difference.

The GRE Literature in English Subject Test is no different from any standardized test in that there are two critical concerns:

1. You must manage a limited amount of time well.

2. You must guess wisely and aggressively.

If you manage your time poorly, you will not get a chance to use your knowledge. Questions you could have easily answered will vanish with the clock, taking their points and your score with them.

Guessing wisely and aggressively calls for the ability (and courage) to use *partial* knowledge. When you fail to guess, you let whatever partial knowledge you have go to waste. For that question at least, it's as though you didn't know a thing. Manage your time poorly or fail to guess, and you withhold exactly what the test wants from you: your knowledge. The test, in turn, withholds points. We're here to make sure that doesn't happen.

GUESSING AGGRESSIVELY BY UNDERSTANDING YOUR RAW SCORE

A successful test comes down to your raw score: how many points you get. More points mean a higher scaled score and a higher percentile ranking. It's that simple. But, because of the marking system—1 point for a correct answer, 0 points for a blank, and –1/4 point for an incorrect answer—there are several ways of arriving at the same raw score.

As an example, let's examine two hypothetical students' scores. Both students arrive at the same raw score of 166 (that's a scaled score of about 670 and a percentile ranking of 94) through different methods.

Out of 230 questions, Student A answers 166 correctly, leaves 64 blank, and answers 0 incorrectly. That's a raw score of 166.

Out of the same 230 questions, Student B answers 179 correctly (guessing correctly on 13 of them), leaves 0 blank, and gets 51 wrong. This also results in a raw score of 166. (Each wrong answer costs an extra –1/4 of a point. 51 divided by 4 rounds up to 13, the guessing penalty. 179 – 13 = 166.)

Let's consider these students. In all probability, Student A above cheated herself out of an even better score. If she knew enough to answer 166 questions without making a single mistake, she must have known *something* about many of those questions she left blank. Where did that knowledge go? Into thin air. Student B was aggressive and answered correctly 78 percent of the questions on which she worked. She has probably maximized her knowledge. In other words, both students received good scores, but whereas Student B maximized her score, Student A blew it. The only really good score is *your best* score. Student A, with just a little more test savvy, could have scored in the 99th percentile.

It is *much* easier to answer a lot of questions and allow for some error than it is to try to answer every question you work on perfectly.

If you can eliminate at least one answer, then you *should* guess. Don't randomly fill in all the bubbles in the last five minutes of the test, but do guess as often as you can.

78% = 90%?

On most tests, answering only 78 percent of the questions correctly results in a mediocre score, but not on the GRE Literature in English Subject Test. Seventy-eight percent correct on the Literature Test puts you in the 90th percentile. The fact that you can miss a lot of questions and still score well has many repercussions for you as a test taker, all of which we will explore, but do not come away from this discussion of scoring thinking that because you can miss some questions the test is easy.

On the contrary, what this fact should alert you to is that the Literature Test is going to *feel* extremely difficult. Be psychologically prepared for a test on which you are going to be challenged, on which you are going to miss many questions. We've talked to several students who came away from the test feeling like they'd just been mugged. It's certain that as their confidence eroded over the course of the test, their performance declined. There was no reason for this to be the case. Don't let the occasional wrong answer alarm you. Don't even let the occasional question about material you've never studied, by someone you've never heard of, alarm you.

THE GUESSING PENALTY SHOULD BE CALLED THE GUESSING BONUS

The numbers above should convince you that the so-called guessing penalty is no penalty at all. If you've spent any time on a question, and have even the slightest twinge of an inkling of what the answer might be, guess! If you can eliminate even one answer choice, guess! Sure, you'll lose a quarter of a point here and there. So what? You'll harvest enough whole points to more than make up the difference. Guessing is the only way to take advantage of your partial knowledge. You may not know enough to be comfortable with an answer, but that isn't the issue. Do you know anything? If so, then guess.

GUESSING WISELY WITH POE

POE is an acronym for the Process of Elimination. You are probably already acquainted with POE in its simplest form: Cross out answers you know are wrong. The Cracking the System approach to POE isn't really different, just more intense.

POE—no longer just a nineteenth-century master of literary suspense.

You'll find that on a number of questions the right answer will jump out at you. You'll be given a literary selection, for example, and find yourself thinking, "Hey, that's my term paper." When that happens, you'll pounce on the right answer, fill in the correct bubble, and move on. Other times, however, the selection will be unfamiliar and the answer choices will only ring vague bells. That's when POE should be a reflex. Through POE, you can take advantage of what partial knowledge you have. Let's look at an example:

> The chateau into which my valet had ventured to make forcible entrance, rather than permit me, in my desperately wounded condition, to pass a night in
> *Line* the open air, was one of those piles of commingled
> (5) gloom and grandeur which have so long frowned among the Apennines, not less in fact than in the fancy of Mrs. Radcliffe. To all appearance it had been temporarily and very lately abandoned.

Which one of the following correctly describes the passage above?

(A) The passage is drawn from Ernest Hemingway's *A Farewell to Arms.*

(B) The passage is drawn from Jane Austen's novel *Northanger Abbey.*

(C) The passage is drawn from Joseph Conrad's *Heart of Darkness.*

(D) The passage is drawn from Horace Walpole's *The Castle of Otranto.*

(E) The passage is drawn from Edgar Allan Poe's "The Oval Portrait."

Here's How to Crack It

Let's look at the answer choices one at a time. You may think you don't know anything about the passage, but it's what you know about the answer choices judged against the passage that counts. It's what you know about the answer choices that allows you to use POE.

(A) The passage is drawn from Ernest Hemingway's *A Farewell to Arms.*

Ridiculous! Sure, *A Farewell to Arms* is set in and around the Apennines, and features a wounded soldier, but Hemingway's style is nothing like that of the passage. Cross it out.

(B) The passage is drawn from Jane Austen's novel *Northanger Abbey.*

Well, *Northanger Abbey* is a parody of Anne Radcliffe's gothic novels, and the passage does mention "Mrs. Radcliffe," but people's bodies aren't wounded in Austen's novels, only their egos are. For these reasons, this answer just doesn't seem right. Cross it out.

> (C) The passage is drawn from Joseph Conrad's
> *Heart of Darkness.*

Heart of Darkness is a story set in colonial Africa and told from aboard a ship. This is neither colonial Africa nor a ship. Cross it out.

> (D) The passage is drawn from Horace Walpole's
> *The Castle of Otranto.*

The Castle of Otranto is the first gothic novel, and predates Anne Radcliffe's writing. It couldn't possibly mention Radcliffe (thank goodness we took that course on the gothic novel).

> (E) The passage is drawn from Edgar Allan Poe's
> "The Oval Portrait."

"Commingled gloom and grandeur..." sounds like Poe. "Desperately wounded..." and a mysteriously abandoned house. Yeah, that sounds like Poe. What's more, it's all that's left. Poe it is. POE.

PHYSICALLY CROSS OUT WRONG ANSWERS

The test booklet is yours to doodle on as much as you like. As you eliminate answers, make sure you physically cross them out in the booklet. Circle the correct answer. That way, if you make a mistake bubbling, it will be easy to correct. Also, when answers are crossed out, you are less likely to mistakenly choose them (don't forget that the test is almost three hours long—even the most attentive brain might wander).

WAIT A MINUTE!

Not so fast, you say. What if you hadn't known anything about Horace Walpole and the *Castle of Otranto*? Then you would have had to guess between D and E. We aren't saying POE always leads you to the single correct answer. POE lets you use what you do know in order to guess aggressively.

By the way, what if the mention of Mrs. Radcliffe had left you certain the passage was from *Northanger Abbey*? Without any surrounding context, you might even have talked yourself into thinking that "desperately wounded condition" indeed referred, with characteristic Austenian irony, to a wounded ego.

Well, then you would have gotten the question wrong, and lost a quarter of a point more than if you'd left it blank, which is no big deal; but more importantly, it won't happen. This was not a real question. ETS would not use an obscure passage with a reference to gothic novelist Anne Radcliffe *and* offer *Northanger Abbey* as an answer choice, unless it were the correct answer choice. ETS does not

Having confidence in yourself will help you guess more aggressively.

want to penalize you for good partial knowledge. If this were a real ETS question, the Jane Austen answer choice would have referred to a different Austen work, perhaps *Emma*, a work they would expect you to know has nothing to do with Anne Radcliffe. We'll have more to say about POE and this sample question in Chapter 4 of this book on Advanced Principles.

TIME MANAGEMENT

Time management is the flip side of aggressive guessing. The principle of aggressive guessing is to answer as many questions as you can using POE. Time management means dealing with the reality that "as many questions as you can" does not mean all 230 questions. Almost everyone runs out of time on the GRE Literature in English Subject Test. Racing through at breakneck speed will not help your score.

Like POE, time management is a means of getting to the knowledge you have, of squeezing every last point out of the test. Knowing the answer to the last question on the test does you no good if you never get to it. Why did you not get to it? Because you struggled pointlessly with earlier questions and they stole your time. Good time management depends on optimizing the speed at which you work, and optimizing the questions you select to work on.

SPEED

The folks at ETS don't tell you that the Literature in English Subject Test is in large part a speed-reading competition, but it is. The GRE Literature in English Subject Test favors the fast reader. The discussion on understanding your raw score should have demonstrated that, all things being equal, the more questions you answer, the better your score will be. But the Literature in English Subject Test is designed to push the average and even the above-average student to the limits of his or her reading ability. Only the most exceptional (or wildly reckless) students answer all 230 questions on the GRE Literature in English Subject Test. Even students scoring in the 99th percentile can find themselves running out of time. If you can get to all 230 questions, great, but don't expect to. If you find yourself racing through and rushing to get to the last question, keep in mind that there is definitely a point at which you are working too fast.

The speed at which you read has already been largely determined, and we definitely don't advocate going out and taking a speed-reading course. We do, however, advocate getting the most out of yourself.

CONCENTRATE

We can't teach you how to concentrate, but we can offer valuable tips. Be strong, brave, and confident—in other words, forewarned. Confidence adds immeasurably to your concentration. You've taken a huge step toward improved confidence by reading this book, because now you know what's in store. We've had more than one student say to us: "I never felt stupid before, not until I took this test." Those students didn't know what to expect. Expect what *feels* like a very hard test; count on it. The *average* student misses slightly more than four out of every ten questions, and that's on a test where the average student is someone intending to apply to graduate school in English. So don't panic, and be prepared to miss a lot of questions; you'll end up with an excellent score.

STUDY

One of the best ways to improve your speed on the GRE Literature in English Subject Test is to know the material. When a question is about material that you are truly familiar with, it will be ridiculously easy. You'll not only get a point; you'll buy time. Just being familiar with the types of reading you'll confront will speed you up. If, for example, you haven't looked at Chaucer since that 8:00 A.M. freshman survey with old professor what's-his-name, 15 minutes spent looking over *The Canterbury Tales* will do you a world of good. Because studying for the GRE Literature in English Subject Test is a peculiar art, we've devoted a whole section to it, and no, we won't ask you to read everything ever written.

THE TWO-PASS SYSTEM

The two-pass system is The Princeton Review's name for judicious skipping. It means working through the test once (the first pass) to gather up all the quick, easy points, and then going back (the second pass) to work on the time-consuming, difficult questions you skipped initially. There is nothing in the GRE Literature in English Subject Test book that says you have to do the questions in the order given, and you shouldn't. Ideally, you would want to attempt every question on the test, but even for the best students, this is often simply not realistic. If you must skip some questions, you want to skip the ones you would have gotten wrong anyway. The two-pass system is the art of eating your dessert first and leaving the gross stuff for last.

The Basic Object of the Two-Pass Style

The object, then, is for you to do all the fast and easy questions first, and the slow and hard questions last. We're going to give you guidelines for how to do that. Keep in mind that these are guidelines, not strict rules. Understanding the point of the two-pass system and using it in a way that makes sense to you is far more important than following the program exactly.

Because there are a variety of forms in which questions are posed on the GRE Literature in English Subject Test, this is a good time to go back to Chapter 2 and briefly review the different types of questions you'll face. It will help you to understand and use some of our guidelines for the two-pass system.

Guidelines For the Two-Pass System

The First Pass
Objective: Collecting the easy and fast points.

1. **Look for questions with short passages or no passage at all.** In general, the less reading you have to do, the less time the question takes. Keep a special eye out for the relatively rare "stand-alones" in which there is no reading selection, just a question and five choices, usually authors or titles. These questions require very little time. Answer them. Guess if need be.

2. **When you recognize a passage, do the question(s) on it immediately.** The questions on a truly familiar passage will be a breeze. Do them in the first pass for sure.

3. **Glance at passages for familiar names.** Most questions involve a reading passage, ranging from a single sentence to several paragraphs. No matter how long the passage, skim for names. If you see names you recognize, do the question or questions. If there are no familiar names and the passage is long, skip it.

4. **Glance at the answer choices for familiar names.** Some answer choices are long reading passages unto themselves; some are just a single name. Either way, look for names you recognize. If most of the answer choices contain familiar names, answer the question. If there are no names, or none are familiar (i.e., "who are these people?"), skip the question on the first pass.

5. **Answer "Super POE" questions.** As explained in the sample questions section (page 15), there are questions formatted in a way that makes the Process of Elimination super effective. These should be first-pass questions.

6. **When several questions are asked on a single reading passage, answer all the questions.** Many passages have more than one question asked about them, and as you might expect, it's the longer passages that tend to have multiple questions. Once you've taken the time to read a passage, answer *all* the questions on it, difficult or not; you don't want to find yourself coming back to it and having to read the passage again. This is not specifically a first-pass technique, but something you should do throughout the test.

7. **Do not skip any of the questions when you have read the passage they ask about.** You will definitely begin questions that look doable only to discover halfway through that they're difficult. It happens all the time. This is exactly the point at which most students decide to skip a question, *and it is exactly the wrong time to skip.* Once you've bothered to read a question, any associated reading, and the answer choices, you've done 95 percent of the work! Don't bail out now. And don't waste time fretting either. Use your partial knowledge and take your best guess.

The Second Pass
Objective: Getting the maximum number of questions right in the time left.

After finishing your first pass, you should be left with the medium and tough questions, the questions you didn't like at first glance. On the first pass, you undoubtedly answered some questions you wish you'd left for later. That's no cause for alarm. On the second pass, you'll find some questions that turn out to be easier than you'd expected. If you've done the first pass well, what you're left with are mostly the tougher questions. Now, grind 'em out, using POE and every ounce of concentration you have. Just keep focused.

You Can Still Skip to Your Heart's Content

There's no law that says you can't do a third or even fourth pass. Skip questions that look like they'll eat up your time without giving you anything back.

The Five-Second Rule

The way to use the two-pass system is to skip questions that *look* hard. This should be a matter of following your instincts and using the guidelines above. It should *not* be a source of anxiety. Deciding whether a question is first pass or not is a snap decision. Five seconds is the absolute longest you should think about whether a question is first pass or not. Use the five-second rule:

- If it takes more than five seconds to decide if it's a first- or second-pass question, it's a second-pass question; skip it.

A Word (or Several) on Bubbling

Bubbling is the art of transferring your answers onto the score sheet. When you bubble, be sure to fill in the oval completely so that you'll receive the credit you deserve. If you follow our advice (and you should), you should be skipping around—so pay special attention to where you bubble. As you skip around different questions on your answer sheet, don't forget to keep track of the question numbers you are bubbling. It is a horrible feeling to get to question 55 and realize you've just bubbled the answer for 54. Check your work every once in a while.

Last Words on the Two-Pass System

There is no magic number of questions to answer on your first pass. You might answer ten questions on your first pass or you might answer 100. Either way is fine. The main point of the two-pass system is to gather up the easy points quickly and efficiently first, and then work through the rest of the test.

Don't ever skip a question once you've put time and thought into it. Remember, guessing helps your score!

"No coward soul is mine
No trembler in the world's
storm-troubled sphere"

Emily Brontë, from
"No Coward Soul Is Mine"

"Make use of time, let not
    advantage slip;
Beauty within itself should
    not be wasted;
Fair flowers that are not
    gather'd in their prime
Rot and consume themselves
    in little time."

Shakespeare,
from *Venus and Adonis*

"Two girls discover
the secret of life
in a sudden line of
poetry."

"The Secret"
Denise Levertov, 1964

4

Advanced Principles

THE BIG MYTH

In writing this book, time and again we encountered students (and even instructors) who said, in one way or another, "A book on the GRE Literature in English Subject Test? But it can't be studied for!"

There was a time when people said just that about the SAT. The Princeton Review proved the SAT (and a host of other tests) could be cracked, and the same is true of the GRE Literature in English Subject Test.

When taking standardized tests, there are two things you must know. First, you must know how the test is written. Second, you must know what the test *actually* tests, because when it comes to standardized exams, in almost every case what is tested differs from what the test writers claim. In the case of the GRE Literature in English Subject Test, much less is tested than ETS leads you to believe.

The big myth of the GRE Literature in English Subject Test is that it tests English literature (all of it, from about the year C.E. 300 up to yesterday), in addition to classical authors (Homer, Virgil, etc.) and "world" authors like Goethe, Dante, Tolstoy, Balzac, and . . . and . . . and . . . . That's when the cold sweat breaks out. We've seen another book on the GRE Literature in English Subject Test that "offers" a seven-page, single-spaced reading list. It doesn't tell you what to look for, it just spews title after title. The list amounts to whole library shelves worth of reading matter—tens of thousands of pages. Clearly the folks who put that list together believed the hype. Suppose you did read and master that list, then *why bother with graduate school*? That list must surely be worth a degree or two.

This myth doesn't reflect reality. Once you understand the severe limitations the test writers face, you'll realize that the GRE Literature in English Subject Test can be studied for, very practically and within a reasonable amount of time.

Although this chapter contains some specific techniques, it is essentially a detailed introduction to our study lists. That said, you might be tempted to go straight to our study lists, but we strongly recommend you follow this chapter closely. It explains how we put our lists together. Read this chapter and you'll understand the rationale behind our materials; you'll understand how the test writers write the test and what the test doesn't test. Knowing these things, you'll be able to take full advantage of what we offer. You'll be able to tailor your studying to the GRE Literature in English Subject Test, and instead of trying to read endless shelves of material, 99.99 percent of which is never tested, you'll study just the right page, the right poem, and sometimes even the right line of a poem.

"THE MASS OF MEN LEAD LIVES OF QUIET DESPERATION" — H. D. THOREAU

Thoreau must have been talking about the ETS test writers, especially the ones responsible for putting together the GRE Literature in English Subject Test.

Imagine trying to write a multiple-choice test that measures a given student's knowledge of literature in English. The test should pertain to the demands of widely differing graduate programs, it should assess the abilities of students who have studied in any one of the thousands of undergraduate English departments around the world, and it should be as valid for the student returning to academia after a decade or more out of school as for the 22-year-old with a newly minted diploma. The task is impossible. No test could take into account the differences in curricula and emphases that so broad a population will have encountered in their four or so years of college study.

This poses something of a bind for the test writers, as they still have to write a test, impossible task or not. Their solution (perhaps the only solution) is to seek the common ground. "What," the test writers ask, "can we reasonably expect *any* semi-recent English B.A. graduate to have studied and know?" Keep that question in mind. It is vital to your study for the GRE Literature in English Subject Test and to your study of this book.

WHAT CAN ETS REASONABLY EXPECT ANY SEMI-RECENT ENGLISH B.A. GRADUATE TO HAVE STUDIED AND KNOW?

The answer is a surprising one—not very much. There is almost no truly common ground that all students cover. The number of different authors and works studied in all the English departments in all the colleges and universities of the United States (and Great Britain, Canada, Australia, New Zealand, South Africa, Jamaica, Belize, etc.) is staggering. Tackling the ridiculous seven-page reading list we mentioned earlier would still only familiarize you with a drop in the bucket of the possible material. Can you think of even one title that has been studied by *every single* English major within the past ten years? We can't, and neither can ETS.

The lack of a standard undergraduate English curriculum works in your favor.

WHAT'S BAD FOR THE TEST WRITERS IS GOOD FOR YOU

The overabundance of material is not a problem for you, it is a problem for the *test writers*. The lack of a standard English curriculum limits the test writers' possibilities dramatically.

ETS compromises by selecting the material it believes (hopes) the majority of students has studied and by selecting material "important" enough to justify its inclusion. Despite the appearance of a world of literature to choose from, there is very little that can be reliably and reasonably tested by the GRE Literature in English Subject Test.

HERE'S WHAT ETS THINKS YOU SHOULD KNOW

Back in Chapter 2, we gave you the ETS spin on what the GRE Literature in English Subject Test covers. Here's our version.

The GRE Literature in English Subject Test covers:

- Reading difficult texts for meaning

- Basic grammar

- Basic differences among some common schools of criticism

- Recognition of some famous authors and knowledge of facts pertaining to those authors

- Recognition of some famous works and allusions to those famous works

- Literary terms

READING COMPREHENSION AND GRAMMAR

Now, as to the first two subjects mentioned—reading comprehension and basic English grammar—we think you should know them, too. This book does *not* include a focused section on reading comprehension, nor one on grammar, because we think you probably already know how to tackle these questions based on your high-school and college education. We will, however, help you out with some of our general test-taking techniques. Here's what we do have to say about those topics.

Reading Comprehension

There is a sizable amount of reading comprehension on the GRE Literature in English Subject Test. Roughly 30 percent of the questions directly ask what a particular passage means or implies, and in many more questions, getting the right answer will in large part depend on understanding what you've read. Some comprehension questions are easy, but many are not. As an aspiring English grad student, you are probably pretty confident of your ability to understand what you read. Keep in mind that the GRE Literature in English Subject Test is designed to tax the abilities of prospective grad students, people who in some sense want to become professional readers. As strong as your reading skills may be, don't be surprised if you are occasionally challenged.

All told, however, reading comprehension is one area of the GRE Literature in English Subject Test that your undergraduate education should have prepared you for, assuming that your course work involved reading difficult texts for meaning.

In terms of The Princeton Review's technique, approach these questions as you would any other multiple-choice question. Use POE. Use the two-pass system. Passages you are familiar with will be far easier than those from authors and eras about which you know little.

Finally, a little practice will go a very long way. If you spent your senior year immersed in a specialty subject, studying just Post-Colonial literature, for example, or if you've simply been out of school for a while, you are probably rusty on the material you studied earlier, and not just on the details (e.g., What's Desdemona's maid's name again?), but on the comprehension end of things as well. The remedy for this is to refresh your skills. This is especially true of pre-nineteenth-century material. If, for example, you haven't read a metaphysical poem in a few years, by all means read one. In all likelihood, there is no need to make a special point of doing this. As you study the materials we present in this book and work through our diagnostic, you'll be presented with an enormous variety of texts. We'll point out the details you need to know, and as you go looking for the details we mention, keep in mind that comprehension does matter. For example, if you're looking over a section of Milton's *Paradise Lost* in order to familiarize yourself with Milton's style, you may find that you aren't sure what he's talking about. When this occurs, slow down and reread until the lines make complete sense, until you can restate them in your own words. Do that and you'll hone your Literature in English comprehension skills and cement your knowledge of the style in question.

Sample Reading Comprehension Questions

The best way to get the hang of reading comprehension test questions is to practice. Please refer to these four sample passages, questions, and explanations that follow.

Passage I:

The reason, then, that ambiguity is more elaborate in poetry than in prose, other than the fact that the reader is
trained to expect it, seems to be that the presence of metre
Line and rhyme, admittedly irrelevant to the straightforward
(05) process of conveying a statement, makes it seem sensible to
diverge from the colloquial order of statement and so imply
several colloquial orders from which the statement has
diverged. But rhythm is a powerful weapon in itself, which
needs to be considered separately…
(10) However, one can oppose the use of rhythm to the use of
ambiguity, because an interest in rhythm makes a poet
long-winded, and ambiguity is a phenomenon of compression. Thus it is seldom that one finds relevant ambiguities
in Spenser or Marlowe, because their method is by a vari-
(15) ety of means to sustain a poetic effect for so long that the
poetic knot can be spread out at length…

1. This passage is taken from a critical work by:

   (A) Kenneth Burke
   (B) Cleanth Brooks
   (C) T. S. Eliot
   (D) William Empson
   (E) Harold Bloom

2. The passage mentions two authors. Which of the following is the name of a work by one of those authors?

(A) *The Duchess of Malfi*
(B) *King John*
(C) *Troilus and Cressida*
(D) *She Stoops to Conquer*
(E) *Tamburlaine*

3. Which of the following does the author of this passage offer as evidence that "ambiguity is more elaborate in poetry than in prose" (lines 1–2)?

(A) A "phenomenon of compression" (lines 12–13)
(B) A "variety of means to sustain a poetic effect" (lines 14–15)
(C) The "poetic knot can be spread out at length" (line 16)
(D) The "straightforward process of conveying a statement" (lines 4–5)
(E) The "presence of metre and rhyme" (lines 3–4)

Here's How to Crack It

1. This passage is pulled from William Empson's *Seven Types of Ambiguity* (1930), so even if you're not familiar with Empson's work (his other big one is *Some Versions of Pastoral* [1935]) in detail, you can still identify this passage by how frequently the word "ambiguity" is used. This work is an important example of 20th century literary criticism. The thing to remember when dealing with literary critics is that they can often be identified by key words they use.

Each of the critics in the answer choices has a special set of buzzwords that show up over and over in their criticism: for Burke, the words are "symbols," "pentad," and the description of literature as "equipment for living." Cleanth Brooks is a famous New Critic, whose major contributions to literary criticism have to do with "paraphrase" (from "The Heresy of Paraphrase" in *The Well-Wrought Urn*), "irony" (from "Irony as a Principle of Structure"), and "paradox." Harold Bloom has been incredibly prolific, but his major work of criticism is *The Anxiety of Influence*, which charts literary influence via what Bloom calls a kind of "misreading" or "misprision." Eliot is the toughest to pin down here—if you see "objective correlative," you know it's Eliot, but otherwise, the ideas contained in "Criticism and the Individual Talent" and "The Metaphysical Poets" are his most famous. It wouldn't be a bad idea to scan over these texts if you haven't already. For cracking this particular passage, note that the buzz word for Empson is "ambiguity," therefore, the answer is (D).

2. Two authors are mentioned in the passage, Spenser and Marlowe. Since none of the answer choices refer to poems, we can eliminate Spenser as a possibility. Thus, the author referred to here is Christopher Marlowe. If you know that Christoper Marlowe wrote *Tamburlaine*, then this question is simple. If you didn't know, or you're not sure, you can still work through this question. *King John* (ca. 1590) and *Troilus and Cressida* (ca. 1602) are both by William Shakespeare. Since

there are two works by the same author, both can't be right and must therefore both be wrong. *She Stoops to Conquer* (1773) is by Oliver Goldsmith, and is considered an example of Restoration comedy, so it is of a different genre than the others. It can be eliminated. *The Duchess of Malfi* (1612–1613) is by John Webster. Even if you were unsure which work was by Marlowe, you should be able to eliminate the two Shakespeare answers, and if you can eliminate even one answer choice, you should guess! The correct answer is (E).

3. This is about as straightforward a Reading-Comprehension question as ETS will give you on this exam. Essentially, you just need to unpack a few clauses in the first sentence, and not get too distracted by the other answer choices. Make sure you are answering the question, and consider the question in its most basic sense: What makes poetry different than prose? The presence of rhyme and rhythm. Done! Answer: (E).

Passage II:

> No worst, there is none. Pitched past with grief,
> More pangs will, schooled at forepangs, wilder wring.
> Comforter, where, where is your comforting?
> *Line* Mary, mother of us, where is your relief?
> *(05)* My cries heave, herds-long; huddle in a main, a chief
> Woe, world-sorrow; on an age-old anvil wince and sing—
> Then lull, then leave off. Fury had shrieked 'No ling-
> ering! Let me be fell: force I must be brief'.
> O the mind, mind has mountains; cliffs of fall
> *(10)* Frightful, sheer, no-man-fathomed. Hold them cheap
> May who ne'er hung there. Nor does long our small
> Durance deal with that steep or deep. Here! Creep,
> Wretch, under a comfort serves in a whirlwind: all
> Life does end and each day dies with sleep.

4. The final line of this poem is an allusion to a line spoken by the character Prospero in which Shakespeare play?

   (A) *Macbeth*
   (B) *The Tempest*
   (C) *Richard III*
   (D) *Cymbeline*
   (E) *All's Well That Ends Well*

5. Which of the following is the antecedent for the word "there" (line 11)?

   (A) "forepangs" (line 2)
   (B) "world-sorrow" (line 6)
   (C) "Fury" (line 7)
   (D) "the mind" (line 9)
   (E) "cliffs" (line 9)

6. The passage is an example of

   (A) mock epic
   (B) villanelle
   (C) sprung rhythm
   (D) Middle English alliterative verse
   (E) imagism

Here's How to Crack It:

4. Prospero is a character in *The Tempest*, but even if you didn't know that, it is possible to make an educated guess. This question provides an excellent example of name recognition as the key to catching Shakespeare allusions. Even if you're not sure where Prospero comes from, you can eliminate (A), (C), and (D) immediately because these plays are set in Anglophone countries—Scotland, England, and Roman Britain, respectively, making the characters unlikely to have an Italian-sounding name like Prospero. Be aware that this is not an exact science (and not totally foolproof, either), but it can be a great way to think about a question you might otherwise have to leave blank. *All's Well That Ends Well* may have caught your eye, but this play is set in southwestern France. This allusion is to *The Tempest*, Act IV, Scene 1, lines 156–157: "We are such stuff/As dreams are made on, and our little life/Is rounded with a sleep." The answer is (B).

5. Use the semi-colon to your advantage here. "O the mind, mind has mountains; cliffs of fall/Frightful, sheer, no-man-fathomed. Hold them cheap/May who ne'er hung there." The question is a bit tricky because the entire passage is all a big metaphor for the mind, the clearest referent for the word is "cliffs." Notice that everything after the semi-colon modifies the word "mountains" (i.e., what the mind "has"), rather than the mind itself. Knowledge of the sonnet form can help here as well: "O the mind" begins the sestet, which you can take as a hint that "O the mind" begins a new unit in the poem (placed alongside the first eight lines of the sonnet, the "octave.") Therefore the answer is (E).

6. If you recognized this poem as "No worst, there is none" by Gerard Manley Hopkins, you've got yourself a pretty safe bet with "sprung rhythm," the weird pattern of stresses that Hopkins developed that basically threw the practice of counting syllables out the window (or cast it into the wreckage in "The Wreck of the Deutschland"). All that counts here are stressed syllables, so even though many of the lines have different numbers of total syllables, the stressed ones are all that count. Even if you weren't able to connect the poem with Hopkins, you should be able to recognize sprung rhythm. The answer here is (C).

For full definitions of sprung rhythm and other literary terms, see our Glossary of Literary Terms in Chapter 5.

Passage III:

Thus I live in the World, rather as a Spectator of Mankind, than as one of the Species; by which means I have made my self a Speculative States-man, Soldier, Merchant, and Artizan, without ever meddling with any Practical Part in Life. I am very well versed in the Theory of an Husband, or a Father, and can discern the Errors in the Œconomy, Business, and Diversion of others, better than those who are engaged in them; as Standers-by discover Blots, which are apt to escape those who are in the Game. I never espoused any Party with Violence, and am resolved to observe an exact Neutrality between the Whigs and Tories, unless I shall be forc'd to declare myself by the Hostilities of either side. In short, I have acted in all the parts of my Life as a Looker-on, which is the Character I intend to preserve in this Paper.

7. This passage was first published in the

    (A) Fifteenth Century
    (B) Sixteenth Century
    (C) Seventeenth Century
    (D) Eighteenth Century
    (E) Nineteenth Century

8. One of the main authors of this publication is

    (A) Joseph Addison
    (B) Samuel Johnson
    (C) Jonathon Swift
    (D) John Donne
    (E) Daniel Defoe

9. One of the major authors of this publication contributed to which other publication?

    (A) *The Review*
    (B) *The Rambler*
    (C) *The Examiner*
    (D) *The Tatler*
    (E) *The Female Spectator*

Here's How to Crack It

7. This passage is taken from the first issue of *The Spectator*, first published in 1711. If you get a question dealing with periodical nonfiction (which is what this is), it's almost certain that it will be from the eighteenth century. *The Spectator*, written and edited by Joseph Addison and Richard Steele, and *The Rambler*, written and edited by Samuel Johnson, are the two most famous "papers" (also commonly referred to as "periodical essays"), and both of these were published in the eighteenth century. Many of the other novelists of the period took up the periodical form (e.g., Defoe, Swift, Pope), but their contributions to the form are not nearly so famous as those of Addison, Steele, and Johnson. The form really took off in this period with the emergence of what Jürgen Habermas has famously called the "public sphere." The periodical essay is an important component of 18th century British literature, and it's as important to know (and fortunately as easy to recognize) as many of the novels and poems. Now that you know all this, you surely know that the answer is: (D).

8. All of these authors, except Donne, were major forces behind some periodical, so even knowing only that you can eliminate John Donne, and following our recommendations, if you can eliminate one answer, you should guess! But if you were able to reason beyond that first step, you should consider that if ETS is going to test any of the other authors, they're likely to test their more characteristic writings, since each has a particular work or two for which he is especially known; for example, if they're going to test Defoe, they're a lot more likely to give you a passage from *Robinson Crusoe* than his tri-weekly periodical *The Review* (1704–1713). Now you've eliminated three choices. Notice now the presence of the word "Spectator" in the first line. This should indicate right off the bat that the author of this passage is Addison if you are at all familiar with 18th century

periodicals. The question says "one of the main authors" because authorship of *The Spectator* is typically credited to both Joseph Addison and Richard Steele. So, the answer here is: (A).

9. Let's look at these answer choices: *The Female Spectator* is the wild card here, but the good news is that if you do get a question about it, it's really easy to identify by its authorship; it's the only one of the major periodical essays written by an explicitly female author. So, for this question, you should be able to eliminate that based on intuition. You're likely to get a question about 18th century periodicals on the test, so let's look closely at these other titles: Richard Steele started *The Tatler* in 1709, and under the pseudonym Isaac Bickerstaff published his "lucubrations" (whatever those are) in this journal until starting *The Spectator* with Addison in 1711. *The Review* was Daniel Defoe's gig; *The Rambler* was Samuel Johnson; *The Examiner* was Jonathan Swift; and *The Female Spectator* was Eliza Haywood. Addison and Steele are almost always referred to together, and they're easy to remember because their major contributions to the literature of the period were all in these periodical essays. Again, if they're going to test an author like Defoe, Swift, or even Johnson, it's likely they'll test from one of these authors' major non-periodical works. So, knowing all that, you should now see that the answer is: (D).

Passage IV:

> "…You've plenty; that's the great thing; you're, as
> I say, damn you, so happily and hatefully young.
> Don't at any rate miss things out of stupidity. Of
> *Line* course I don't take you for a fool, or I shouldn't
> (05) be addressing you thus awfully. Do what you like
> so long as you don't make my mistake. For it was
> a mistake. Live!"…Slowly and sociably, with full
> pauses and straight dashes, Strether had so deliv-
> ered himself; holding little Bilham from step to step
> (10) deeply and gravely attentive. The end of all was that
> the young man had turned quite solemn, and that
> this was a contradiction of the innocent gaiety the
> speaker had wished to promote. He watched for a
> moment the consequence of his words, laying a hand
> (15) on his listener's knee as if to end with the proper
> joke: "And now for the eye I shall keep on you!"

10. The author of this passage is also the author of

(A) *Howards End*
(B) *The Bostonians*
(C) *The Age of Innocence*
(D) *A Hazard of New Fortunes*
(E) *Nostromo*

11. In context, the word "consequence" in line 14 most nearly means

(A) import
(B) meaning
(C) humor
(D) effect
(E) ending

12. What is the purpose of the quotation in lines 1–7 in
the context of the passage?

  (A) Strether jokes with Bilham regarding his own
      mistakes but it becomes clear that he dislikes
      Bilham intensely.
✓ (B) Strether laments the loss of his youth and takes
      on an unexpectedly serious tone in encourag-
      ing Bilham to enjoy his own.
  (C) Strether warns Bilham that Bilham will be
      closely watched to ensure that he acts properly
      and makes no mistakes.
  (D) Strether snubs Bilham, insisting that Bilham not
      trouble him with his mistakes again. (E)
      Strether chides Bilham for being irresponsible
      and looks to make Bilham atone for his mis-
      takes.

10. This passage comes from *The Ambassadors* (1903). This passage is part of the climactic scene in the book during which the main character, Lambert Strether, urges Little Bilham to live his life to the fullest. While we do not advocate trying to spot all authors by their style, there are some characteristics unique to certain authors that make them identifiable. The passage is characteristic James in that the sentences are long, with clause piled upon clause and heavy use of pronouns without obvious antecedents (though the pronouns do have antecedents). Along with Isabel Archer (from *The Portrait of a Lady*), Maggie Verver (from *The Golden Bowl*), and Daisy Miller, Lambert Strether is probably the most famous of all James's characters. In any case, James was also the author of *The Bostonians*. The other novels listed in the answer choices are more or less contemporary with *The Ambassadors* (or the authors were James's contemporaries), but the novels are by different authors: *Howards End* (1910) is by E. M. Forster; *The Age of Innocence* (1920) is by Edith Wharton; *A Hazard of New Fortunes* (1890) is by William Dean Howells; and *Nostromo* (1904) is by Joseph Conrad. If you are not familiar with any of these works or their authors, this would be a difficult question to answer. Remember that if you run across a question like that on the test, don't be afraid to skip it and come back to it. The answer to this question is (B).

11. This question can be answer simply by logically working through the material in the passage. Strether watches "for a moment the consequence of his words"; in other words, he watches to see the effect his words have on Bilham. Unfortunately, the effect is not as intended; while Strether had meant to promote "innocent gaiety" (but did he really mean it?) Bilham has "turned quite solemn." The answer is (D).

12. There are about six sentences and the single word command, "Live!" in this quotation. Only one of these sentences really gets at what Strether is trying to say: "Don't at any rate miss things out of stupidity," and he sums it all up in the command, "Live!" When you put the pieces together, it becomes clear that Strether's "mistake" is that he didn't enjoy things while he was young, and he is trying to prevent Bilham from making the same mistake, pointing to (B) as the answer. *The Ambassadors* is "late James." It's usually lumped together with *The Wings of the Dove* and *The Golden Bowl* in what's called James's "Major Phase," his

period of greatest achievement but greatest difficulty. For the latter reason especially, these are highly likely to show up on Reading Comprehension questions.

Grammar for the Literature in English Subject Test

The GRE Literature in English Subject Test does not test esoteric grammar. You will not be asked anything like, "What are three examples of the dative case in English?" Your knowledge of grammar will be tested at about the same level as it was tested in high school. You need to know the basic parts of speech: noun, verb, adjective, and adverb. You need to know the difference between a direct object and an indirect object, a subject and a predicate, a dependent and an independent clause. If that sounds like a piece of cake, well, there is just one catch.

Literature in English grammar questions are actually a disguised kind of reading comprehension question. ETS likes to ask its grammar questions on long, tangled, difficult sentences, usually from verse. It's one thing to know what a direct object is, but it's quite another to find the direct object in a sentence you don't understand. To answer Literature in English grammar questions, make sure you comprehend the selection.

Here's an example:

> My vouch against you, and my place i' th' state
> Will so your accusation overweigh,
> That you shall stifle in your own report
> And smell of calumnie.

The controlling verb of the main clause is:

(A) Vouch
(B) Overweigh
(C) Stifle
(D) Report
(E) Smell

Here's How to Crack It

POE lets you get rid of "vouch" and "report" (both of which are used as nouns, not verbs), but you should see that this question is more about comprehension than it is about grammar. The best way to go about tackling it, if the answer isn't immediately obvious, is to rephrase and translate the sentence into a more manageable form. Something like this:

"My claim and position will so outweigh your accusation that you will choke on your own words and be the one slandered."

From this, you should be able to see the compound subject "My claim and position" takes the verb "outweigh." This corresponds to "overweigh" in the original passage. (B) is the correct answer. (By the way, the passage is from Shakespeare's *Measure for Measure*, II. iv.)

If you find you do need to review basic grammar, we recommend *Grammar Smart*, by the staff of The Princeton Review.

AUTHORS, TITLES, ALLUSIONS, AND LITERARY CRITICISM

"Thou art my father, thou my author, thou my being gav'st me; whom should I obey but thee, whom follow?"

Paradise Lost *Book 2, lines 864–865, John Milton, 1667*

This book concentrates on the areas that cause the vast majority of students problems (and anxiety) on the GRE Literature in English Subject Test: identifying authors, works, allusions, and (to a lesser extent) critical schools.

QUANTITY VS. QUALITY

In our advice on reading comprehension, we mentioned that you should read the first book of Milton's *Paradise Lost* in order to familiarize yourself with that poem. You will not have to read all of *Paradise Lost* in order to study for the Literature in English Test. In college, you may well have studied the poem's larger philosophic import, the implications of Milton's profound and idiosyncratic Christianity, and the effect of his thought on writers of later generations. *None of that is tested*. This information, of course, does not apply solely to *Paradise Lost*. It applies to all of the literature tested on the subject test.

None of the deeper issues of any work is tested on the GRE Literature in English Subject Test.

No matter what masterpiece we're talking about, when it comes to the subject test, the deepest you'll be required to go will be to identify from among five answer choices what one tiny portion of that masterpiece (a portion right there in front of you) means.

Read *Paradise Lost* while you're waiting for those acceptance letters to come pouring in; write a brilliant dissertation on it in grad school. Go ahead, study all the great works of every culture and of all time; but don't do it for the GRE Literature in English Subject Test.

The GRE Literature in English Subject Test wants quantity, not quality.

> You will never be tested on the deeper issues of literature.

THE WORST PARTY YOU'LL EVER ATTEND

The GRE Literature in English Subject Test is like a horrible cocktail party full of insufferable poseurs intent on name-dropping while grilling you on trivial gibberish ("I was over at Billy's little soiree the other night at the Globe, private screening of his latest, Hamlink or something, anyway it's just faboo, *very* artistic . . . and who's sitting next me? Dicky Burbage, that's who. . . ."). Your job is to keep up with the chatter.

As we mentioned, you don't need to know very much about literature in any scholarly sense, but you do need to know the cocktail-party details. Take Shakespeare's *Hamlet*, for example: You might need to know that it was first performed at the Globe Theater. You should also know the principal characters of the play, and the barest outlines of the plot. We used *Hamlet* as an example here because we're pretty sure anyone reading this book knows something about it. The truth is Shakespeare is a special case and we'll talk about how to deal with him specifically later.

The point we want you to hold onto is this:

> ETS is never going to ask you anything that requires true depth. As you study, ask yourself, "What do I need to know in order to fake it at the cocktail party?" If you can catch the right name, nod at the right time, *pretend you've read the book when all you've read is the review* . . . you'll ace this test.

HEY, NORTON!

Remember when we said that there is no standard curriculum for English majors and that this fact makes your life easier and the test writers' much harder? Well, there is one near standard factor: *The Norton Anthology of English Literature*. It is a required text for the vast majority of English majors. If you sold yours back to the bookstore (for what? $2.00 or something?), borrow one immediately. Other than this book, *The Norton Anthology* is your best friend on the GRE Literature in English Subject Test. The ETS writers consider everything in volumes I and II of *The Norton Anthology* fair game. Does this mean we're saying you have to read the entire Norton collection: *The Norton Anthology of Poetry* and the *Norton Anthology of Modern Poetry*, etc., etc.? No! Don't panic.

You need a copy of *The Norton Anthology of English Literature* (or other comparable anthology) because it is a handy place to find almost everything we will suggest you read. Leave it around, and in your spare time, read the introductory chapters, starting with what you know least well. Don't know much about Old English? Read the introduction to the Middle Ages. Don't know much about Victorian essayists? Read the introductory chapter to the Victorian Age. Much of what you read will be reiterated here, but the reinforcement is valuable, and though the Norton can be dry, its introductions do an excellent job of contextualizing writers and their times. The more context you have, the easier it is to remember details.

Norton is great, but what may be even more helpful are references—quick sources for identifying key facts about authors. We recommend *Benet's Reader's Encyclopedia*, the *Oxford Guide to Literature in English*, and even Wikipedia can be a good reference!

FLASHCARDS

Because so much of this test has to do with the minutiae of literature rather than big narrative arcs or movements, flashcards can be extremely valuable in helping you to remember many of the details of works, literary terms, concepts, and authors. As you'll see reading through this book, different literary time periods are tested differently, but keep in mind that flashcards are important tools no matter what genre or time period.

At some point in your career as a student you've probably used flashcards as study tools, but, in case you haven't, we've given you a few examples of how you might use them for this test. If you are concerned about literary terms, you could make card with the term on the front. On the back would be its definition and at least one example of a work where this term is used. It should look something like this:

FRONT OF CARD: Caesura

BACK OF CARD: Pause in the middle of a line of poetry. Used in
Old English verse. EXAMPLE: See Beowulf.

It's likely that by the time you are done, you'll have a ton of them, so remember less is more on each individual card. As you're making these flashcards, always remember that this is a basic knowledge test, and that you do not have to learn every detail to do well on this test. To help remind yourself of this, have a look at some of the questions in your own area of specialization. You'll probably find that everything you love about these works, the nuances and details, has been stripped from the questions and passages.

The easiest flashcards to make and memorize are the ones that have to do with literary terms. Use the glossary we've given you in this book. Our glossary is fairly exhaustive, but if you feel like you need more practice, flip through a dictionary of literary terms to catch any others you think might be useful. Make sure you understand the terms: a good flashcard will contain the definition and a quick example.

For Classical literature, your primary goal is to be able to spot allusions, and the most important thing in spotting an allusion is to spot names. As such, make sure you've got a basic sense of those on the Greek Gods cheat sheet. See our section on the Greek gods in Chapter 7. A great flashcard on Hestia, for example, would look like this:

FRONT OF CARD: Hestia

BACK OF CARD: Greek goddess of the hearth (and the home).
Roman name: Vesta.

Whenever possible, also include an example of an allusion to the god or goddess that is made in a later work of literature.

A bad flashcard (bad insofar as it won't be useful to you) might say this: "Hestia is the goddess of the hearth. She's the daughter of Cronus and Rhea and was the first to be swallowed by Cronus and then spit out. Apollo and Poseidon wanted to marry her, but she swore to remain a virgin forever. Hestia/Vesta was believed to have invented the art of building houses and, because of the altar's association with the hearth, was also believed to preside over all sacrifices…" Hyperbole, yes, but such hyperbole is indicative of exactly the kind of thing you don't want to do. Focus on the main points, NOT details.

Names are very important in catching allusions to the Bible as well, although at least a short passage from the Bible is likely to show up in Reading Comprehension. Flashcards for biblical names should include a brief summary of that name's story:

FRONT OF CARD: Abraham

BACK OF CARD: Abraham had a son named Ishmael with his
wife's servant Hagar and then a son named Isaac
with Sarah. God asked A. to sacrifice Isaac but
stopped him at the last minute. From: Genesis

Flashcards that chart allusions can be useful as well. These allusion flashcards are extremely useful because it's like killing two birds with one stone, but they are a lot harder to track down:

FRONT OF CARD: *The Sun Also Rises*

BACK OF CARD: by Hemingway. Novel about a group of Americans dealing with post-WWI life, living in Europe. Allusions: The title is a biblical allusion to "Ecclesiastes."

All other flashcards will be doing some version of the above. For some of the bigger name authors (Chaucer, Milton, Shakespeare, Austen, etc), make a bunch of flashcards listing key terms, allusions, characters, and titles of major works associated with these authors. Shakespeare's major plays, for example, warrant a flashcard each. Even here, though, don't overdo it. A flashcard shouldn't have much more on it than a sentence plot summary, major characters, and any heavily alluded-to lines. For example:

FRONT OF CARD: King Lear

BACK OF CARD: King asks his daughters who loves him more, and they all fawn over him in a big power play. King goes nuts out on the heath. Daughters: Regan, Goneril, Cordelia (the good one). Other characters: Gloucester, Edmund, Edgar, Albany. Big quotes: 'Nothing shall come of nothing.

Similar cards can be useful for the major Canterbury Tales, Austen's novels, etc. For the authors who aren't so heavily tested, flashcards that give the author's dates (really just the author's century of most productivity is fine), major titles, major characters, and a line or two about that author's style:

FRONT OF CARD: Thomas Pynchon

BACK OF CARD: Late twentieth century. The Crying of Lot 49; Gravity's Rainbow; V. Oedipa Maas (49); Tyrone Slothrop (GR). Encyclopedic, heavily allusive (to literature, history, and pop-culture), dense prose. Postmodernism.

The key is, however you make your flashcards, don't overdo it. You can't learn everything, but you can learn a little bit about a whole lot if you use your flashcards strategically.

NAMES

Now that you've mastered the art of using flashcards as study tools, you're ready to start prioritizing the study material. So here it is: the most important details to keep track of in your study for the GRE Literature in English Subject Test are names. Pay attention to the names—of authors, of characters, anybody of importance mentioned within a text. Many, *many* of the questions on the GRE Literature in English Subject Test are a piece of cake if you can just recognize a *name*. Are we being too emphatic? *No, we are not being too emphatic!!!* NAMES.

This brings up an extremely important point regarding guessing: Don't guess obscure names for the sake of obscurity. Obscure names are more often wrong than right. The test writers' goal is to test you on what you can reasonably be expected to know. If, after four years of college, you find an answer choice totally unfamiliar, then chances are it isn't something you "should" know. When you get down to two answers and with nothing else to go on are faced with a choice between a major author (or work) and Mr. X, *pick the major author*. Are we saying never pick the obscure answer choice? No. When you can eliminate the other choices, go ahead and take the one that's left.

DATES

Knowing the period during which an author wrote is important. As you use POE to answer questions, you will often find yourself eliminating choices because they are chronologically impossible. While working on a question, you might find yourself saying something like, "No, Dryden could not be the answer here because the passage states that the author in question influenced Marlowe, and Dryden is too late a figure for that to be possible." In the explanations to the questions on the diagnostic (in Part V), we'll point out several instances where reasoning this way can eliminate several choices.

At the same time, many students make the mistake of studying dates too closely. You do not need to memorize the birth and death dates of important authors, and it is an utter waste of time to do so.

Instead, you should know the chronology of important phases in English literature. You should know with which broad period any given author is associated. You should know when Old English and Middle English were being written. Essentially, given two authors or works, you should be able to identify the period of each, and say whether one precedes the other or that they are contemporaries. Our outline of English literary history, provided in Chapter 8, will give you just that information.

LITERARY TERMS

The GRE Literature in English Subject Test also includes some questions on literary terms. You do not need to know the specialized terminology of individual critical schools. You needn't sweat what Derrida means by "différance," nor what a postcolonial critic means by the "colonial other." The literary terms ETS queries are the old-fashioned kind, such as metaphor, metonymy, and enjambment. Because the majority of these terms are used in the discussion of poetry, so you may already be familiar with them. Whether or not that is the case, these terms will absolutely show up on the exam. That said, learning literary terms is simply a study of vocabulary. In Chapter 5, we offer a glossary of the literary terms that frequently appear on the GRE Literature in English Subject Test. Absolutely study them; they're free points. Use your flashcards to maximize your study time.

> Q: The following titles allude to other famous works. Can you identify those works?
>
> *The Sound and The Fury* by William Faulkner
>
> *Tender Is the Night* by F. Scott Fitzgerald
>
> *For Whom the Bell Tolls* by Ernest Hemingway
>
> *Things Fall Apart* by Chinua Achebe

> Study the terms and examples laid out in our glossary on pages 52–66.

CROSS-REFERENCES

ETS's favorite game is catch the reference. (They'll often call it an allusion.) Basically, many of the questions on the GRE Literature in English Subject Test will involve a passage that refers in some way to another work. The reference might be a quoted line or the mention of an author. The reference might be that the selection for a particular question is a parody of another work, or (and this is a favorite) that a relatively modern selection harkens back to an earlier form. ETS seems to think it says wonders about your education if you can spot a nineteenth-century author using the conventions of the Homeric epic. ETS loves it when you can catch an oblique reference to Andrew Marvell's "To His Coy Mistress."

We're going to use the same passage you saw when we explained our approach to POE, but now we're going to turn that passage into four super POE questions, with three of the four questions we ask relying on your ability to cross-reference the passage to another author's work. The point here is to show you the kinds of cross-references and allusions the test writers use to come up with questions.

If you paid attention to our discussion of the wrong answers in the POE section on pages 22–23, you should have no problems here. If you have trouble finding the answers to questions 1–4 below, return to that section and look over our explanations.

Questions 1–4 refer to the passage and answer choices below.

> The chateau into which my valet had ventured to
> make forcible entrance, rather than permit me,
> in my desperately wounded condition, to pass a
> night in the open air, was one of those piles of
> commingled gloom and grandeur which have
> so long frowned among the Apennines, not less
> in fact than in the fancy of Mrs. Radcliffe. To
> all appearance it had been temporarily and very
> lately abandoned.

(A) Ernest Hemingway's *A Farewell to Arms*
(B) Jane Austen's *Northanger Abbey*
(C) Joseph Conrad's *Heart of Darkness*
(D) Horace Walpole's *The Castle of Otranto*
(E) Edgar Allan Poe's "The Oval Portrait"

1. Which novel of war is set in the same locale as that of the passage?

2. The passage mentions an author parodied in which work?

3. The passage alludes to conventions first found in which work?

4. From which work is the passage drawn?

A: *The Sound and The Fury* alludes to the lines: "it is a tale Told by an idiot, full of sound and fury, Signifying nothing," from Shakespeare's *Macbeth*.

Tender Is the Night alludes to a phrase from Keats's "Ode to a Nightingale."

For Whom the Bell Tolls alludes to: "Do not ask for whom the bell tolls. It tolls for thee," from a sermon by John Donne.

Things Fall Apart alludes to the line, "Things fall apart; The center cannot hold," from William Butler Yeats's "The Second Coming."

Any of these questions might appear on the GRE Literature in English Subject Test. The most unlikely is question 4. "The Oval Portrait" is too obscure a work for ETS to realistically expect you to identify it (although you could identify it using POE). Expect to see questions like 2 and 3; the questions that deal with Anne Radcliffe and the conventions of the gothic novel. Both these questions involve exactly the kind of cross-reference material ETS loves. You would not have needed to have read *Northanger Abbey*, or *The Castle of Otranto*. Either question could have been faked if you'd read the review.

A FEW MORE WORDS TO THE WISE:

MAKE SURE YOU LOOK AT THE QUESTIONS BEFORE YOU READ A PASSAGE

Sometimes questions only ask you about a couple of lines of a poem. You don't have to read the whole poem to find the answer, just those lines. Save yourself time and energy by reading only what you need to solve the question. Similarly, if the question asks who wrote a passage, and a name from the passage (say, "Pip") catches your eye, you don't have to read the passage. You know that Pip was a character in Dickens's *Great Expectations*. So make sure you look at the questions before you read a passage.

WHEN POSSIBLE, THINK OF YOUR OWN ANSWER BEFORE LOOKING AT THE BOOK'S OFFERINGS

On questions that test reading comprehension or grammar, cover the answer choices. Think of your answer first, jot it down in the margins, and then see which answer choice matches yours. This method ensures that you won't get swayed by answer choices that "feel right."

PART ◆ III

Cracking the System by Cracking the Books

5

Literary Terms,
Verse Forms, and
Schools of Criticism

INTRODUCTION TO LITERARY TERMS, VERSE FORMS, AND SCHOOLS OF CRITICISM

This chapter contains material selected specifically for the Literature in English Subject Test. There are, of course, entire books on literary terms and verse forms. As for literary criticism, it is an entire literature unto itself. We've made no attempt to write a reference work. We've pared the mass of information available down to the bleached bones; what remains is information you *must* know for the Literature in English Subject Test. Think of this chapter as some of the highest points-to-pages ratio study material you'll see.

A GLOSSARY OF LITERARY TERMS

ALEXANDRINE

A line of iambic hexameter. The final line of a Spenserian stanza is an alexandrine.

Example: "A needless alexandrine ends the song/that like a wounded snake, drags its slow length along." The second line of this couplet from Alexander Pope's "Essay on Criticism" is an alexandrine.

ALLITERATION

The use of a repeated consonant or sound, usually at the beginning of a series of words.

Example: "I have stood still and stopped the sound of feet/When far away an interrupted cry/Came over houses from another street..."
"Acquainted with the Night" by Robert Frost

ALLUSION

A reference to someone or something, usually literary.

Example: "Call me Ishmael." This opening line from *Moby-Dick* by Herman Melville is alludes to the biblical figure of Ishmael.

Example: The title of William Faulkner's novel, *The Sound and the Fury* is an allusion to Shakespeare's *Macbeth*: "...it is a tale/told by an idiot, full of sound and fury,/signifying nothing."

ANTAGONIST

The main character opposing the protagonist. Usually the villain.

Example: Iago, from Shakespeare's *Othello*, is the quintessence of an antagonist.

ANTHROPOMORPHISM

The assigning of human attributes, such as emotions or physical characteristics, to nonhumans, most often plants and animals. It differs from personification in that it is an intrinsic premise and an ongoing pattern applied to a nonhuman character throughout a literary work.

Example: The character of Aslan in C. S. Lewis' s *The Chronicles of Narnia* is a lion, but is addressed and behaves as a human.

Example: All the characters of George Orwell's anti-Communist novel *Animal Farm* are anthropomorphic.

Example: The Greek god Zeus is supposed to be superhuman but is often given to human emotions and behaviors.

APOSTROPHE

A speech addressed to someone not present, or to an abstraction. "History! You will remember me..." is an example of apostrophe. The innate grandiosity of apostrophe lends itself to parody.

Example: John Donne, in his poem "The Sun Rising," directly addresses the sun itself: "Busy old fool, unruly sun,/Why dost thou thus,/Through windows, and through curtains call on us?"

BILDUNGSROMAN

A German term meaning a "novel of education." It typically follows a young person over a period of years, from naïveté and inexperience through the first struggles with the harsher realities and hypocrisies of the adult world.

Example: *A Portrait of the Artist as a Young Man* by James Joyce and *The Catcher in the Rye* are both classic examples of coming-of-age novels.

CAESURA

The pause that breaks a line of Old English verse. Also, any particularly deep pause in a line of verse.

Example: "Hwæt! we Gar-Dena || on geardagum..." ("Lo! we Spear-Danes, in days of yore...") —*Beowulf*

Example: "Arma virumque cano, || Troiæ qui primus ab oris..:" ("I sing of arms and the man, who first from the shores of Troy...") —*Aeneid*

Decorum

One of the neoclassical principles of drama. Decorum is the relation of style to content in the speech of dramatic characters. For example, a character's speech should be appropriate to his or her social station.

Example: In Oscar Wilde's *The Importance of Being Earnest*, the characters regularly exhibit decorum in the way they speak.

Doggerel:

A derogatory term used to describe poorly written poetry of little or no literary value.

Example: Shakespeare is known to have purposely employed doggerel in dialogue between the Dromio twins in *The Comedy of Errors* for comedic effect.

Epithalamium

A work, especially a poem, written to celebrate a wedding.

Example: Edmund Spenser's "Epithalamium":

> Song! made in lieu of many ornaments,
>
> With which my love should duly have been dect,
>
> Which cutting off through hasty accidents,
>
> Ye would not stay your dew time to expect,
>
> But promist both to recompens;
>
> Be unto her a goodly ornament,
>
> And for short time an endlesse moniment.

Euphuism

A word derived from Lyly's *Euphues* (1580) to characterize writing that is self-consciously laden with elaborate figures of speech. This was a popular and influential mode of speech and writing in the late sixteenth century.

Example: The character of Polonius in Shakespeare's *Hamlet* demonstrates this literary device, exemplified by his most famous lines:

"To thine own self be true."

"Neither a borrower nor a lender be."

"Brevity is the soul of wit."

Q: The stanza below comes from which poem? Who wrote it?
"Young Juan wandered by the glassy brooks
Thinking unutterable things; he threw
Himself at length within the leafy nooks
Where the wild branch of the cork forest grew;
There poets find material for their books,
And every now and then we read them through,
So that their plan and prosody are eligible
Unless, like Wordsworth, they prove unintelligible."

Feminine Rhyme

Lines rhymed by their final two syllables. A pair of lines ending "running" and "gunning" would be an example of feminine rhyme. Properly, in a feminine rhyme (and not simply a "double rhyme") the penultimate syllables are stressed and the final syllables unstressed.

Example: Sonnet 20 – "A woman's face with nature's own hand" by William Shakespeare:

> A woman's face with Nature's own hand painted
>
> Hast thou, the master-mistress of my passion;
>
> A woman's gentle heart, but not acquainted
>
> With shifting change, as is false women's fashion...

Flat and Round Characters

Terms coined by E. M. Forster to describe characters built around a single dominant trait (flat characters), and those shaded and developed with greater psychological complexity (round characters).

Example of flat: The character of Mrs. Micawber in Charles Dickens' *David Copperfield* is a flat character.

Example of round: Anna Karenina in Leo Tolstoy's *Anna Karenina* is a round character.

Georgic

Not be confused with pastoral poetry, which idealizes life in the countryside, georgic poems deal with people laboring in the countryside, pushing plows, raising crops, etc.

Example: The work from which this term was derived is an excellent example of the term itself: Virgil's *Georgics*. Essentially, it's a poem about the virtues of the farming life.

Hamartia

Aristotle's term for what is popularly called "the tragic flaw." Hamartia differs from tragic flaw in that hamartia implies fate, whereas tragic flaw implies an inherent psychological flaw in the tragic character.

Example: Oedipus, in his hasty temper, is tragically flawed. Macbeth, in his lust for power, is also tragically flawed.

A: The stanza comes from *Don Juan*, Lord Byron's long, comic masterpiece. The verse form employed is ottava rima. By the way, Byron (and his pals Keats and Shelley) genuinely disliked Wordsworth; they felt betrayed by the political turnabout that saw the once freethinking Wordsworth become a crusty reactionary in his later years.

HOMERIC EPITHET

A repeated descriptive phrase, as found in Homer's epics.

Example: "Rosy-fingered dawn," "the wine-dark sea," and "the ever-re-sourceful Odysseus" are all examples.

HUDIBRASTIC

A term derived from Samuel Butler's *Hudibras*. It refers specifically to the couplets of rhymed tetrameter lines (well, eight syllables long, anyway), which Butler employed in *Hudibras*, or more generally to any deliberate, humorous, ill-rhythmed, ill-rhymed couplets. Butler had a genius for "bad" poetry.

Example:

> We grant, although he had much wit
> He was very shy of using it
> As being loathe to wear it out
> And therefore bore it not about,
> Unless on holidays, or so
> As men their best apparel do.
> Beside, tis' known he could speak Greek
> As naturally as pigs squeak.

HYPERBOLE

A deliberate exaggeration.

Example: "Here once embattled farmers stood/ And fired the shot heard round the world." This line from Ralph Waldo Emerson's "The Concord Hymn" denotes obvious exaggeration, employed for the purpose of highlighting the importance of that battle.

LITOTES

An understatement created through a double negative (or more precisely, negating the negative). It sounds more complicated than it is.

Example: From the Book of Acts in the Bible: "Paul answered, 'I am a Jew, from Tarsus in Cilicia, a citizen of **no ordinary city**. Please let me speak to the people.'" (Acts 21:39)

MASCULINE RHYME

A rhyme ending on the final stressed syllable (aka, regular old rhyme).

Example: Robert Frost's "Stopping by the Woods on a Snowy Evening" illustrates this term:

Whose woods these are I think I know.

His house is in the village though;

He will not see me stopping here

To watch his woods fill up with snow.

METONYMY

A term for a phrase that refers to a person or object by a single important feature of the person.

Example: The famous line, "The pen is mightier than the sword," from Edward Bulwer-Lytton's play *Richelieu*, is an example of metonymy. The sentence is essentially saying that the written word is often more powerful and influential than acts of war and violence, but it uses the pen to represent the written word, and the sword to represent violent acts.

NEOCLASSICAL UNITIES

Principles of dramatic structure derived (and applied somewhat too strictly) from Aristotle's *Poetics*. They are called the neoclassical unities because of their popularity in the neoclassical movement of the seventeenth and eighteenth centuries. The essential unities are of time, place, and action:

- To observe unity of time, a work should take place within the span of one day.
- To observe unity of place, a work should take place within the confines of a single locale.
- To observe unity of action, a work should contain a single dramatic plot, with no subplots.

PASTORAL ELEGY

A type of poem that takes the form of an elegy (a lament for the dead) sung by a shepherd. In this conventionalized form, the shepherd who sings the elegy is a stand-in for the author, and the elegy is for another poet.

Example: Milton's "Lycidas" and Shelley's "Adonais" (a lament for John Keats).

PASTORAL LITERATURE

A work that deals with the lives of people, especially shepherds, in the country or in nature.

Example: Christopher Marlowe's poem "The Passionate Shepherd to his Love" is a classic example of pastoral literature.

PATHETIC FALLACY

A term coined by John Ruskin. It refers to ascribing emotion and agency to inanimate objects.

Example: Ruskin's famous line: "The cruel crawling foam."

PERSONIFICATION

Giving an inanimate object human qualities or form.

Example: This except from "The Train" by Emily Dickinson demonstrates this, as the train in the poem is said to "lap," "lick," and "step":

> I like to see it lap the miles,
> And lick the valleys up,
> And stop to feed itself at tanks;
> And then, prodigious, step…

PICARESQUE

A novel, typically loosely constructed along an incident-to-incident basis, that follows the adventures of a more or less scurrilous rogue whose primary concerns are filling his belly and staying out of jail.

Example: Mark Twain's *Huckleberry Finn*. Also, Defoe's *Moll Flanders* is a rare example of a female picaresque.

PROTAGONIST

The main character, usually the hero.

Example: In Shakespeare's *Othello*, Othello is the protagonist.

SKELTONICS

A form of humorous poetry, using very short, rhymed lines and a pronounced rhythm, made popular by John Skelton. The only real difference between a skeltonic and doggerel is the quality of the thought expressed.

Example: From "How the Doughty Duke of Albany" by John Skelton:

> O ye wretched Scots,
> Ye puant pisspots,
> It shall be your lots
> To be knit up with knots.

SPRUNG RHYTHM

The rhythm created and used in the nineteenth century by Gerard Manley Hopkins. Like Old English verse, sprung rhythm fits a varying number of unstressed syllables in a line—only the stresses count in scansion.

Example: From "Pied Beauty" by Gerald Manley Hopkins:

> Glory be to God for dappled things—
> For skies of couple-colour as a brinded cow;
> For rose-moles all in stipple upon trout that swim
> Fresh-firecoal chestnut-falls; finches' wings;
> Landscape plotted and pieced—fold, fallow, and plough;
> And áll trades, their gear and tackle and trim.

SYNAESTHESIA

A term referring to phrases that suggest an interplay of the senses. "Hot pink" and "golden tones" are examples of synaesthesia.

Example: From John Keats' "Ode to a Nightingale":

> Tasting of Flora and the country green,
> Dance, and Provencal song, and sunburnt mirth!
> O for a beaker of the warm South...

SYNECDOCHE

Synecdoche is a phrase that refers to a person or object by a single important feature of that object or person.

Examples: Take the following lines from T. S Eliot's "The Love Song of J. Alfred Prufrock: "I should have been a **pair of ragged claws**/ Scuttling across the floors of silent seas." Because the "pair of ragged claws" only references the claws, but is used to mean the whole animal, it is an example of synecdoche.

VOICE

The perspective from which a story is written. Literature is most often written from the first person or the third person, though there are rare instances of artists utilizing the second person or the first-person plural. It is difficult to find an entire literary work that exemplifies each, as voice often changes within a particular literary work.

First person

The work is narrated using the pronoun "I." The narrator can be the protagonist. The narrator can also be an omniscient speaker who is not even a clear character in the story. There can also be multiple "I" narrators in the same work.

Example: "I met a traveler from an antique land who said: Two vast and trunkless legs of stone/stand in the desert." Percy Shelley's "Ozymandias" is narrated from the first person in the first two lines, though the narrator later changes to the voice of Ozymandias himself.

Example: Edgar Allen Poe's "The Tell-Tale Heart" is a perfect example of first person voice. The reader feels what the narrator is feeling as the story unfolds.

Example: William Faulkner's *As I Lay Dying* is an example of a first-person narrative told from multiple perspectives with multiple first-person narratives.

Third person

The work is narrated using a name or a third-person pronoun (he, she, etc).

Example: "It is an ancient mariner, And he stoppeth one of three." Samuel Taylor Coleridge's "The Rime of the Ancient Mariner" is narrated from the third person.

Example: Most of Jane Austen's novels, including *Pride and Prejudice* and *Persuasion,* are narrated from the third person.

Second person

In this rarely utilized voice, the author speaks using the pronoun "you," making the reader an active participant in the work.

First-person plural

Another rarely used point of view where the work is narrated using the pronoun "we." This voice forces the reader to concentrate more on what the story is about than who is telling it.

A GLOSSARY OF VERSE FORMS

STANZA TYPES

Ballad

The typical stanza of the folk ballad. The length of the lines in ballad stanzas, just as in sprung rhythm poetry and Old English verse, is determined by the number of stressed syllables only. The rhyme scheme is *abcb*.

Example: "The Rime of the Ancient Mariner" by Samuel Taylor Coleridge

In Memoriam

The stanza composed of four lines of iambic tetrameter rhyming *abba*.

Example: This can be found in a stanza of Tennyson's "In Memoriam A.H.H."

Ottava Rima

Eight-line stanza (usually iambic pentameter) rhyming *abababcc*.

Example: Lord Byron's *Don Juan*

Rhyme Royal

Seven-line iambic pentameter stanza rhyming *ababbcc*.

Example: "They Flee from Me That Sometime Did Me Seek" by Sir Thomas Wyatt:

> They flee from me that sometime did me seek
>
> With naked foot stalking in my chamber.
>
> I have seen them gentle, tame, and meek,
>
> That now are wild, and do not remember.

Spenserian

It is a nine-line stanza. The first eight lines are iambic pentameter. The final line, in iambic hexameter, is an alexandrine. The stanza's rhyme scheme is *ababbcbcc*.

Example: This is the stanza Spenser created for *The Faerie Queene*. The definitive example is, therefore, Edmund Spenser's *The Faerie Queene*.

Terza Rima

This form consists of three-line stanzas with an interlocking rhyme scheme proceeding *aba bcb cdc ded*, etc.

Example: Terza rima was invented by Dante for his *Divine Comedy:*

> Midway on our life's journey, I found myself
>
> In dark woods, the right road lost. To tell
>
> About those woods is hard—so tangled and rough...

VERSE TYPES

Blank Verse

This is unrhymed iambic pentameter verse.

Example: Alfred Lord Tennyson's "Ulysses":

> One equal temper of heroic hearts,
>
> Made weak by time and fate, but strong in will
>
> To strive, to seek, to find, and not to yield.

Free Verse

Unrhymed verse without a strict meter.

Example: "Song of Myself" by Walt Whitman:

> I celebrate myself, and sing myself,
>
> And what I assume you shall assume,
>
> For every atom belonging to me as good belongs to you.
>
> I loaf and invite my soul,
>
> I lean and loaf at my ease observing a spear of summer grass.

Old English Verse

Verse characterized by the internal alliteration of lines and a strong midline pause called a caesura.

Example: *Beowulf:*

> Protected in war; so warriors earn
>
> Their fame, and wealth is shaped with a sword.

SONNET TYPES

The sonnet, as a rule, is a 14-line form composed of rhyming iambic pentameter lines. From Spenser to the modern era, virtually every poet has attempted this form.

Italian, or Petrarchan

A 14-line poem rhyming *abbaabba cdecde*. The first eight lines are called the octave. The final six lines (composed of two groups of three, or *tercets*) are called the sestet.

Example: John Milton's "When I Consider How My Light Is Spent":

When I consider how my light is spent *a*
Ere half my days, in this dark world and wide, *b*
And that one talent which is death to hide *b*
Lodged with me useless, though my soul more bent *a*
To serve therewith my Maker, and present *a*
My true account, lest he returning chide; *b*
"Doth God exact day-labor, light denied?" *b*
I fondly ask; but Patience to prevent *a*
That murmur, soon replies, "God doth not need *c*
Either man's work or his own gifts; who best *d*
Bear his mild yoke, they serve him best. His state *e*
Is kingly. Thousands at his bidding speed *c*
And post o'er land and ocean without rest: *d*
They also serve who only stand and wait. *e*

English, or Shakespearean

A 14-line poem rhyming *abab cdcd efef gg*.

Example: Shakespeare's "Sonnet 73":

That time of year thou mayst in me behold, *a*
When yellow leaves, or none, or few do hang *b*
Upon those boughs which shake against the cold, *a*
Bare ruined choirs, where late the sweet birds sang. *b*
In me thou seest the twilight of such day, *c*
As after sunset fadeth in the west, *d*
Which by and by black night doth take away, *c*
Death's second self that seals up all in rest. *d*
In me thou seest the glowing of such fire, *e*
That on the ashes of his youth doth lie, *f*
As the deathbed, whereon it must expire, *e*
Consumed by that which it was nourished by. *f*
This thou perceivest, which makes thy love more strong, *c*
To love that well, which thou must leave ere long. *c*

Spenserian

A 14-line poem rhyming *abab bcbc cdcd ee.*

Example: "One Day I Wrote Her Name Upon the Strand" by Edmund Spenser:

> One day I wrote her name upon the strand, *a*
> But came the waves and washed it away: *b*
> Again I wrote it with a second hand, *a*
> But came the tide and made my pains his prey. *b*
> Vain man (said she), that dost in vain assay *b*
> A mortal thing so to immortalise; *c*
> For I myself shall like to this decay, *b*
> And eke my name be wiped out likewise. *c*
> Not so (quod I); let baser things devise *c*
> To die in dust, but you shall live by fame; *d*
> My verse your virtues rare shall eternise, *c*
> And in the heavens write your glorious name: *d*
> Where, when as death shall all the world subdue, *e*
> Our love shall live, and later life renew. *e*

The three main schools of literary theory are Marxist, Linguistic, and Psychological.

Quick Tip

How do you tell these sonnets apart without memorizing the rhyme schemes? Note the presence of couplets in each form. (Also note that, conveniently, the names are in alphabetical order.)

- *Petrarchan*—0 final couplets
- *Shakespearean*—1 final couplet
- *Spenserian*—1 final couplet plus 2 couplets in the body

OTHER VERSE FORMS

Villanelle

A 19-line form rhyming *aba aba aba aba aba abaa.* Its most noticeable characteristic is the repetition of the first and third lines throughout the poem: *aba ab1 ab3 ab1 ab3 ab13.*

Example: Dylan Thomas's "Do Not Go Gentle Into That Good Night"

Sestina

This is a 39-line poem of six stanzas of six lines each and a final stanza (called an envoi) of three lines. Rhyme plays no part in the sestina. Instead, one of six words is used as the end word of each of the poem's lines according to a fixed pattern. If you see a poem of six-line stanzas based on a pattern of repeated end-words, it is a sestina.

Example: In "Sestina of Tramp-Royal" by Rudyard Kipling, the word "die" is used in each stanza. The first two stanzas are shown below:

> Speakin' in general, I 'ave tried 'em all,
> The 'appy roads that take you o'er the world.
> Speakin' in general, I 'ave found them good
> For such as cannot use one bed too long,
> But must get 'ence, the same as I 'ave done,
> An' go observin' matters till they die.
> What do it matter where or 'ow we die,
> So long as we've our 'ealth to watch it all —
> The different ways that different things are done,
> An' men an' women lovin' in this world —
> Takin' our chances as they come along,
> An' when they ain't, pretendin' they are good?

Marxist theory concentrates on the economic situation in which literature is written and read.

A BRIEF GRAMMAR REVIEW

A couple of grammar questions usually crop up on the Literature in English Subject Test. Here's a review of the more obscure grammar terms (we'll assume you remember what verbs and nouns do):

Term	Definition	Example
Auxiliary	"helping verb" (often a form of "be," "have," or "do")	"I am working on it."
Gerund	a verb acting as a noun clause (usually the "-ing" form of the verb)	"Eating worms is bad for your health."
Imperative	verb used for issuing commands	"Do it now!"
Indicative	plain old verb in present tense	"John plays with the ball."
Infinitive	an unconjugated verb with "to" in front of it	"To be, or not to be."
Participle	the "-ed" form of a verb	"John has played with the ball many times."
Predicate	further information about the subject (a verb and its cohorts)	"This test is really bogus."

Term	Definition	Example
Subjunctive	verb used to express conditional or counterfactual statements	"If I were a rich man…"
Subordinate Conjunction	a word that introduces a subordinate clause	"Since you're awake, I'll just turn on the TV."
Substantive	a group of words acting as a noun	"Playing the banjo is extremely annoying."
Vocative	expression of direct address	"Sit, Ubu, sit!"

Psychological criticism investigates the personality and the biography of author and reader as sources of overarching meaning.

SCHOOLS OF TWENTIETH-CENTURY LITERARY CRITICISM

Literary criticism, as practiced in the graduate schools of today's universities, is about as brain-bending a discipline as one can pursue. The undergraduate version of criticism is typically far more generalized and far less taxing. ETS knows this. They do not expect you to be intimately familiar with any particular school of criticism. The exam is not likely to have more than three or four questions dealing with this material. That said, it is very important to familiarize yourself with the basic ideas and key names and terms pertaining to each school in order to be able to differentiate amongst them.

In general, modern criticism makes use of insights drawn from three broad schools of theory: Marxist, Linguistic, and Psychological. Some earlier twentieth-century schools were drawn purely from one of these three approaches; however, recently these once-hostile camps have tended to converge. The best example of this is probably contemporary feminist theory, which draws profoundly on all three major strains of theory.

Much of the thought we mention here is difficult and subtle. On the GRE Literature in English Subject Test, however, ETS typically gives you an extreme, dogmatic, blunt example of a critical approach, with a bit of identifying jargon thrown in, and then presents you with five answer choices, each with the name of a different school of thought. If you can identify the jargon or the broad outlines, you're in great shape. As always with the GRE Literature in English Subject Test and this book, the idea here is to give you a basic understanding of these schools of thought so that you will get more points on the test. We are not to trying to teach you entire schools of criticism in two hundred words or less.

You will definitely see pre-twentieth century critical writing on the Literature in English Subject Test, but when you do, the questions asked will be about identifying a specific author's writing or identifying a specific term rather than identifying the critical school itself.

Linguistic criticism examines the philosophy of language and linguistics.

LACANIAN CRITICISM

Jacques Lacan's particular brand of literary criticism has come into favor and is now taught in most undergraduate literature programs. You may be familiar with Lacan's famous essay "The Mirror Stage in the Formation of the I" in which he makes a claim about the word "I," suggesting that a child's first (mis)recognition (méconnaisance) of him- or herself in the mirror is the point at which the child becomes alienated from him- or herself, because it is the point at which the child enters the symbolic order. For Lacan, the endless chain of signifiers has its analogue in Freud's theory of the interpretation of dreams, which are themselves a chain of substitutions, often with no clear referent. Essentially, the major difference between Lacan and Freud is kind of a chicken-egg thing. For Freud, the unconscious comes first and language is mapped on to it. For Lacan, language comes first and shapes, or "structures," the unconscious. So, if it's helpful for you to think of him in terms of other theorists, Lacan is in some ways the perfect bridge between psychoanalytic criticism and linguistic criticism; he might best be thought of as Freud and Hegel read through Saussure. As in Saussure, there is a discontinuity between signifiers and signifieds, and the signifiers "float" in an endless chain of substitution.

As with other critics, Lacan is most easily spotted through his singular language—his particular set of keywords: mirror, phallus, signifier/signified, substitution, desire, jouissance, objet petit a, and the three orders: imaginary, symbolic, and real, to name a few.

MARXIST CRITICISM AND ITS INFLUENCE

In its dullest sense, **Marxist criticism** is a left-wing view of literature. ETS will occasionally throw some of this your way. Look for all the buzzwords of socialism: *base and superstructure* (that is, material economic reality and the cultural superstructure built upon it), *class, proletariat, means of production, bourgeoisie, imperialism, dialectical materialism,* etc. Basically, the Marxist criticism ETS presents will grossly emphasize the economic situation from which literature emerges and in which it was and is consumed.

The **Marxist influence on criticism** cannot be over-emphasized. The central insight of Marxist thought for literary criticism is that texts are *not* timeless, fixed creations subject to universal standards of evaluation and interpretation, nor does Man possess essential, unchanging qualities that works of "great literature" address across the ages. Rather, a given individual, his consciousness, and the products of that consciousness are themselves the products of a specific cultural and historical context, and thus that context must be addressed; exactly how and to what purpose is the big question. This mode of analysis is the jumping-off point for dozens of critical approaches and micro-approaches, but for the GRE Literature in English Subject Test, the most important of these are New Historicism and its related schools.

New Historicism argues that the specifics of culture matter profoundly: The institutions (in the broadest sense—for example, language is an institution) of a given society produce discernible effects in the consciousness of society's members, and therefore in the products of consciousness, such as literature. The major term for the social-institutional presence in consciousness is *ideology*. According to

New Historicists, the presence and effects of ideology in literature are not artificial layers of fluff to be stripped away in order to get at the essential and "the real," rather, the cultural–ideological layer is the proper object of analysis itself. What the perceptive critic finds in a text, above all, is the *encoded ideology supporting the dominant class* and also the struggling voice of the oppressed ideological subject.

Feminist criticism, Black criticism, and **Post-Colonial criticism** all partake of a New Historicist-influenced critical mode, each with its own particular emphasis. By way of example, a feminist critic might deplore our *patriarchal* language in the paragraphs above on the Marxist influence on criticism (e.g., "Man" as a synonym for all humanity and the use of the pronoun "his." As you may have noted in this and other TPR books, we interchange "he," "she," "his," and "her," when used as impersonal pronouns. This sensitivity to the latent ideological nature of language is directly attributable to the influence of New Historicism/ Feminist criticism on our culture). All three schools would surely note that although some schools of criticism here get separate entries, these three have been lumped together—*Euro-American patriarchy's* typical *marginalization* of the *other*. Actually, it just made a good example, and all three critical schools really do share a common bond, precisely because of the historic status of women, African Americans, and occupied people as disenfranchised in the European *phallocratic hegemony* (white male dominance of systems of power). As these types of criticism often investigate definitions (aka, constructions) of self, they are sometimes called **Identity criticisms**.

Note that in our examples above, we've focused on language, and in the case of "phallocratic," the language implies both Freudian psychological theory and the Marxist preoccupation with ideological consciousness. This word provides a striking example of a contemporary theory's intermingling of Freudian, Marxist, and Linguistic approaches.

PSYCHOLOGICAL CRITICISM

Psychological criticism, in its broad outlines, examines and emphasizes precisely those things Marxist-influenced criticism does not (although, as we've just noted, those hostilities have relaxed somewhat). First, Psychological criticism is concerned with universals of human consciousness and the ways in which essential aspects of the human psyche manifest themselves in literature. Secondly, Psychological criticism considers the personality and biographical particulars of the individual author as legitimate fields of inquiry, something both the Marxist-influenced and linguistic critics typically do not.

Freudian criticism sometimes appears on the test. Like Marx, Freud has a continuing influence on other thinkers, even as the particulars of his theory have fallen into disuse. Again as with Marx, when ETS wants you to spot what they call a Freudian or **Psychoanalytic critic**, they won't be subtle about it. Look for the familiar jargon of Freudianism: *Oedipal complex, libido, id, ego, superego, subconscious, repression, resistance*, et al.

One Freudian critic, Harold Bloom, is worthy of special attention. His theory of authorial production states that authors subconsciously position their work against that of another, earlier author who functions as a kind of literary father figure. Look for the term *strong-poet*, which refers to those writers whose works (particularly the style of those works) exert this powerful influence on writers who follow them.

Archetype or **Myth criticism** is a still-vital school of criticism, drawn from the theories of Freud collaborator Carl Jung and from the work of anthropologist James G. Frazer, particularly his encyclopedic study of myth and ritual, *The Golden Bough*. Critics Joseph Campbell and Northrop Frye are important figures in the subsequent development of this school. Myth criticism looks for recurring symbols, motifs, character types, and plots, finding them in sources as disparate as "The Epic of Gilgamesh", Superman comics, Arthurian legend, and T. S. Eliot's *The Waste Land*. Campbell's *The Hero with a Thousand Faces* is a transcultural examination of the surprisingly consistent figure of the mythic hero. Myth critics believe that the existence of these persistent, powerful, ever-repeated stories and characters points to needs and urges deep within the human psyche, and that the study of such stories can reveal the *collective unconscious* of humankind.

LINGUISTIC CRITICISM

By **Linguistic criticism**, we mean that broad area of critical thought concerned primarily with language. In the cases of Formalism and New Criticism, that concern is with the particulars of literary language. In the cases of structuralism and deconstruction, the concern is more with a philosophy of language than with literature per se.

Linguistic criticism has its roots in the early twentieth century, when critics felt the need to professionalize their discipline, to make its methodology more rigorous and less speculative. To do this, critics developed a number of strategies.

Formalist criticism, a predominantly Russian school of the 1920s, attempted to discern the underlying laws that shape a literary text, the objectively discernible features that make it, in fact, literature. Much of this analysis centered around the concept of *defamiliarization*. Literature, the Formalists found, employed *devices* of plot, story, and voice, that made language unfamiliar, and thus signaled to the reader that the writing was an aesthetic—literary—object.

New Criticism, another critical approach with roots in the beginning of the century, is no longer new at all. This mode has a very strong chance of showing up on the GRE Literature in English Subject Test because of its dominance in American and English universities for several decades at mid-century. This dominance can be at least partly explained by the fact that several of the New Critics were not only penetrating scholars, but formidable stylists in their own right. T. S. Eliot, Robert Penn Warren, Cleanth Brooks, I. A. Richards, John Crowe Ransom and F. R. Leavis were all New Critics.

Like the Formalists, New Critics thought earlier critical approaches were polluted by unsustainable speculations about authorial intent and subjective effusions about the beauty and emotion of the work. Indeed, the New Critics coined terms—*the intentional fallacy* and *the affective fallacy*—to describe such errors. The New Critics also had an absolute loathing for criticism that attempted to extract the germ of content from what "Great Writer X was trying to say," a flawed method the New Critics called *the heresy of paraphrase*. For New Critics, the words were there on the page; one only need examine them closely. If a phrase or word is found to be ambiguous, a New Critic doesn't ask what the author "actually" meant but rather studies the ambiguity in order to discern how the several readings affect the totality of the piece. This method of analysis is called *close reading* and it remains a staple of Lit-Crit method even as New Criticism has faded from the academy. Close reading takes writing and subjects it to a word-by-word scrutiny, showing how the words of a poem (New Criticism was most successful with poetry) bounce off one another within the poem to create dense packages of irony, ambiguity, symbol, and meaning.

Structuralism is the school that dominated continental Europe while New Criticism was all the rage in England and the U.S. It is derived from the theories of linguist Ferdinand de Saussure, among others. Structuralism is closely related to **semiotics**. Both are complex, difficult, and influential fields of study. ETS does not expect you to have a detailed knowledge of the linguistic underpinnings that buttress Structuralism or to be able to differentiate among the overlapping theories and counter theories of its varied schools.

Essentially, structuralism holds that meaning is never or rarely intrinsic—meaning is only produced by structure. The fundamental unit of structure is relative difference. The ramifications of this simple insight have carried critics into the theoretical stratosphere.

For the purposes of the GRE Literature in English Subject Test, you need only be able to recognize some jargon. The terms *sign, signifier,* and *signified* are clear indicators of the structuralist/semiotic mode of criticism. Also, structuralist literary criticism will often describe a text in terms of binary oppositions, often spatial metaphors: for example, the center and the periphery, or the vertical axis and horizontal axis.

Post-Structuralism is the name for those schools that both make use of structuralist theory and critique it. The most important of these schools for the test is **deconstruction**. Whereas structuralism posits a tidy, orderly structure to meaning, deconstruction focuses on the displacements, the excesses, and the gaps, that structuralists dismiss as exceptional. Deconstructionists hold that these "exceptions" are absolutely integral to the creation of meaning. This theory, as you are no doubt aware, gets pretty heady.

Again, ETS doesn't expect you to be a deconstructionist, just to be able to spot one. In the case of deconstructionists, the jargon is a dead giveaway. Key terms of deconstruction are: *erasure, trace, bracketing, differance, slippage, dissemination, logocentrism, indeterminacy, decentering.* Key terms of post-structuralism in general are *mimesis, alterity, marginality, desire,* and *lack.*

Reader-Response criticism makes an occasional appearance on the test. Reader-Response criticism insists that the reader's experience of a text is the literary event—literature is what happens inside a reader's head, not what occurs on the page. Another Reader-Response notion is that literary works involve an *implied,* or *ideal reader.* Some Reader-Response criticism, in a literary-history mode, examines the aesthetic impact of a work, judging whether the work broke with the aesthetic *horizon of expectations* of its time. This school is closely allied with Reception Aesthetics. Individual Reader-Response critics make use of Marxist, Psychological, and Linguistic theory, so just look for the distinctive Reader-Response jargon, and its signal concern with the effect literature has on the reader.

6

What You Should Study

THE MAKE-YOU-OR-BREAK-YOU POINTS

If you try to study for every question on the GRE Literature in English Subject Test you will either drive yourself mad, or more than likely just give up. Please take note:

> Room for error is deliberately figured into the test.

Q: Whose epitaph is this? Good friend for Jesus' sake forbeare, To digg the dust encloased heare. Blese be ye man yt spares thes stones. And curst be he yt moves my bones.

One of the ways ETS makes up for the lack of a standard English curriculum is to ask way too many questions, assuming (correctly) that even the very best students haven't studied everything. You could leave one-fourth of the test blank and still score above the eighty-eighth percentile! You could leave more than two-fifths of the test blank and still score in the fifty-fifth percentile, that is, slightly above average!

This book does not attempt the impossible task of preparing you for every question. You don't need it. What you need are the "make you or break you points," the points that can be prepared for. That's where our study materials and the practice test come in.

THE POINTS-TO-PAGES RATIO

The question now is, what exactly should you study? This chapter provides the answer in the form of study lists. They've been put together according to a simple concept we call the "points-to-pages ratio." We figure you don't want to devote the rest of your life to studying for this test. You just want a high score. In order to help you get that, we've put our study material together according to a points-to-pages ratio: The more GRE Literature in English Subject Test points that reading a page can earn you, the more strongly we suggest you read it. If a single ten-line poem is likely to be tested, we suggest you read it. It has a high points-to-pages ratio. If reading the complete works of Dickens is worth a point or maybe two, well, it would be absurd to waste valuable study time doing so. The points-to-pages ratio would be one to several thousand.

THE MISSING PERSONS REPORT

As you look over our study materials and lists, you may find yourself wondering, "So, what happened to Shakespeare?" "What happened to the Bible?" "What happened to most of the twentieth century?" You may even have thought, "What century do these Princeton Review people live in? These lists are 99 percent dead white European males. Women and people of color are badly underrepresented!"

These omissions are not oversights, and neither are we trying to defend the "traditional literary canon." The study materials have been put together according to the points-to-pages ratio. We aren't trying to be comprehensive and we aren't trying to be fair. We are preparing you for the GRE Literature in English Subject Test working under the assumption that you do not have unlimited time available for study.

You may be surprised to find that we've de-emphasized Shakespeare, the Bible, and "world" literature, especially because ETS makes a point of mentioning there will be questions on these topics. The reasoning behind our decisions and what to expect regarding these topics is discussed below.

THE BIBLE AS LITERATURE

You will see roughly two questions directly concerning the Bible, one of which will be easy if you are in any way familiar with the Judeo-Christian tradition, the other of which will be less easy. You will also probably see several questions dealing with biblical allusions. To study the thousands of pages of the Bible does not make sense, so we have condensed the material in these manageable summaries.

Note: In the context of this book and this exam, the Bible is a work of literature. Literature itself is a secular discipline, and so the people in the Bible are here regarded as literary characters and not as religious figures. No offense is intended in this characterization.

Old Testament

Genesis

If we were to recommend that you read one book of the Bible, that book would certainly be Genesis. On its own terms, Genesis is one of the most plot-driven books of the Old Testament, but more importantly for this test, it's also the source of many of the literary allusions that show up in later texts. Here are a few highlights:

A: William Shakespeare's

- The creation: "In the beginning God created the heaven and the earth," reads the opening line, thus setting in motion a quick cycle of creation ("And God said, 'Let there be light,' and there was light."), assessment ("And God saw the light, that it was good..."), and classification ("And God called the light day..."). According to Genesis, God created the different parts of the earth as follows:
  Day 1: Light and Darkness (aka, day and night)
  Day 2: Heaven (firmament)
  Day 3: Earth (dry land), complete with grass, herbs, trees
  Day 4: Lights in the firmament of heaven (sun, moon, stars)
  Day 5: Animals of sea and sky
  Day 6: Beasts of the earth and man in God's own image
  Day 7: Rest

- The fall: God creates all of this, and tells the newly created Adam ("formed…of the dust of the ground, and breathed into his nostrils the breath of life…") that Eden is his for the taking, and he can do pretty much whatever he likes except eat from the tree of the knowledge of good and evil. Adam consents, and all is well and good until Eve, created from Adam's rib, comes along and gets duped by a serpent (Satan in disguise) into eating from the tree. Adam and Eve are cast out of the garden of Eden for good. You may have heard this referred to as the "Fall of Man," and it is generally read as the Judeo-Christian interpretation of the fall of all humankind. To further cement the idea, Adam itself is a Hebrew word meaning "the man." Although, as Samuel Johnson admits of Milton's *Paradise Lost*, "none ever wished it longer," Milton's epic is entirely concerned with these that come only from the first two chapters or so of Genesis.

- Cain and Abel: Eve eventually bears two sons, Cain ("a tiller of the ground") and Abel ("a keeper of sheep"). After the Lord appreciates one of Abel's offerings more than Cain's, Cain gets very angry and slays Abel. As a punishment, Cain is driven out of God's sight to take up residence in the east of Eden, but Cain is marked for protection ("the mark of Cain"), and God warns, "whosoever slayeth Cain, vengeance shall be taken on him sevenfold." Eve has another kid named Seth, but his life is not nearly so eventful. John Steinbeck's *East of Eden* (1952) is a retelling of the Cain and Abel story.

- The flood: After some generations had passed, God decides he doesn't like the way things are going, seeing that "the wickedness of man was great in the earth, and that every imagination of the thoughts of [man's] heart was only evil continually." The solution? A huge flood to kill everyone and start over. He picks Noah to assemble his family, build an ark, and to collect "two and two of all flesh" to restart all life once everything dries out. After all is said and done, God seems to regret his decision in the wake of all the destruction and vows, "neither will I again smite any more every thing living, as I have done." The rest of the book details the events of Noah and his family, but the flood is what's most important.

- The Tower of Babel: Some generations later, the people of Shem decide to build a tower that will reach up to heaven. The Lord is very angry at the arrogance of idea, and decided that as a punishment, he would scatter the generations all over the earth. In doing so, he "confound[ed] the languages of the earth." This, according to the Bible, is why people in different parts of the world speak different languages and cannot communicate with each other.

- Abraham and Isaac: Abraham and Sarah, two very devout people, are having a tough time conceiving. They try and try but to no avail. Finally, Sarah recommends that Abraham try to conceive with her Egyptian maid Hagar. That works, and they have a son named Ishmael, but no one really thinks much of him (cf., Melville's narrator of the same name in *Moby-Dick*). After this, God comes to Abraham and tells him that he's going to be the "father of many nations" and that his generations will inherit the land then known as Canaan. When Abraham and Sarah are both old, Sarah finally gets pregnant and gives birth to Isaac. Then one day, God comes and asks Abraham to sacrifice Isaac as a burnt offering. Abraham unflinchingly sets out to do so, but God stops him at the last minute. This event often comes up in discussions of religious faith; in fact, this single event was the single subject of Danish philosopher Soren Kierkegaard's meditations in *Fear and Trembling*.

As you can see, there's a great deal of information in Genesis (all of the above comes from about the first 20 chapters), but so much of what you'll need to know for the GRE Literature in English Subject Test just has to do with name recognition. We've given these mini-stories because they're so important, but the main things you need to make sure you know here are the names. A name will almost always be the way to spot an allusion. Other big names from Genesis include: Nimrod, Ham, Lot, Lot's wife, Sodom, Gomorrah, Jacob (later Israel), Esau (later Edom), Joseph (and of course his coat of many colors), Judah.

Exodus

Exodus is important mainly for documenting the major events in the life of Moses, the central prophet in Judaism. In fact, the first five books of the Bible can be referred to either as the Torah or as the "five books of Moses."

At the time of Moses's birth, the Egyptian Pharaoh ordered that all Hebrew children be killed. To protect her son, Moses's mother Jochebed hid Moses for three months and when she could no longer hide him, she put him in a mini-ark and sent him down the river. Who should pick him up but the daughter of Pharoah. She knew the child was a Hebrew, but was moved by compassion and eventually adopted him. Moses grows up as an Egyptian prince until one day he sees an Egyptian slave-driver whipping a Hebrew slave. Moses kills him, then escapes to live in the countryside as a herder.

Later, God appears to Moses in the form of a burning bush. He tells Moses to lead the Hebrew people out of bondage. To help Moses convince the Hebrew people that he has the support of the Lord, God gives Moses two miracles: a rod that turns into a snake, and a hand that goes from leprous to non-leprous in the blink of an eye. After a lot of convincing, the Hebrew people are ready to follow him, and Moses goes to Pharaoh and speaks the famous line, "Let my people go." Pharaoh won't, and so begin the "Ten Plagues," highlights among which are all pools of water (rivers, lakes, seas, hot tubs) becoming blood, plagues of frogs, locusts, hail mixed with fire (aka, "fire and brimstone"), and all kinds of other hideousness. The most notable of these plagues was the last one, the death of the first born, where God sends an angel of death to kill the first born children of all the houses who have not marked their doors with lamb's blood. Hebrews and Hebrew sympathizers were the only ones who did this, and so their houses were passed over. This is the origin of the Jewish holy day Passover, celebrating when the angel of death passed over their homes.

After Pharaoh's first born son dies, he gives up, frees the Hebrews, and Moses and his people set out for Canaan. Ever fickle, though, Pharaoh then decides that he doesn't want to let the Hebrew people go after all, and he sends a large army to pursue them. Seeing that the Hebrews were hemmed in by the Red Sea and Pharaoh's army, God gave Moses the power to part the sea so that the Hebrews could pass through it, and then brought the sea down on the Egyptians.

The rest of Exodus is concerned with the laws that God gave to the Hebrews, such as the Ten Commandments ("Thou shalt not kill," etc.), and the challenges that the Hebrew people faced in their journey through the desert. The 1956 film *The Ten Commandments* starring Charlton Heston is actually a great way to plug some holes in your Exodus knowledge. If you can't get your hands on the film, some names and concepts that might help: Aaron, the golden calf, the ark of the covenant, manna, "Eye for eye, tooth for tooth," Mount Sinai, ram's blood, the casting down of the first two tablets of laws.

Other biblical books are not very likely to show up on the exam (with the exception of Samuel and Kings) as they often deal predominantly with familial lineage.

Samuel and Kings

These four books (both Samuel and Kings are split into two books) detail the doings of the first kings of Israel, anointed by the prophet Samuel, himself the last of the Hebrew judges. Saul is the first of these kings, followed by David when Saul is killed in a battle with the Philistines.

Even before he is crowned king, David makes an early name for himself, defeating the giant Goliath by felling him with a stone shot from a sling. David is also important as the credited composer of many of the Psalms. The later king and wise man Solomon was David's son by Bathsheba. David's son Absalom rebels against David and tries to usurp his throne (a similar power struggle takes place between Saul and David). This rebellion has been a particularly attractive topic for authors, and is told allegorically in John Dryden's satirical long poem *Absalom and Achitophel* (1681-1682) and William Faulkner's novel *Absalom, Absalom!* (1936).

Job

Job's story is fairly simple. Satan proposes to God that God's loyal subject Job is only loyal because of God's protection. To test the hypothesis, God begins to strip away Job's health, wealth, and family to tempt Job to curse God. He doesn't, and God, in admiration of his perseverance ("the patience of Job") restores all his riches. Artists and philosophers are particularly drawn to this chapter because it is so heavily invested in dialogue. Job looks to understand his situation through dialogue with his friends, and while many hold Job up as an Abraham-like figure for his unshakable faith, many others see the book of Job as an important moment of uncertainty in the Old Testament.

Daniel

The book of Daniel is brief but incredibly dense. It is set during the Babylonian captivity of Jerusalem, and can be split into two main parts: the "court tales" of Daniel, Shadrach, Meshach, and Abednego, and Daniel's interpretation of dreams (psychoanalysts, enter at your peril). Daniel rises from the position of a servant to aid and confidant of the king because of his famed skill at interpreting dreams. He is called to interpret several reccurring dreams that king is having and ends up predicting an upcoming famine, allowing his kingdom to store enough grain in advance to insure their survival. Daniel is then appointed by King Darius of Babylon to be one of three presidents of the kingdom, and the others, jealous of the king's preference for a Hebrew, cast Daniel into a den of lions. Daniel survives, ascribing his safety to the Lord's protection; this is where the phrase "Daniel in the lion's den" comes from. The book of Daniel is also the source of the "writing on the wall," referring to a prophecy that Daniel must interpret for the drunk and terrified Belshazzar the King.

Jonah

God orders Jonah to "go to Nineveh, that great city, and cry against it; for their wickedness come up before me." Jonah apparently doesn't want to, so he tries to escape the "presence of the Lord" by boarding a ship headed for Tarshish. God, of course, is not fooled, and sends out a mighty tempest. The other sailors get suspicious, and when Jonah admits that he's the reason for all the boat-rocking (literal and figurative), the other sailors cast him overboard where he is promptly swallowed by a fish (probably a whale), in whose belly he spends three days and three nights. Because there's not a ton to do in the belly of a whale, Jonah repents, and God orders the whale to spit Jonah out safely on the shore. The book of Jonah is of particular interest to authors writing about the sea. Although the narrator of Melville's *Moby-Dick* is named Ishmael (who, I'm sure you remember, is Abraham's first son by the servant Hagar), the novel as a whole is deeply engaged with the book of Jonah.

The New Testament

The New Testament is in some ways harder to quantify because so much of it is just about one person. Of course, that person did quite a lot, of which we will give some examples below, but catching references to the New Testament can often depend more on your knowledge of the author making the reference than on your knowledge of the New Testament itself. In the most basic sense, you should know that the most important and commonly referenced books of the New Testament are the Gospels: the books of Matthew, Mark, Luke, and John.

Authors like Dante (*The Divine Comedy*, *Vita Nuova*), John Milton (*Paradise Lost*, et al.), and John Bunyan (*Pilgrim's Progress*) were such profound scholars of the Bible in general and the New Testament in particular that often single words or turns of phrase will be pulled from some part of the testament. Many authors, such as Jonathan Swift and John Donne, were themselves clergymen and thus were arguably more engrossed in the study of the Bible than in their own writing.

Even so, here are some of the basics. We'll start with the life of Jesus, pulled from, as Joyce's *Finnegans Wake* would call them, Mamalujo (The Gospels of Matthew, Mark, Luke, and John).

Joseph and Mary are newlyweds, but they haven't consummated their marriage. You can imagine Joseph's surprise, then, when Mary comes to him and tells him that she is pregnant, even though she's still a virgin. In fact, the angel Gabriel came to her and told her that she would bear a son and that her son would be the son of God. His name: Jesus, the would-be King of the Jews. This event is what is referred to as the Immaculate Conception.

Three Wise Men (aka, the "Magi") travel from far away, bearing gifts to celebrate the birth of the King of the Jews. King Herod hears about this new king, and he promptly orders that all children under the age of two be killed in what has since been known as the "Massacre of the Innocents." Mary and Joseph flee with the child and he is protected until after Herod's death.

There is little in any of the Gospels about the events of Jesus's childhood and adolescence. We hear little of his life at all until many years later when he encounters John the Baptist, who recognizes Jesus as the Son of God without being introduced and promptly baptizes him. After the baptism, Jesus spends forty days and forty nights in the desert fasting (notice this was the same amount of time Moses spent on the mountain), and while he's there, the Devil tempts him three times but Jesus is not won over and is nourished by God instead.

Much else happens to Jesus along the way (he turns water to wine, raises Lazarus from the dead, and feeds five thousand people with five loaves and three fish, to name a few key events). For purposes of this exam, however, nothing is so well known and heavily alluded to as his death. At a Passover meal Jesus is sharing with his disciples, commonly known as the "Last Supper," Jesus prophesies that one of his disciples will betray him. After they eat, Jesus and his disciples go to pray in the Garden of Gethsemane. In the garden, Jesus is arrested, having been betrayed by Judas Iscariot, who identifies Jesus by kissing him in plain sight of the soldiers who arrest him. For this betrayal, Judas is paid thirty pieces of silver. Thus any literary reference to someone being paid thirty pieces of silver most likely denotes that a betrayal has taken place. After this, the apostles go into hiding, and Judas eventually kills himself from guilt. Jesus is crucified in Golgotha, but resurrected shortly thereafter.

Other important names in the New Testament include Salome, the daughter of a later Herod, who requested the head of John the Baptist on a plate (and got it); Lazarus, whom Jesus resurrected; and Mary Magdalene, a prostitute whom Jesus reformed.

Clearly you won't have time to read the whole New Testament, but there are three short sections of it that are worth a quick look: the Sermon on the Mount (Matthew Ch. 5-7), Parable of the Prodigal Son (Luke 15:11-32), and the Parable of the Sower, which appears in all the Gospels except John (Mark 4:1-20, Matthew 13:1-23, Luke 8:1-15). These three parts thrust you right into the often elliptical language of the New Testament, and the use of the parable has been a particularly powerful didactic tool in literature since.

Biblical Allusions in Literature

Because the Judeo-Christian Bible was the foundational text for over a thousand years, allusions to it can show up in countless ways. We've already mentioned several of them in the course of our biblical summaries. The easiest way to spot a biblical allusion is to familiarize yourself with the names in this summary.

The *King James Bible*, still the standard Bible in literary studies, was first issued in 1611 by the Church of England. As such, if you familiarize yourself with the language of the edition, you can often see where certain lines are out of place in a poem or novel. Take the last line from Charlotte Bronte's *Jane Eyre*:

> No fear of death will darken St. John's last hour: his
> mind will be unclouded, his heart will be undaunted,
> his hope will be sure, his faith steadfast. His own
> words are a pledge of this—
>
> "My Master," he says, "has forewarned me. Daily He
> announces more distinctly,—'Surely I come quick-
> ly!' and hourly I more eagerly respond,—'Amen;
> even so come…'"

You don't need to know the last line comes from the book of Revelation 22:20 to see that it is clearly a biblical allusion. The word "amen" should put you on the scent, and then the odd formation of "even so come" indicates a kind of forcibly archaic wording, distinct from the author's own. In this instance, the last sentence of the book actually ends "…and hourly I more eagerly respond,--'Amen, even so come, Lord Jesus!'", but ETS is good at carefully omitting material that might make you more familiar with the text.

Just as often, the allusion will be contained in the title, and these are often easier to spot. Obvious examples are Toni Morrison's *Song of Solomon*, William Faulkner's *Absalom, Absalom!*, and Marcel Proust's *Sodom and Gomorrah*. Possibly less obvious examples are Hemingway's *The Sun Also Rises*, Samuel Butler's *The Way of All Flesh*, Henrik Ibsen's *The Master Builder*, and Jean Toomer's *Cane*.

SHAKESPEARE

There will be six or seven questions that deal with Shakespeare's work directly, and several more that have some connection to him. That's a large number of points. Though you should already have enough familiarity with Shakespeare to answer some of the questions, we think it's important to do a brief review.

There will also be one or two very difficult Shakespeare questions. In order to study for these questions, you would need to know all of Shakespeare's plays and poems thoroughly, because they are all fair game as far as ETS is concerned. It does not make sense to try and cram the whole body of Shakespeare's works into your brain for an insignificant number of points (this is the points-to-pages idea again), but hopefully these little snippets will be able to help.

If you're a Shakespeare person, the summaries below will make you want to scream, but as with anything else on the GRE, the key is be able to spot the basics: skeleton of the plot, major characters, and important moments. If you don't have much familiarity with Shakespeare, and you don't have time to read any of the plays, watch movies! Shakespeare's plays are performance texts, so it's never a bad thing to see them performed. It's important that you be careful which movies you see, but as long as they're in the original English (Kurosawa's Shakespeare adaptations are great, but they won't help you here) and not too cut down (or spliced together, as in Orson Welles's *Chimes at Midnight*), you should be fine. Be on the lookout especially for Kenneth Branagh's Shakespeare adaptations as they are famously faithful to the material. Laurence Olivier's films often involve cuts, but many would argue that this is how Shakespeare was meant to be performed.

Shakespeare is an especially important author to know for this test not only because of the frequency with which he shows up on the test but also because of the allusions concentrated in his works. On the one hand, Shakespeare had a profound knowledge of the Bible and Roman mythology and incorporated both regularly into his work. On the other hand, Shakespeare's works themselves became the source of regular reference and allusion. As such, Shakespeare really is the central figure in the history of English literature given both his own importance and the historical link he provides between classical antiquity and modernity.

For your studying convenience, we have chosen theatrical works from each of Shakespeare's thematic categories: tragedy, comedy, and history.

Tragedies

Romeo and Juliet

The prologue to *Romeo and Juliet* gives a very basic outline of the plot:

> Two households, both alike in dignity
>
> In fair Verona, where we lay our scene,
>
> From ancient grudge break to new mutiny,
>
> Where civil blood makes civil hands unclean.
>
> From forth the fatal loins of these two foes
>
> A pair of star-crossed lovers take their life,
>
> Whose misadventured piteous overthrows
>
> Doth with their death bury their parents' strife.

The two households, the Montagues and the Capulets, have had, to put it mildly, tense relations since time immemorial. Romeo of the Montagues and Juliet from the Capulets fall in love with each other and are married on the sly. They want to be together, so like any pair of young lovers they concoct a scheme of faked death involving this potion that makes you look dead for forty-two hours. Romeo doesn't get the memo that Juliet's death is fake, though, and he kills himself from grief. When Juliet wakes up from her death-nap, she sees that Romeo is dead and kills herself with a dagger, thus ending this season's romantic comedy smash. "For never was a story of more woe/Than this of Juliet and her Romeo." No kidding.

- Major characters: Romeo, Juliet, Friar Laurence, Juliet's nurse, Benvolio (Romeo's cousin), Mercutio (Romeo's friend; the Riff to his Tony, if you're familiar with *West Side Story*), Tybalt (Juliet's cousin; the Bernardo to her Maria)

- Famous moments: the prologue (above); Mercutio's Queen Mab speech (I.4); the balcony scene (II.1): "But soft, what light through yonder window breaks?", "wherefore art thou Romeo?"

Hamlet

Hamlet is the Prince of Denmark. His father recently died, leaving the kingdom to Hamlet's uncle Claudius, who thought it would only be proper to marry Hamlet's mother Gertrude. One night, the ghost of Hamlet's father appears and says he was poisoned by Claudius and that Hamlet must avenge his death. Hamlet is not sure at first that the Ghost is telling him the truth, and in order to find out he stages a play re-enacting the murder scene to monitor Claudius's reaction. Claudius, not a subtle man, rises in anger and leaves the room during the play, convincing Hamlet of Claudius's guilt. In the bloodbath at the end of the play, involving poison in all kinds of standard and not-so-standard places (in a drink and on the tips of fencing swords), Gertrude drinks a poisoned cup intended for Hamlet, and Hamlet is felled by the poison-tipped swords but not before he kills Claudius.

Other characters:
- Ophelia – The object of Hamlet's affection, though also the recipient of the famous "Get thee to a nunnery!" command. Her father is Polonius (whom Hamlet kills by accident), and her brother is Laertes (who kills Hamlet in the duel). She eventually goes bonkers, singing songs to herself, and in the end, she drowns in a lake. The "Goonight" lines in Eliot's The Waste Land allude to some of Ophelia's final, and craziest, lines before she drowns (the jury is still out on whether it was a suicide).
- Horatio – Hamlet's best friend and confidante. It is suggested at the end of the play that Horatio will tell Hamlet's story: "And let me speak to th' yet unknowing world/How these things came about."
- Rosencrantz and Guildenstern – Also Hamlet's "friends," important because they are sent to England with Hamlet with instructions that the recipient of the letter should kill him. Rosencrantz and Guildenstern are not too bright, though, and Hamlet alters the letter so they are killed. You may know their names from Tom Stoppard's 1966 play Rosencrantz and Guildenstern are Dead.
- Fortinbras – The "strong-armed" Prince of Norway who is constantly pressing on the Danes from without. He appears at the end looking to meet with Claudius, but finds only the results of the deadliest fencing match ever. Hamlet crowns Fortinbras king of Denmark just before his death, and Fortinbras orders an honorable burial for Hamlet.

Important moments and quotes in addition to those mentioned above: "Something is rotten in the state of Denmark." (I.4) "To be, or not to be: that is the question…" (III.1) Other key concepts include the play within a play, alternately called "The Murder of Gonzago" and "The Mousetrap" (III.2).

Macbeth

In some ways, the plot of *Macbeth* is incredibly simple, especially as it relates to the title character. Prodded by his own ambition and (even more so) by his wife's, Macbeth murders his way to the top of the Scottish monarchy. Early in the play, Macbeth hears a prophesy from three witches predicting his meteoric rise to power. He tells Lady Macbeth about the prophecy, and she gets pretty fired up about it. They plot together to kill King Duncan on his return from the battlefield, setting into motion a ruthless and relentless chain of death. Macbeth is elected King but becomes increasingly guilty and insecure, and is eventually undone by Macduff, the Thane of Fife. Lady Macbeth also is eventually overcome with guilt and kills herself.

Macbeth has a pretty small cast of characters relative to the other tragedies. All of the play's major characters have been mentioned in the summary above.

Famous quotes: "Yet I do fear thy nature./It is too full o'th' milk of human kindness/To catch the nearest way." (I.5) And a long one, but full of important allusions: If you're going to remember one thing from *Macbeth*, it should be Macbeth's famous speech (V.5):

> Tomorrow, and tomorrow, and tomorrow
>
> Creeps in this petty pace from day to day
>
> To the last syllable of recorded time,
>
> And all our yesterdays have lighted fools
>
> The way to dusty death. Out, out, brief candle.
>
> Life's but a walking shadow, a poor player
>
> That struts and frets his hour upon the stage,
>
> And then is heard no more. It is a tale
>
> Told by an idiot, full of sound and fury,
>
> Signifying nothing.

Othello

As in *Macbeth*, the plot is relatively simple and the cast of characters relatively small. Othello, a war hero, and Desdemona, daughter of the Duke of Venice, have recently been married. The Duke initially disapproved of the marriage but has come to accept it as Othello and Desdemona have proven their love to him. Othello has recently promoted Cassio to be his lieutenant, and this action, for all intents and purposes, is what starts the villain Iago's machinations. Iago wanted the job, and so he first sets up a plot to get Cassio removed from the position (via a drunken, staged fight with Roderigo), and then moves on to the bigger prey: Othello. Through a series of deceptive ploys, the coup de grâce famously involving a handkerchief, Iago convinces Othello that Desdemona and Cassio are getting down, "beast with two backs" style. Long story short, it works, and overwhelmed by jealousy, Othello strangles Desdemona in a series of gut-wrenching scenes that mix tenderness and brutality in pretty unprecedented ways. Realizing that he's been duped, Othello kills himself, and Iago is carried off for, we hope, the gallows.

Othello has drawn lots of critical attention for two main reasons: first, and perhaps most importantly, it is the play in which Shakespeare engages most directly with issues of race (*The Merchant of Venice* is a close second, as we'll see). Othello is a "Moor" in Venice, a black man ruling white subjects. Second, the character of Iago is a quintessential example of a literary antagonist. The search for Iago's motivations in his ultimate betrayal have been of interest to artists and writers. For Harold Bloom in *The Anxiety of Influence*, for example, Iago becomes the prototype for a kind of evil or rebellion so profound as to be the object of endless conjecture; Iago, says Bloom, is the forebear of another memorable character: Milton's Satan.

Famous quotes:

- "For when my outward action doth demonstrate/The native act and figure of my heart/In compliment extern, 'tis not long after/But I will wear my heart upon my sleeve/For daws to peck at. I am not what I am." (Iago, I.1)
- "She swore in faith 'twas strange, 'twas passing strange,/'Twas pitiful, 'twas wondrous pitiful." (Othello, I.3)
- "I hate the Moor..." (Iago I.3) "Men should be what they seem;/Or those that be not, would they might seem none!" (Iago, III.3)
- "O! beware, my lord of jealousy;/It is the green-ey'd monster which doth mock the meat it feeds on..." (Iago, III.3)
- "Put out the light, and then put out the light..." (Othello, V.2)
- "I kissed thee ere I killed thee, no way but this,/Killing myself, to die upon a kiss." (Othello, V.2)

Comedies

The Taming of the Shrew

Like Chaucer's "Wife of Bath's Tale," *The Taming of the Shrew* has drawn attention for its portrayal of a proto-feminist character, Kate, and in this portrayal, seems to one of a number of extended Shakespeare meditations on women in society. It's impossible to know, of course, what Shakespeare himself intended with this "comedy." Modern eyes often see Kate's "taming" as a downfall and a clear instance of patriarchy pummeling independent women.

Baptista, a merchant in Padua, has two daughters, Bianca and Katherina. Bianca is clearly a babe and has a bunch of suitors (the most recent of whom is Lucentio), but the problem is that Baptista won't let Bianca marry until her older sister, the "shrew" Kate, is married. Petruccio, the proto-macho-man to Kate's proto-feminist, swoops in and convinces Baptista to let him woo and marry Kate. They are married, and they leave for Verona shortly after the wedding. In what amounts to pretty much long-form torture, Petruccio breaks Kate down (read: he "tames the shrew") until she accepts the subservient position she's "supposed" to have. In the end, Kate is the best "wife" of all the women in the play.

The main characters are, of course, Baptista, Bianca, Katherine (Kate), and Petruccio. This play has a lot of fun with the Italian-sounding names ending in –io (Petruccio, Lucentio, Grumio, Gremio, Hortensio, Tranio, Vincentio), and so if one of these names does show up, the odds are in your favor that it's from this play.

Famous quotes:
- You lie, in faith, for you are called plain Kate,
  And bonny Kate, and sometimes Kate the curst,
  But Kate, the prettiest Kate in Christendom,
  Kate of Kate Hall, my super-dainty Kate—
  For dainties are all cates, and therefore 'Kate'... (Petruccio II.1)

This exchange is from the end (V.2), where Kate is completely "tamed," and gives a good sense of the change that has taken place in her character:
- Kate:...Then vail your stomachs, for it is no boot,
  And place your hands below your husband's foot,
  In token of which duty, if he plase,
  My hand is ready, may it do him ease.
  Petruccio: Why, there's a wench! Come on, and kiss me,
  Kate.

The Tempest

The Tempest, typically regarded as the last play Shakespeare wrote alone, has emerged as one of the most studied Shakespeare plays since the Culture Wars of the 1980s. For many critics, *The Tempest* is Shakespeare's most direct engagement with the burgeoning colonial expansion of his day (the play was originally performed in 1611). Although we're classifying it as a comedy here, *The Tempest* is also commonly referred to as a "romance," a designation given to some of Shakespeare's later plays, including *The Winter's Tale*, *Cymbeline*, and *Pericles*. The "romances" are so named because of the distinction many scholars see between these late plays and the earlier Shakespeare comedies, and because of the common characteristics many of these plays share with the Medieval romance tradition.

As for the plot, Alonso, king of Naples, and many of his subjects are returning from Tunis, where Alonso's daughter has recently been married. The tempest destroys their boat, and the crew is shipwrecked on a mysterious island. Meanwhile, on the island, Prospero, former duke of Milan, is telling his daughter Miranda his own story essentially about how his brother Antonio had usurped him and forced him to flee. He escaped to this island with his infant daughter and his books about magic. The only inhabitants of the island are Caliban, whom Prospero eventually enslaves, and many spirits, such as Ariel, whom Prospero also more or less enslaves after freeing Ariel from a tree in which he was imprisoned by Sycorax (Caliban's mother and former head of the island).

There are many interactions among the characters but no single plot-arc: at one point, Caliban and some of his newfound cronies from the shipwreck look to overthrow Prospero but are thwarted when Ariel tells Prospero what's going on. One of the people shipwrecked, Ferdinand, falls in love with Miranda, and the two are eventually married (after Ferdinand's long servitude to Prospero). Ariel is set free. Caliban is forgiven. The ship is not wrecked after all, and everyone's able sail back to old Italia.

Although so much of the action seems to revolve around Prospero, the most discussed character in recent criticism has certainly been Caliban, particularly because of his position as "colonized" to Prospero's "colonizer." Margaret Paul Joseph's 1992 critical work *Caliban in Exile: The Outsider in Caribbean Fiction* gives a good sense of this. Interestingly, Caliban was a much-studied figure even before the emergence of postcolonialism as a discourse. In Robert Browning's dramatic monologue "Caliban in Setebos" (1864) champions Caliban as a "natural man" in Rousseau's sense of the term.

Famous quotes:
- "All lost! to prayers, to prayers! All lost!" (Mariners, I.1).
- "I, thus neglecting worldly ends, all dedicated/To closeness and the bettering of my mind..." (Prospero, I.2)
- "...All the charms/Of Sycorax, toads, beetles, bats, light on you;/For I am all the subjects that you have,/Which first was mine own king..." (Caliban, I.2)
- "You taught me language, and my profit on't/Is I know how to curse. The red plague rid you/For learning me your language!" (Caliban, I.2)
- "O wonder!/How many goodly creatures are there here!/How beauteous mankind is!/O brave new world/That such people in't!" (Miranda, V.1)

The Merchant of Venice

The Merchant of Venice has also been interesting to critics in recent years because of its own portrayal of race, this time in the form of the Jewish moneylender, Shylock. As with Caliban in *The Tempest*, Shylock is the not the play's "main character," but he has drawn more interest in criticism and in allusions to the play (in painting, literature, music, etc.) than any other character.

Bassanio, a young Venetian, decides to try and marry Portia, a beautiful Venetian heiress, upon hearing that her fortune would be his. He needs three thousand ducats to woo Portia. He asks Antonio (the "merchant"), who himself has to borrow the money from Shylock. Shylock is not a big fan of Antonio, mainly because Antonio is openly anti-semitic, but he lends him the money nonetheless, although with the odd caveat that if he can't pay the money back in three months, Shylock gets to extract a pound of flesh from Antonio. Antonio agrees.

In another weird deal, Portia's father says in his will that any of his daughter's suitors must choose from one of three casks before he can marry Portia. One of these casks has Portia's picture in it, and if the suitor picks that one, Portia is his; if not, he doesn't get Portia or anyone ever. Harsh. Fortunately, Bassanio draws the right cask, and Portia agrees to marry him immediately.

Meanwhile, Shylock's daughter Jessica has run off with Lorenzo, so he's in a rather foul mood when three months roll around and Antonio can't pay. Bassanio rushes to Venice and offers to overpay the loan, but all Shylock can think about is how much he'd love to take a pound of flesh from a Christian. In a clever, gender-bending disguise, Portia returns to save Antonio and, disguised as a lawyer, rules that Shylock can have his pound of flesh as long as he doesn't draw blood. Tough deal for the Shylock, who can't think of a way to make that work. Adding insult to injury, Shylock is found guilty of conspiring to murder a Venetian and has to give up all his wealth: half to Antonio and half to Venice. Antonio offers to give half of the half back as long as Shylock gives it to his estranged daughter and converts to Christianity. Shylock assents and everyone lives happily ever after (well, except Shylock).

Famous quotes:
- "I will buy with you, sell with you, talk with you, walk with you, and so following, but I will not eat with you, drink with you, nor pray with you." (Shylock, I.3)
- "The devil can cite Scripture for his purpose./An evil soul producing holy witness/Is like a villain with a smiling cheek,/A goodly apple rotten at the heart./O, what a goodly outside falsehood hath!" (Shylock, I.3).
- "But love is blind, and lovers cannot see/The pretty follies that themselves commit...What, must I hold a candle to my shames?" (Jessica, II.6)
- "I am a Jew. Hath not a Jew eyes? Hath not a Jew hands, organs, dimensions, sense, affections passions...If you prick us, do we not bleed?" (Shylock, III.1)

Histories

Richard III

We're including *Richard III* here because it's the most heavily tested of Shakespeare's histories, but equally important are *Henry IV* (especially Part I) and *Henry V*. Just because these are called "histories," though, don't get the impression that these are Shakespeare's only plays that deal with historical events. Usually lumped in with tragedies or romances, plays like *Julius Caesar*, *Antony and Cleopatra*, and *Pericles* are also based directly on historical sources. Even plays like *Macbeth* and *King Lear*, while not considered explicitly historical, have their roots in history. *Richard III* is often studied because of its long meditation on evil, especially the way this meditation is complicated by putting an evil character at the center of the history and, dare I say it, making the reader/audience sympathize with him.

Richard is Duke of Gloucester at the beginning of the play, and he states at the outset his intention to wrest the kingship from his brother King Edward IV. In the first of a string of killings, Richard arranges for the murder of his brother George, Duke of Clarence. Well, after this, things pick up, and Edward falls ill, but the crown will not pass to his brother but to one of his sons. As the princes are still children, Richard is appointed regent to govern in their stead until they are of age, and keeps them locked up in the Tower of London as "protection." While the children are in the tower, Richard begins to consolidate his power and, upon Edward's death, is crowned king. Thus it is all the more vile that Richard kills the two young princes in the Tower of London, seeing as he already has the crown. Edward's widow Elizabeth flees with her children from her first marriage (the princes were her children as well, of course). Elizabeth's own daughter Elizabeth (go figure) has become the apple of Richard's eye in the meantime, and Richard sees her as a great way to marry royal blood. In the end Henry Tudor, Earl of Richmond, declares war on Richard. Richard is killed in battle, and Henry Tudor is crowned Henry VII.

Aside from some cruel killing, the plot is not quite so overwrought as many of Shakespeare's later plays. Even so, Richard continues to be a compelling figure, and many of his lines are of the most famous in Shakespeare. Take these lines from the opening monologue:

> Now is the winter of our discontent
> Made glorious summer by this son of York;
> And all the clouds that loured upon our house
> In the deep bosom of the ocean buried...
> But I, that am not shaped for sportive tricks
> Nor made to court an amorous looking-glass,
> I that am rudely stamped and want love's majesty
> To strut before a wanton ambling nymph,
> I that am curtailed of this fair proportion,
> Cheated of feature by dissembling nature…
> And therefore since I cannot prove a lover
> To entertain these fair well-spoken days,
> I am determined to prove a villain
> And hate the idle pleasures of these days.

The first 40 lines of the play take exactly this form: Richard III's direct address to the audience with no one else on stage, announcing that the play is much more about Richard himself than about the narrative action of the play. There are many meditations on Richard's own evildoing, and these are often the most famous lines of the play, so if you get something that looks like Shakespeare with a character plotting or evildoing (and proud of it), chances are it's spoken either by Richard or, the most villainous of all, Iago.

Sonnets

Finally, while Shakespeare is mainly known as a dramatist, his sonnets have been equally influential. There are 154 sonnets, so you can't know all of them, but there are at least a few that you should read: 18 ("Shall I compare thee to a summer's day?"), 116 ("Let me not to the marriage of true minds"), and 130 ("My mistress' eyes are nothing like the sun"). These are the most cited of Shakespeare's sonnets on the exam, and they can give you a good sense of how the Shakespearean sonnet is structured and how it differs from the Petrarchan and Spenserian sonnets. You can see full examples of this in our glossary of literary terms on page 52.

Hopefully with these summaries, along with your previous knowledge of Shakespeare, you certainly already know enough about Shakespeare to use POE and arrive at a reasonable guess even on the most difficult questions .

HEY, WHAT ABOUT WORLD LITERATURE?

ETS mentions that it will test some important world literature. What ETS means by this is that you will see some questions on the great nineteenth-century French and Russian novelists. Then there's German literature, which can be summed up with two authors, Goethe and Brecht. Italian literature is even easier: Dante.

We're aware that Europe isn't the world. ETS probably doesn't think so either. But the test must contain questions that a statistically significant portion of students can answer. Despite the progress being made in multicultural education, so few students can answer a question on Middle Eastern or Asian literature that questions about authors from those parts of the world are not asked. When it comes to Latin American and African authors, only questions about the most famous writers have any likelihood of showing up. How famous? Gabriel García Márquez, Jorge Luis Borges, Chinua Achebe, Athol Fugard, Nadine Gordimer, and so on.

ETS's worst nightmare is the increasing trend toward multicultural education. This isn't because ETS is a political dinosaur (well, not entirely anyway), but because the more multicultural education becomes, the less standardized the curricula at different institutions become. Without something at least close to a standard curriculum, the test is impossible to write. ETS is aware that students are reading and studying writers like Leslie Marmon Silko, Louise Erdrich, Maxine Hong Kingston, and Derek Walcott. But, ETS wonders, which of these authors exactly, what books exactly, and how many students are reading them? ETS needs answers to these questions before it can include significant amounts of test material on non-canonical writers.

WHERE DO WE GO FROM HERE?

Now let's get down to business and look at what you definitely should study.

AN OUTLINE OF BRITISH AND AMERICAN LITERARY HISTORY

We'll start with a brief outline of British and American literary history to help you place writers and works in the appropriate historical periods. We've covered only British and American writers because they are the most likely to appear on the test. All writers in the outline are British unless otherwise noted. The British, after all, had a lot longer to write than did American writers.

As we demonstrated in Chapter 4, knowledge of general dates can be crucial to your scoring more on the test. So take a look at the outline below and keep the general periods in mind as you study.

Note that we have placed authors in this chart according to when they were most active as authors, not to when they were born and have done our best to place authors in chronological order within each time period.

Date	Period / Notes	Representative Authors
400–1300	Old English (c. 1000, the English language became strongly influenced by medieval French) Battle of Hastings (1066)	Caedmon c. 670 Author of Beowulf c. 750
1300–1500	Middle English Battle of Agincourt (1415) Gutenberg Bible (1456)	William Langland (1380) Geoffrey Chaucer (1380) Thomas Malory (1450)
1500–1558	Early Tudor period Reigns of Henry VII, Henry VIII, Edward VI, and Mary	John Skelton Thomas More
1558–1603	Elizabethan period Reign of Elizabeth I	Philip Sidney Edmund Spenser John Lyly Christopher Marlowe William Shakespeare
1603–1625	Jacobean period Reign of James I	Ben Jonson
1625–1649	Caroline period Reign of Charles I	John Donne John Webster
1649–1660	Charles I executed (1649) Cromwell and the Interregnum	John Milton Robert Herrick Andrew Marvell

1660–1714	Restoration Reign of Charles II (1660–1702)	William Congreve George Etherege John Bunyan John Dryden
1714–1727	Reign of Anne (1702–1714), the last Stuart monarch	Daniel Defoe Alexander Pope
1727–1760	Reign of George I of the House of Hanover	Jonathan Swift Henry Fielding Thomas Gray
1760–1790	Reign of George II The Enlightenment First 30 years of reign of George III American Revolution (1775–1783) The Gothic Novel	Samuel Johnson Lawrence Sterne Horace Walpole Thomas Chatterton Mary Wollstonecraft William Cowper
1790–1820	Early Romantic pe- riod Second 30 years of reign of George III Sturm und Drang in Germany	Anne Radcliffe William Blake William Wordsworth Samuel Coleridge Percy Bysshe Shelley Lord Byron John Keats
1820–1837	Middle Romantic period Reign of George IV (1820–1830) Reign of William IV (1830–1837)	Charles Lamb Jane Austen British: Thomas Carlyle Alfred Tennyson American: Washington Irving Edgar Allan Poe
1837–1869	Late Romantic and Victorian periods First 32 years of reign of Victoria	British: Thomas Macaulay Emily Brontë Charlotte Brontë Charles Dickens Robert Browning

	Transcendentalism in the United States	American: Nathaniel Hawthorne Ralph Waldo Emerson Henry David Thoreau Walt Whitman Herman Melville
1869–1901	Second 30 years of reign of Victoria Realism	British: John Ruskin George Meredith Charles Swinburne George Eliot Gerard M. Hopkins Thomas Hardy American: Mark Twain Henry James
1901–1939	Modernism	British: William Butler Yeats Joseph Conrad D. H. Lawrence W. H. Auden James Joyce Virginia Woolf American: Ernest Hemingway F. Scott Fitzgerald Gertrude Stein T. S. Eliot Ezra Pound W. E. B. Du Bois

7

Homer and
Other Masters

ANCIENT GREEK LITERATURE AND MYTHOLOGY

You are no doubt aware that classical literature, especially the literature of ancient Greece, has exerted a powerful influence on English-language authors. As we mentioned in Chapter 4, one of ETS's favorite games is "catch the reference." Given the influence of ancient authors on English letters, it should come as no surprise that many of the cross-references on the test are to authors like Homer and figures like Aeneas.

Homer's *Iliad* and *Odyssey* are the ultimate source of the majority of the questions on classical topics. Ideally, if you haven't read one or both of these works, you should do so. The points-to-pages ratio is very high. If, however, you are pressed for time, or if you have developed a phobia of the ancient Greeks in general (or Homer in particular), there is hope. The knowledge of just a few topics will clear up the lion's share of any weakness you have concerning classical Greek literature.

The material that follows presents the information about classical literature we think you must know for the GRE Literature in English Subject Test.

> Homer is the source of most questions about classical literature.

EPICS, ENGLAND, AND ETS

It is crucial that you know the conventions of the epic form. From the Renaissance through the Victorian age, English authors often assumed their readers were familiar with the epic form. An allusion to Achilles was hardly more esoteric to a university-educated English reader than an allusion to Arnold Schwarzenegger movies would be today. English authors, ever ready to display their wit and verbal virtuosity, were particularly fond of poking fun at the treasured works of the past by parodying the distinctive features of the Homeric epic in their own writing. None of this is lost on ETS. They expect you to know the conventions of the epic and to be able to recognize the look of its peculiar devices when borrowed or parodied by an English author.

An epic, in the most general sense, is a long narrative about sustained heroism. But the epic, in the sense derived from Homer's *Iliad*, has several distinct features. Not every epic modeled after Homer's has every feature. Below, we describe the classic conventions of an imaginary ideal epic:

- The epic begins with the invocation of the muse. This is called the **epic invocation** or **epic question**, as the address to the muse is often in the form of a request for the muse to help the poet remember the past.

- The action is then begun in the midst of things—*in medias res*. For example, the *Iliad* begins with the siege of Troy already ten years old. Background information is supplied as the narrative unfolds.

- The background information and the descriptions of equipment or participants are often in the form of long lists, called **epic catalogs**.

- Some descriptions are highly stylized in a form called the **epic simile**. This, like any simile, is a comparison (almost always beginning with *like* or *as*), but the epic simile carries the comparison to an extraordinary length. For example, in Milton's *Paradise Lost* one finds:

> Now gentle gales,
> Fanning their odoriferous wings, dispense
> Native perfumes, and whisper whence they stole
> Those balmy spoils. *As when to them who sail*
> *Beyond the Cape of Hope, and now are past*
> *Mozambic, off at sea northeast winds blow*
> *Sabean odors from the spicy shore*
> *Of Araby the Blest, with such delay*
> *Well pleased they slack their course, and many a league*
> *Cheered with the grateful smell old ocean smiles;*
> So entertained those odorous sweets the fiend . . .

As epic similes go, the one above is fairly restrained. They can get much more involved. Two more characteristics are:

- Epics also typically involve interfering or interested supernatural beings who, in some sense, toy with the human participants.

- Finally, the epic is usually resolved by a great battle, contest, or deed.

THE *ILIAD*

If there is one epic to know for the test, it is the *Iliad*. Tradition has it that the *Iliad* was composed by a blind man named Homer sometime around the eighth century BCE. (For the test, that this is probably not actually the case does not concern us beyond the fact that you should know that the details of the authorship of the *Iliad* and the *Odyssey* are in permanent dispute.) The events that Homer describes took place during the twelfth century BCE. Historically, the city of Troy stood on the eastern side of the Hellespont in what is now Turkey. Following is a brief summary of the work.

Background: The city of Troy, ruled by Priam, is under siege from a massive army led by the Spartan Agamemnon. Priam's son, Paris, has stolen Helen, the wife of Agamemnon's brother, Menelaus, which led to the hostilities. As the *Iliad* opens, Troy has been under siege for ten years and the conflict remains deadlocked.

The *Iliad* begins, "This is the story of an angry man." The angry man referred to is Achilles. Achilles is by far the ablest warrior on the Greeks' side, and his men, the Myrmidons, are some of the fiercest fighters. Agamemnon, by abusing his privileges as commander-in-chief and taking Achilles's favorite woman, Bryseis, has angered the great warrior. Achilles refuses to take part in the siege any longer and goes to his ships, taking the Myrmidons and his best friend, Patroclos, with him. While Achilles broods, the siege continues.

The *Iliad* in 39 words: Agamemnon and Achilles of Sparta besiege Troy because Paris of Troy stole married Helen of Sparta. Achilles's best friend dies as the Trojans beat back the Spartan Greeks (including Odysseus). Achilles avenges his death by killing Paris's brother, Hector.

The Trojans, under the guidance of their champion, Hector (brother of Paris and son of Priam), turn the tide of the battle and drive the Greeks from around the walls of Troy, pushing the fight all the way back to the Greek ships at the shore. For the Greeks, the situation is dire. Leading Greek captains, Odysseus among them, implore Agamemnon to apologize to Achilles. Agamemnon relents and offers to compensate Achilles for the wrongs the hero has suffered, but Achilles will not be appeased. Eventually, however, Achilles allows his friend Patroclos to participate in the defense of the ships. Patroclos dons Achilles's magnificent armor and enters the battle. The ships are saved, but Patroclos is killed by Hector, and the armor is lost.

Enraged (to put it mildly) at the death of his best friend, Achilles decides to fight, but he cannot fight without armor. Achilles calls on his mother, the demigod Thetis, and through her obtains a fantastic suit of armor crafted by the god Hephaestus. Achilles finally takes the field and quickly avenges the death of Patroclos by killing Hector and dragging the Trojan hero's corpse through the dirt behind a chariot. Priam, mourning the loss of his valiant son, enters the Greek camp and begs Achilles for the body. Achilles, moved by Priam's grief, returns Hector's body to the old man.

Throughout the story, the gods above are as divided in Olympus as the Greeks and Trojans are below, and they take sides, helping their favorite mortals when the opportunity arises. By working at cross purposes to each other, the gods seem blithely bent on provoking the greatest possible mayhem among the mortal troops of both sides.

Greek God Cheat Sheet

Greek God	aka Roman Name	Job Title/Job
Zeus	Jupiter	chief god, god of the sky
Poseidon	Neptune	lord of the sea
Hades	Pluto	lord of the dead, the underworld (but not death itself)
Hestia	Vesta	goddess of the hearth
Hera	Juno	protector of marriage
Ares	Mars	god of war
Athena	Minerva	goddess of wisdom
Aphrodite	Venus	goddess of love and beauty
Hermes	Mercury	messenger god (leads dead to underworld; inventor of music)
Artemis (twin of Apollo)	Diana	goddess of the hunt
Apollo	Phoebus	god of healing, intellectual pursuits, fine arts, prophesy, and, in later years, sun and light

Greek God	aka Roman Name	Job Title/Job
Hephaestus	Vulcan	god of smiths and weavers
Demeter	Ceres	goddess of the harvest
Persephone	Proserpine	goddess of the underworld
Dionysus	Bacchus	god of wine
Eros	Cupid	god of love
Eris		goddess of strife
Pan		god of goatherds and shepherds (plays the fife and has a goat-like appearance)
The Graces:		daughters of Zeus and Eurynome
Aglaia		Splendor
Euphrosyne		Mirth
Thalia		Good Cheer
The Muses:		daughters of Zeus and Mnemosyne; known for their music, which brings joy to any who hear it. Each of the nine muses has her own specialty:
Clio		History
Urania		Astronomy
Melpomene		Tragedy
Thalia		Comedy
Terpsichore		Dance
Calliope		Epic Poetry
Erato		Love Poetry
Polyhymnia		Songs to the Gods
Euterpe		Lyric Poetry
The Furies		punish crime
The Fates		choose a man's destiny and life span
Titans		ruled the earth before the Olympians overthrew them
Chronos	Saturn	ruler of the Titans
The Naiads		one of three classes of water nymphs, along with the Nereides and Oceanides

The following family tree is a helpful reference list. Although you won't be tested on the information below, it is good to review the relationships in classical mythology, as later writers make extensive references to them.

Greek God Family Tree

We have included the entire lineage for your personal edification, and the names most likely to show up on the test are printed in bold.

THE ODYSSEY

Like the *Iliad*, the *Odyssey* begins *in medias res* and backtracks to the beginning of the tale only after a significant amount of action has already unfolded. It is far simpler to tell the story chronologically; for the GRE Literature in English Subject Test, this approach is completely adequate. Following is a brief summary.

Odysseus, after the sacking of Troy, attempts to return to his home, Ithaca, with his men and twelve ships. Things go well for a short while, but then Odysseus and his men encounter the Cyclops Polyphemus and blind him, which enrages the Cyclops's father, Poseidon, god of the sea. Eleven of the twelve ships, and the men on them, are soon after lost in a battle with giants. Odysseus and his remaining men come to the island of Aenea, where the witch Circe turns Odysseus's men into pigs. Odysseus manages to have his men returned to human form, and after a year, Circe allows them to leave the island.

Odysseus successfully sails between Scylla and Charybdis, two monsters, and resists the Sirens' song, but when his men commit sacrilege and kill the sacred cows of Helios, Zeus strikes them down. Only Odysseus survives. He drifts at sea and washes up upon the shore of Ogygia, the island home of the goddess Calypso. She detains him for seven years (it is at this point in the story that Homer's narrative of the *Odyssey* begins), but finally releases him at Zeus's command. Odysseus builds a raft and, after a mishap at the hands of Poseidon, who holds a grudge, gets to the land of Scheria. Odysseus is received kindly, catches up on news he's missed, and discovers that his and his companions' exploits in the plains around Troy have already become the stuff of legend. Odysseus recounts his subsequent adventures to the Scherians, and they bring Odysseus to Ithaca by ship.

In tandem with the tale of Odysseus's adventures is the story of what occurs in Ithaca during his long absence. Penelope, Odysseus's wife, has been beset by suitors, but she manages to put them off with ruses and sheer obstinacy. The suitors plot to have Telemachus, Odysseus's son, murdered, but Telemachus evades their schemes.

With Odysseus's return to Ithaca, the story's threads of Odysseus's attempt to return home and Penelope's stalling of the suitors are united. Odysseus, in disguise (his dog recognizes him, though), finds his domain overrun by the riotous debauched suitors, who are eating him out of house and home. With Telemachus's aid, Odysseus slaughters the lot of them and, for good measure, executes those servants who had been in cahoots with the suitors. Odysseus's martial competence and the intervention of the goddess Athena prevent the suitors' relatives from pressing for revenge against Odysseus. The story ends with Odysseus restored to his home and his faithful wife.

The *Odyssey* in 45 words: Odysseus tries to return home after sacking Troy (see the *Iliad*). Cursed by Poseidon, he drifts at sea for ten years, has various adventures, and finally gets home to find wife Penelope fending off avid suitors. He and son Telemachus get rid of the lot.

The Aeneid

Agamemnon in 26 words: Clytemnestra, angry with husband Agamemnon for sacrificing their daughter and for bringing home his prescient love slave Cassandra, conspires with her lover Aegisthus to murder Agamemnon.

Choephoroe ("The Libation Bearers") in 36 words: Based on the advice of an oracle, Orestes (Agamemnon and Clytemnestra's exiled son) decides to avenge his father's murder. He and sister Electra murder Clytemnestra and her lover Aegisthus, but Orestes is tormented by the Furies.

The Eumenides ("Benevolent Ones") in 41 words: Athena presides over a precedent-setting murder trial: Orestes vs. the Furies for the murder of Clytemnestra and Aegisthus. The jury is hung. Athena decides in favor of Orestes but placates the Furies by offering to share the ruling of Athens.

Virgil (or Vergil) was a great admirer of Homer, and he wanted to write an epic poem that could be for the Romans what the *Iliad* and the *Odyssey* had been for the Greeks. As such, Virgil was not merely an admirer of Homer, but very much a student, and for this reason, much that can be said for the formal qualities of Homer's epics is true of Virgil's, as well.

Because of the Catholic church's profound sway throughout much of Europe— at least until the end of the nineteenth century—Latin has historically been more widely studied and read than Greek. Although today we may think of Homer as the greatest epic poet, many generations of writers and scholars have given this honor to Virgil, and his *Aeneid* has arguably had more direct influence of pre-twentieth century artworks than Homer's two major epics have ever had. After all, it's not Homer who leads Dante through the *Inferno* and *Purgatorio*, but Virgil. The XII¬-book structure of Milton's *Paradise Lost* is lifted from the XII¬-book structure of the *Aeneid*. Greek made a big comeback in the eighteenth and nineteenth centuries, but even later writers such as George Bernard Shaw were more familiar with Virgil than Homer, and Shaw's play *Arms and the Man* takes its title from the first line of Virgil's epic: "I sing of arms and the man…" In this sense, James Joyce's use of Homer in *Ulysses* (1922) was somewhat of an anomaly (and even here, notice the book uses the Latin name of the hero Odysseus).

We'll now move on to the summary. As in Homer, things begin *in medias res*. Also as in Homer, Juno (Hera in Homer's works) resents the Trojan people and wishes destruction upon them. Aeneas, a Trojan soldier and son of the goddess Venus, is leading a fleet to find a new home after their defeat at the hands of the Greeks. It has been foretold that they will found a great nation in Italy, but because of Juno's wrath, they are blown to the shores of Carthage. Here, Aeneas woos the Carthaginian Queen Dido and wins her favor.

In Carthage, Aeneas recounts the events between the end of the *Iliad* and the present. He tells the story of the "Trojan Horse," a ruse created by Ulysses as a surprise attack on the Trojans. The Trojan priest Laocoon warned against accepting the gift but was eaten, pretty much out of nowhere, by two giant sea snakes. (NB: Friedrich Schiller's famous essay "Laocoon" is not about Virgil specifically, but about a statue that was inspired by Virgil's description of Laocoon's cruel fate.) The Greeks proceeded to massacre the Trojans, and although Aeneas fought bravely, his mother Venus intervened and told him to flee. Aeneas flees with his father Anchises on his back.

However, Aeneas hasn't quite made it to Italy as he's telling the story, and only after a fiery love affair with Dido is he reminded by Jupiter and Mercury of his purpose. Dido, wrought with grief, kills herself and vows that Carthage will avenge her. For Virgil's contemporary audience, Rome's recent wars with Carthage (known as the Punic wars) are clearly invoked here. Many subsequent authors, though, have been most taken with the character of Dido, and allusions to her have been plentiful. There are allusions to Dido in Mercutio's "Queen Mab" speech in *Romeo and Juliet*; Dante's *Inferno*, in which she appears in the second circle of hell, punished for all eternity for her lust; Christopher Marlowe's *Dido, Queen of Carthage*; even T. S. Eliot's Lil in the "A Game of Chess" section of *The Waste Land* is a composite of abandoned lovers, including Dido. She is quite often made just such a composite with other famously tragic women from the classical era such as Eve, Philomela (from Ovid's *Metamorphoses*), Cleopatra, and Ophelia.

The second half of the epic deals mainly with Aeneas's battles as he and his men land on the Italian shores and begin to fulfill their destinies. Aeneas teams up with Evander, king of the Latins, to combat Turnus and the Rutuli. Lots of blood is spilled, including Turnus's (a lot of it), and Aeneas and his men can peacefully set up shop in Italy, comfortable in the knowledge that their descendents will have pretty much the biggest empire ever.

THE CURSED HOUSE OF ATREUS

The Greek tragedian Aeschylus drew upon a set of stories concerning an ancient familial curse, the curse upon the House of Atreus, to write the *Oresteia* trilogy—*Agamemnon, Choephoroe* (The Libation Bearers), and *Eumenides*—in the fifth century BCE. You needn't be concerned with the origins of the curse upon Atreus and his lineage. The important part of the story—for our purposes—picks up with the curse's effect on Atreus's sons, Agamemnon and Menelaus. As those names should signal, the story of the House of Atreus intersects with that of the Trojan War (cf. the *Iliad*). The following family tree is a quick overview of the relationships between these characters.

Family Tree of Characters in Aeschylus's Trilogy of Tragedies

Aegisthus married Clytemnestra, whom Orestes overthrew.

Oedipus the King in 56 words: The Oracle prophesies that King Laius will have a son who will kill Laius and marry Queen Jocasta. But instead of killing newborn Oedipus to avoid the prophesy, they give him up for adoption. Grown-up Oedipus solves a sphinx's riddle and marries the Queen. When the incest is revealed, Jocasta commits suicide and Oedipus blinds himself.

Oedipus at Colonus in 21 words: Oedipus goes to Colonus with daughters Antigone and Ismene. His sons fight each other to the death for his vacated throne.

Antigone in 33 words: Despite penalty of death, Antigone attempts to bury her brother Polyneices. King Creon, her uncle, banishes her to a cave where she hangs herself. Creon's son Haemon, her lover, stabs himself in grief.

The Trojan War is, in one sense, thought to have been triggered by the abduction of Menelaus's wife Helen by the Trojan, Paris. In another sense, the original cause is Zeus himself, who takes on the form of a swan and rapes the mortal woman Leda. Yeats's poem "Leda and the Swan" makes just this point. But, in still another sense, the curse on the House of Atreus is a cause both of the war and of the problems that hound the Greeks, particularly Agamemnon, at every turn. Everything connected to Atreus's line eventually falls to bloody shambles. Menelaus's wife is abducted, which starts the war. The Greek fleet, amassed at Sparta under Agamemnon's command, cannot sail against Troy because of an ill wind. Eventually, Agamemnon sacrifices his daughter Iphigenia in order to turn the wind, a crime which will lead ultimately to his own death. First though, he manages to offend Achilles, a misstep which leads to the slaughters recounted in the *Iliad*.

With the "successful" conclusion of the Trojan War, Agamemnon returns to Sparta with Cassandra, the daughter of Priam (King of Troy), as his mistress. Back in Sparta however, Agamemnon's wife Clytemnestra has taken a lover, Aegisthus. Despite having a lover, she is consumed with jealousy at the sight of Cassandra. Clytemnestra and Aegisthus murder Cassandra and Agamemnon, an act they justify as revenge for Agamemnon's sacrifice of Iphigenia.

It's at this point that the curse proceeds down the line. Orestes, Agamemnon's son, picks up where dad left off. He kills the usurper Aegisthus as well as his own mother, Clytemnestra, who begs eloquently and *almost* successfully for mercy. The Furies, Greek divinities of pitiless and relentless revenge (particularly of murder within families), shriek down on Orestes for his crime and drive him partly mad. Orestes pleads to Apollo for protection and is granted a trial; the Athenian citizens (as well as Athena herself) are the judges, and the Furies prosecute. The vote on Orestes's guilt is split, and Athena declares that a tie goes to the defendant. The Furies aren't happy about the verdict, but here the curse on the House of Atreus is finally laid to rest.

OEDIPUS

Sophocles dramatized the story of Oedipus and his offspring in the tragedies *Oedipus the King, Oedipus at Colonus,* and *Antigone* in the fifth century BCE. You should know the outlines of the legend related in those plays. However, for the purposes of this test, the Oedipus story is much less important than the material concerning the Trojan War. We do not suggest you put more time into studying the Oedipus legend than reading the following summary.

The Oracle prophesies that the king of Thebes, Laius, will have a son who murders his father and marries his mother. When an infant son is born to Laius's wife, Jocasta, he orders the child slain. The child's feet are pierced, but instead of being abandoned in the wilderness, the child is given to a shepherd and eventually taken in by the childless king and queen of Corinth. When Oedipus (in Greek, the name refers to his injured feet) matures, he learns from the Delphic Oracle that he will kill his father and marry his mother. He vows never to set foot in Corinth again. Wandering, Oedipus comes to a crossroads where he kills a stranger after an argument. The stranger, of course, turns out to be Laius.

Oedipus eventually wanders to Thebes, a city suffering a plague that will only be relieved when the riddle of the sphinx is solved. Oedipus solves the riddle and wins the grand prize. He is made king of Thebes and Jocasta becomes his wife. Oedipus fathers four children, the sisters Antigone and Ismene, and brothers Eteocles and Polyneices, before the truth comes out. When Oedipus learns his true parentage he blinds himself; Jocasta hangs herself.

Following King Oedipus's death, his children debate the succession. Eteocles and Polyneices agree to share rulership of Thebes, alternating active command yearly. Eteocles reigns first, and when his year is up he refuses to yield the throne. Polyneices organizes an army against Eteocles and attacks Thebes (this is the story behind *Seven Against Thebes* by Aeschylus). Polyneices and Eteocles die at one another's hands. Creon, brother of Jocasta and acting regent of Thebes, decrees that because Polyneices has waged war against his own city, he will not be buried, an act that will prevent Polyneices's spirit from finding peace. Antigone defies the decree and performs the burial ceremonies for her brother. For this, Creon has Antigone entombed alive within a cave. There, she commits suicide, and Haemon (Creon's son), her lover, finds her body and commits suicide beside her.

House of Thebes

HOMER AND OTHER MASTERS ◆ 103

8

The A, B, and C Lists

HOW TO USE THE A, B, AND C LISTS

For the GRE Literature in English Subject Test, you want to have your head crammed with tons of tidbits, with that right "little something" about every author on the test. Hence, we've come up with lists of the most important works, those that will almost certainly be on the test and have a high points-to-pages ratio.

We have by no means covered, or even attempted to cover, *every* author who might appear on the test in these lists. The A, B, and C lists are those authors and works that we think have a high degree of likelihood of appearing on the test. If we tried to cover all authors whose work might appear on the GRE Literature in English Subject Test, you would spend more time reading this book than their works. Authors we think are less likely to appear on the test are covered in the explanations to the practice test questions in Part V. This is another reason why it's important that you read all the explanations.

The A list has the highest points-to-pages ratio; with a copy of *The Norton Anthology of English Literature* (volumes I and II) handy, you could work through the whole A list in about half an hour and pick up a number of points.

The B list is a little more unwieldy. It contains notes to important older (and longer) works. Ideally, you should refer to those works, but in a pinch, just reading the B list itself should give you much of what you need.

The C list is like a menu. It presents works, authors, and periods that are very likely, but not certain, to be on the test. You should pick through this list and bone up on those places where you find a gap in your knowledge.

Each list has an introduction which goes into more detail on how to use that particular list. Within the lists, the works are given in *chronological* order, not in order of importance.

Finally, remember that quantity, not quality, is what you need. Don't obsess about any one work. You're looking for names, a sense of the style, and the specific points we mention you should note. Be careful when you're reading or you'll find yourself hooked; these works are called masterpieces for a reason.

THE A LIST

This list contains those very short works that you should read *in their entirety*. These works are poems that are often studied and that contain lines frequently alluded to by other poets—considerations that make them favorites of the ETS writers. These are works that have a very high probability of getting you some of those make-or-break points, with very little study time. The notes that follow each entry tell you exactly what you should pay attention to in these works.

Christopher Marlowe's "The Passionate Shepherd to His Love" (1599)

Know this poem's opening lines—"Come live with me and be my love/And we will all the pleasures prove"—by heart. They have been quoted or alluded to by many English poets over the years. Sir Walter Raleigh, John Donne, Robert Herrick, and C. Day Lewis are just a few of the poets who have used Marlowe's poem as a starting point for verses of their own. Raleigh's, called "The Nymph's Reply to the Shepherd," is the most notable of these responses.

Ben Jonson's "To the Memory of My Beloved Master William Shakespeare" (1623)

This poem is so chock-a-block full of references to other poets that it's hard for the ETS folks to resist. It's not a poem you need to study so much as you need to be able to recognize it. The line, "He was not of an age, but for all time!" is particularly famous. "He" refers to Shakespeare (but you knew that).

Robert Herrick's Julia Poems: "Upon Julia's Breasts," "Upon Julia's Clothes," "The Night Piece, to Julia" (1648)

The point here is to familiarize yourself with the Julia Poems, which are in themselves famous, and which have inspired other poets to follow Herrick's lead and invent mistresses for themselves about which to write poems. If a poem mentions Julia, chances are it is at least a nod in Herrick's direction.

You might also want to glance at Herrick's "To the Virgins, to Make Much of Time," because it has the same theme as "To His Coy Mistress."

Andrew Marvell's "To His Coy Mistress" (1681)

It's hard to imagine a GRE Literature in English Subject Test that doesn't somehow include a question on this poem.

The poem's theme is: Come and have sex with me immediately because before you know it, we'll all be rotting in our graves. This theme was the rallying cry of the perpetually randy cavalier poets, and it is almost certain to make an appearance on your test. ETS will rephrase it to something like, "make the best use of your time while you can."

Almost every one of the poem's 46 lines is famous, but be sure you recognize "But at my back I always hear/Time's wingèd chariot hurrying near;/And yonder all before us lie/Deserts of vast eternity."

Thomas Gray's "Elegy Written in a Country Church Yard" (1751)

This almost qualifies as a long poem for the purposes of our list, but along with Marvell's "To His Coy Mistress," it is one of the works most likely to show up on your test.

You should know that the poem is a meditation upon death, especially death without worldly fame, or (to be more fair to Gray) death without recognition or full expression of one's gifts. Many of the poem's lines are famous (or once were famous—the poem was tremendously popular in its time), but for the subject test, just be sure you can recognize the epitaph that closes the poem (probably for Gray's friend, the sometime poet Richard West), and above all the lines "Some mute, inglorious Milton here may rest,/Some Cromwell guiltless of his country's blood."

William Wordsworth's "She Dwelt Among the Untrodden Ways" (1800)

There are just two things to pay attention to here, but either could be worth a point. First, the subject of the poem is a girl named Lucy. Wordsworth wrote several poems about her, which are called, naturally enough, the Lucy Poems. Secondly, all 12 lines of "She Dwelt Among the Untrodden Ways" are well known and often alluded to, so read them.

As you read these works, pay attention to the author's style. Writers often will have distinguishing characteristics that will help you recognize their other works.

The poem's theme, though much more compactly expressed, is very much like that of Gray's "Elegy Written in a Country Church Yard"—the death of one lovely person unknown to larger society.

The other Lucy Poems are "Strange Fits of Passion Have I Known," "Three Years She Grew," "A Slumber Did My Spirit Seal," and "I Traveled Among Unknown Men."

Alfred Lord Tennyson's "Ulysses" (1842)

This is a great poem and an ETS favorite because of its classical references. You should read it once so that you can recognize it when you see it. The poem's conceit is that Odysseus is hanging around Ithaca, very old and very bored. He gazes out over the water and contemplates sailing with his companions off "beyond the sunset" because "Old age hath yet his honor and his toil./Death closes all; but something ere the end,/Some work of noble note, may yet be done,/Not unbecoming men that strove with gods."

Another Tennyson work shows up with regularity on the test—"In Memoriam A.H.H." Although it's too long to justify a thorough read for the test, you should be at least somewhat familiar with this very popular and influential poem, particularly its stanza form, which we discuss in our section on verse forms for the GRE on page 59. You should also know that the line "Nature, red in tooth and claw" comes from "In Memoriam A.H.H."

William Butler Yeats's "The Second Coming" (1921)

How many book titles, allusions, and morbid epigrams have come from this poem's 22 lines? It is probably the most quoted poem of the twentieth century. Read it.

THE B LIST

This is a list of Old English and Middle English works that *will* make an appearance on the GRE Literature in English Subject Test.

ETS tries to provide a rough balance in the number of questions it asks about any given time period. Unlike other eras, there is only a small body of important work to study in Old and Middle English. At the same time, so many students are weak on pre-Elizabethan literature that the questions ETS asks aren't particularly tough if you're the least bit familiar with the material. These considerations make it a virtual guarantee that studying these works will *not* be a waste of time.

Old English verse has a unique form. Lines are structured according to the number of accented syllables only. Unaccented syllables are not counted. Furthermore, rather than rhyming, individual lines alliterate across a mandatory central pause called a *caesura*. By 1100, Old English verse had fallen into disuse.

Old English gave way fully to Middle English around 1350, but at the same time, literary production picked up and a style of verse bearing important similarities to Old English verse (the element most obviously missing was the formal central *caesura*) had a brief but brilliant resurgence. During the Middle English revival of alliterative verse, *Piers Plowman* and *Sir Gawain and the Green Knight* were produced.

The two most important entries for you in this list are *Beowulf* and Chaucer's *The Canterbury Tales*, and these entries are also the longest. The Chaucer entry is particularly long. Don't go crazy and think this means the GRE Literature in English Subject Test is actually the GRE *Canterbury Tales* Subject Test; it isn't. We just wanted to provide enough information about the *Tales* that you could study from our notes without going directly to the source if you were pressed for time.

Beowulf (ca. 750)

Beowulf was sung by *scops* (Anglo-Saxon bards) for several centuries before being put to paper sometime around CE 750. Beowulf is a Swedish hero who, at the request of the Danish king Hrothgar, slays the monster Grendel (and Grendel's mother, after she comes around to avenge her son's death). Beowulf then returns home famous, rich, and respected, and ultimately becomes king of his people, the Geats. Years pass. Older and weaker but still fearless, he is called to duty again, this time to slay a dragon. Beowulf kills the dragon but is mortally wounded in the combat. During the fight a young warrior, Wiglaf, proves his worth. Beowulf appoints Wiglaf his successor and dies.

Beowulf in 19 words: Beowulf slays monster Grendel and becomes king. Years later, he is killed by a dragon and Wiglaf becomes king.

You can count on some questions about both the content of *Beowulf* and its formal qualities in Old English. A bare-bones knowledge of the plot will suffice to answer the content questions, but familiarize yourself with the Old English of the original. You *might* be given one question that asks you to translate an Old English line. Studying Old English in order to answer one possible question is insane. Just sound the words out and you should be able to make a reasonable guess. Much more important, be able to recognize the characteristics of Old English verse and the Old English poetic line. Here's an example:

> *Beowulf wæs breme*   —*blæd wide sprang*—
> Beowulf was famous   [his] fame wide sprung

Beowulf is written in strong stress verse, which is characteristic of Old English verse. Lines are not organized from one to the next by rhyme; instead, they are internally organized by alliteration. Furthermore, an Old English line is based not on a pattern of stressed and unstressed syllables (called accentual-syllabic meter), but on the number of stressed syllables only. Unstressed syllables are not counted in the rhythm. Finally, note the gap in the middle of the line given above. The gap represents a deep pause called a *caesura*. This regularly occurring gap is a special characteristic of the Old English verse line.

Names from *Beowulf* you should know include: Beowulf, Grendel, Grendel's mother, Hrothgar, Beaw, Scyld Scefing, Heorot (not a person—Beowulf's mead-hall), and Wiglaf.

William Langland's *Piers Plowman* (ca. 1380)

This long poem is composed of a series of eight allegorical visions, wherein Will, in dreams, seeks out Truth. You should know that Langland's *Piers Plowman* was written at the same time as Chaucer's *The Canterbury Tales*, but unlike *The Canterbury Tales*, *Piers Plowman* is written in alliterative verse. *Piers Plowman* is the masterpiece of the revival of the alliterative verse form in the fourteenth century.

The Canterbury Tales (1387)

The Canterbury Tales were composed by Geoffrey Chaucer sometime around 1387. They were written in Middle English.

There are a lot of pages to *The Canterbury Tales*, but a lot of points as well. Ideally, you would read *The Canterbury Tales* when studying for this test and use our notes, below, for assistance. If you don't have time for Chaucer, however, our notes should suffice. We suggest at least (re)reading the general prologue to the *Tales*, in which the character of each pilgrim is introduced. ETS thinks you should be able to identify both the tellers of tales and the tales they tell. You also need to be able to make some sense of unmodernized Middle English, so make sure you look at *The Canterbury Tales* in the original as well as a translated version.

The general plot is as follows: A group of pilgrims (including the author) journeys to the religious shrine at Canterbury. On the way, they tell stories to pass the time.

The poem is written in several different meters (depending on whose tale is being told), but the rhyming couplet form used in the general prologue predominates.

Here are the characteristics of the more important of the 24 pilgrims, and synopses of the more important tales:

- **The Knight**

  Valorous, chivalrous, and polite, he's a portrait of what you'd expect a knight to be.

  The knight's is the first tale told following the general prologue. ("The Miller's Tale" is the second, but the ordering of most of the other tales is problematic.) It concerns Arcite and Palamon, a pair of friends, who, while held in a tower as prisoners of war, fall in love with a woman (Emily) they see from the window. After a number of vicissitudes, the story reaches its climax when the two former friends organize an enormous battle to see who is deserving of Emily's hand. Arcite prays to Mars for help, Palamon to Venus, and each god answers its supplicant with what seems an assurance of victory. As it turns out, Arcite wins the battle, but he dies in the process, and thus Palamon gets Emily.

> "Authors, like coins, grow dear
> as they grow old
> It is the rust we value, not
> the gold
> Chaucer's worst ribaldry is
> learn'd by rote
> And beastly Skelton heads of
> houses quote."
>
> Alexander Pope

> "The Knight's Tale" in 13 words: Arcite and Mars fight Palamon and Venus for Emily. Arcite wins but dies.

- **The Prioress**

  She is dainty, materialistic, and sentimental about her little dogs. She wears a well-pleated wimple, a rosary made of coral, and a golden brooch with "Love conquers all" inscribed upon it. Her tale, told in a staid rhyme royal, concerns the murder of a little boy by Jews for singing the Christian hymn *Alma Redemptoris* while walking in a Jewish neighborhood. The murder is discovered because the boy miraculously continues singing despite having had his throat slit. The phrase "murder will out" comes from this story. Some apologists have suggested Chaucer intended to critique the prioress by having her recount this offensive tale, but such a view is almost surely revisionist. Stories of Jewish atrocities were standard fare of the time, and no doubt served as convenient pretexts for the Christians' periodic slaughter of their Jewish neighbors.

  > "The Prioress's Tale" in 14 words: Jews kill a Christian boy; he continues to sing after his throat is slit.

- **The Nun's Priest(s)**

  In the general prologue, a nun and three priests are mentioned as pilgrims accompanying the prioress. The priests are not described individually, and later Chaucer refers to only a single "Nun's Priest." This three-into-one prestidigitation is not considered deliberately symbolic of the unity of Father–Son–Holy Ghost (though someone has probably written a thesis along those lines); it seems that at some point Chaucer decided two of the priests were superfluous.

  > "The Nun's Priest's Tale" in 22 words: Chaunticleer the rooster is kidnapped by Sir Russell, a sweet-tongued fox. Chaunticleer gets away when the fox opens his mouth to brag.

  "The Nun's Priest's Tale" is one of the most frequently studied of *The Canterbury Tales*, and, more important for our purposes, is one of ETS's favorites. It is a fable about Chaunticleer, a handsome, vain rooster noted for his singing; the beautiful Perteltote, Chaunticleer's favorite hen; and Sir Russell, a fox. Chaunticleer dreams he'll be eaten by a strange creature (he describes a fox). Perteltote upbraids Chaunticleer for being a coward who believes in dreams. The fox comes along, flatters Chaunticleer into singing (with his eyes closed), and snatches him away. Just as the fox is about to finish Chaunticleer off, however, he gloats over his victim. In opening his mouth to say a few choice words, the fox allows Chaunticleer to escape. The fox tries to dupe Chaunticleer again, but the rooster has learned his lesson and rebukes himself for having listened to Sir Russell in the first place. The fox learns in turn that he, the fox, was foolish to blab when he should have been eating.

  The story is a favorite of ETS's for a number of reasons (not the least being the "G" rating the story gets as opposed to the "X" rating of some of the other tales). But in terms of the test, it is important to know that "The Nun's Priest's Tale" is mock-heroic; that is, it parodies some of the conventions of classical epic poetry such as *The Iliad*.

- ## The Merchant

The merchant wears motley and a beaver hat, and he talks about little else but his business concerns, which he unfailingly points out are profitable. He's actually in debt, but he bears himself with such calculated dignity that no one suspects it. The general prologue's description of the merchant, which is only 15 lines long, serves as an excellent example of Chaucer's ability to sketch a memorable, witty, psychologically acute portrait in less space than an ordinary writer might take to catch his breath.

"The Merchant's Tale" is a bawdy one. January, an old knight, marries May, a beautiful young girl. At first, January enjoys his young wife greedily (in fact, relentlessly), by night in the bedroom and by day in the garden; which is not bad for a scrawny old fellow with a flappy neck. But one day he suddenly goes blind and finds himself overwrought with jealousy. He keeps May within arm's reach at all times. May contrives to meet her young lover, Damian, in January's garden. She and Damian manage to consummate their passion up in a tree while the blind January remains on the ground holding onto the trunk. In the midst of May and Damian's fun, the god Pluto decides to restore January's sight. Caught in the act, quick-thinking May manages to convince January that she committed adultery only as a cure to restore his vision.

- ## The Wife of Bath

The Wife of Bath is an essential character to know for the GRE Literature in English Subject Test. Read the description of her given in the general prologue and familiarize yourself with the narration she gives of herself ("The Wife of Bath's Prologue") just prior to telling her tale. She's a bit deaf, gap-toothed, plump, ruddy, and not bad-looking in her preposterous way. She wears scarlet stockings, an enormous hat, and is comfortable both riding a horse and swapping jokes with the boys. She's had five husbands and that's "not counting other company she had in youth/but there's no need to speak of such things now." The wife of Bath is the embodiment of an outsized vision of womankind, a partly grotesque character, but one redeemed by the unselfconscious gusto with which she plays her part. Her prologue recounts the story of her five husbands, and more important, her uniquely feminist philosophies of love, sex, and (re)marriage, such as:

If you have enough, why care you how merrily the
other folks fare? For certain, old dotard, you'll have
the fill of my thighs come evening. The man's too
great a miser who won't let another man light a
candle at his lantern. For he'll have no less the light,
by heaven.

"The Wife of Bath's Tale" takes up her pro-woman theme, but
with far more gentility. One of King Arthur's knights rapes a
maiden (so much for the chivalrous days of Camelot), and
Arthur sentences the knight to death. The queen and some
of her ladies protest, and Arthur delivers the knight unto the
queen's justice. She tells the knight that she will spare his life if
he can return with an answer to the question, "What do women
desire most?" After some travail, the knight encounters a repulsive and sinister-seeming witch, who promises to reveal the
answer if the knight will marry her. The knight, not altogether
happily, agrees. The answer, *sovereignty*, is revealed, and the
witch turns into a beautiful maiden once the knight marries her.

- **The Miller**

The miller is a huge, strong, hard-drinking, rough-talking, fight-
picking, unpleasantly coarse fellow, with a shovel-sized red
beard and a big, hairy wart on his nose. He knows and uses the
tricks of the trade when it comes to weighing out grain.

He's quite drunk when he tells his tale ("I am drunk, I know it
by the sound of my voice"), which is perhaps the most vulgar
story of all *The Canterbury Tales*. A well-off carpenter with a
pretty young wife has a boarder named "Handy" Nicholas.
Nicholas is a good-looking, clever young scholar whom the
carpenter respects as one learned in astrology. Nicholas and
the carpenter's wife, Alison, contrive to spend a night of sin together by convincing the carpenter that an apocalyptic flood is
coming and that he should spend the night on the roof sleeping
in the washtub.

The ruse succeeds, but Nicholas and Alison's revels are somewhat interrupted by another of Alison's suitors, the ridiculously
lovelorn Absalom, who comes crooning at the window. Alison
promises Absalom a kiss, and in the darkness she has him kiss
her ass (which she hangs out the window). Infuriated, Absalom
fetches a hot poker and returns. When the lovers try to trick
Absalom a second time (this time it's Nicholas's butt slung out
the window), Nicholas gets the scalding poker across his but-
tocks. The carpenter on the roof awakens to Nicholas's shrieks
of "Water! Water!" Thinking the flood has come, the carpenter
cuts the rope tethering his washtub and so comes clattering
down.

"The Miller's Tale" in 19
words: A cuckold is tricked
into sleeping on his roof in a
washtub while his wife consorts
with various suitors.

- **The Pardoner**

"The Pardoner's Tale" in 16 words: Three drunkards search for death but instead find a treasure, over which they murder each other.

He is a thin, vain, smooth-skinned blond with a bag full of pardons "all hot from Rome." The host calls him a pretty boy, and Chaucer suggests that the pardoner isn't "all man." Chaucer also makes no disguise of portraying the pardoner as nothing more than a successful huckster, with bits of the true-cross, a scrap of St. Peter's sail, and a holy sheep bone that when dunked in a well turns the water into a cure-all potion.

The host, apparently after hearing one of the ribald tales, asks the pardoner to tell a story with a moral, an edifying story. The pardoner offers as prologue to his story an utterly frank confession of his own hypocrisy that is simultaneously an act of perfect hypocrisy itself, for he explains that his bogus wheelings and dealings make him an expert on his chosen theme: *Radix malorum est Cupiditas*. (Translated, this means "The love of money is the root of all evil.")

"The Pardoner's Tale" is a simple one. Three immoral drunkards set out to find Death, who has taken one of their drinking buddies. They're told to look for Death under a certain tree, but instead they find a large pile of treasure there. The three eventually manage to murder each other treacherously in trying to get an increased share of the booty. At the conclusion of the tale the pardoner tries to get the host to pay for the opportunity to handle some of the relics. The host responds that he'd rather have the pardoner's severed testicles so that he might bury them in pig shit. The pardoner begins to pitch a hissy fit at this, but the knight steps in, and the two are reconciled.

- **Other Pilgrims and Tales**

There are a total of 24 stories told, and 29 pilgrims (31 if you count the two mysterious missing priests). It isn't absolutely necessary to know them all, but connect the following names: The franklin, a wealthy landowner, tells a romantic tale about a lover, Aurelius; a faithful wife, Dorigen; and Dorigen's husband, Arveragus.

The reeve, a kind of administrative overseer, tells a tale of how a greedy miller named Simkin has his wife and daughter enjoyed by a pair of clerks, John and Alan, whom he'd swindled earlier. The story is the reeve's (a sometime carpenter) response to the miller's tale of the foolish flood-fearing carpenter.

The clerk tells the tale of Griselda, a patient wife, who endures the trials of her needlessly jealous husband, the Marquis Walter.

The doctor's tale is of a woman, Virginia, who has her father kill her in order to avoid falling into the clutches of Apius, an evil judge.

If you find this five-page summary of one of the greatest works in the history of literature reductive, well, take it up with ETS. This is all they expect you to know about Chaucer, and anything more is simply . . . knowledge.

Sir Gawain and the Green Knight (ca. 1380)

Sir Gawain and the Green Knight is a long poem that draws on the legend of Arthur and the court of Camelot. An enormous, mysterious, entirely green knight intrudes on a New Year's banquet and sets out a bizarre challenge. He will allow any one of the knights present to strike off his head, but if he survives the blow, the knight who failed to behead him must, exactly one year later, submit to being beheaded in turn. Gawain accepts the challenge, lops off the Green Knight's head, and watches in dismay as the Green Knight picks up his head and puts it back on.

After a year, Gawain sets out to keep his side of the bargain. On his journey, he is taken in by a lord and given hospitality at the lord's castle. After three days at the castle, Gawain is told the way to the Green Chapel where he is to meet his fate. At the Green Chapel, Gawain finds the Green Knight, who ultimately spares Gawain's life. He tells Gawain that he is the lord of the castle in another form and that he has spared Gawain because of Gawain's honorable conduct both at the castle and for keeping his bargain. (Because Gawain's conduct was not perfect—during his stay at the castle, he tried to keep a magic girdle that would supposedly protect him when, according to the rules of the castle, he should have returned it to the lord—the Green Knight does cut Gawain's neck slightly.)

The poem is written in distinctive verse stanzas, which can be used to identify the poem and distinguish it from Malory's *Morte D'Arthur*. The body of each stanza is composed of long alliterative lines, but the stanzas end with a peculiar form called "bob and wheel." The "bob" is a single very short line (one foot) and the "wheel" that follows is a short quatrain of trimeter lines rhyming (with the bob) *ababa*. Here's a portion of a stanza from *Gawain and the Green Knight*. Note the alliterative structure of the lines, and note as well the concluding "bob and wheel," which begins at the one-foot line "ill-sped."

The boar makes for the man with a mighty bound
So that he and his hunter came headlong together
Where the water ran wildest—the worse for the beast,
For the man, when they first met, marked him with care,   } quatrain in trimeter
Sights well the slot, slips in the blade,
Shove it home to the hilt, and the heart shattered,
And he falls in his fury and floats down the water,
         ill-sped. ← bob
      Hounds hasten by the score
      To maul him, hide and head;   } wheel in trimeter
      Men drag him in to shore
      And dogs pronounce him dead.

The unknown poet who composed *Sir Gawain and the Green Knight* is also believed to be the author of the poems *Pearl*, *Patience*, and *Cleanness*. The poet is sometimes referred to as "the *Pearl* poet."

Gawain in 52 words: A Green Knight shows up at a New Year's party and issues a challenge: Anyone who desires can behead him, but he who fails must in turn be beheaded. Gawain succeeds, but the knight re-heads himself. Gawain shows up for his own beheading, but the Green Knight (really a lord) spares him.

Sir Thomas Malory's *Le Morte D'Arthur* (1470)

Despite Malory's French title (by which he acknowledged his French source), *Le Morte D'Arthur* was written in Late Middle English. It recounts the legends surrounding King Arthur. In most cases, you shouldn't have any trouble identifying *Le Morte D'Arthur*, but you should be able to differentiate between it and the banquet scene in *Sir Gawain and the Green Knight*. The easiest way to distinguish between the two is formally: *Morte D'Arthur* is prose. Malory wrote the work while in prison and seems to have drawn from English sources as well as the "French book" he acknowledges.

THE C LIST

This is a list of important authors and works and a few periods and schools of literature. Unless we specifically suggest it in the notes, *we are not recommending you read these works in their entirety*. You should take a look at them, especially those by authors less familiar to you, and read just enough to be able to observe the points we note. In the vast majority of cases, what text you need can be found in *The Norton Anthology of English Literature* (volumes I and II).

The idea is to get a sense of the writer's or the work's style and themes and pick up a few names. The notes also point out some less obvious things that we think you should pay attention to, and offer other miscellaneous details we hope will prove valuable. The great majority of the authors on this list *will* appear on the GRE Literature in English Subject Test.

Edmund Spenser's *The Faerie Queene* (1590–1596)

The Faerie Queene is written in Spenserian stanzas: ababbcbcc. Verse forms are discussed in detail in Chapter 5.

Typically, ETS will give you a stanza of *The Faerie Queene* and ask you one or more of the following questions: Who wrote it? When was it written? What is the stanza's form called? What is the term used for the last line of this stanza form?

To answer these questions, you need to look over *The Faerie Queene* just enough to be able to recognize it, which isn't at all difficult, and memorize a few simple points.

Spenser deliberately used an archaic orthography and diction in order to give his epic an antique flavor. Keep in mind that Spenser was a close contemporary of Shakespeare, despite the older-looking English syntax. That alone is often enough to spot *The Faerie Queene*, but don't jump the gun; check the stanza form. Spenser wrote *The Faerie Queene* in what we call Spenserian stanzas (he invented them, and we don't know what he called them). The Spenserian stanza is a nine-line stanza rhyming *ababbcbcc*. The first eight lines are in iambic pentameter, but the final line is in iambic hexameter. An iambic hexameter line is called an *alexandrine*. ETS loves to see if you can identify an alexandrine. You don't have to memorize the rhyme scheme in order to identify a Spenserian stanza. A nine-line stanza with a patterned rhyme scheme that ends in an alexandrine is distinct enough.

Keep in mind that the Spenserian stanza has been used by notable poets up into the twentieth century, so don't assume that a Spenserian stanza must have been written by Spenser; look for his weird stylings.

Christopher Marlowe (1564–1593)

We mentioned Marlowe's "The Passionate Shepherd to His Love" on the A list, but you should also be familiar with his *Tamburlaine* and *Dr. Faustus*. *Tamburlaine the Great*, Parts I and II, is the story of a Scythian shepherd, Tamburlaine, who becomes an extraordinarily ferocious and successful conqueror in Asia Minor. Zenocrate is the main female character.

Dr. Faustus is the story of a sorcerer who sells his soul in return for power. In Marlowe's telling of the tale, Faustus is served and persecuted by Lucifer, Beelzebub, and Mephistopheles. Goethe also wrote a version of the tale called *Faust*. In the Goethe telling, the protagonist's soul is bartered in exchange for knowledge and Faust deals with a single satanic agent, Mephistopheles.

John Donne (1572–1631)

Expect to see Donne's name in more than a few answer choices, often the correct ones. If you're not up on Donne, look over the poems we suggest. Keep in mind that the poetry of Donne as a young man is very different from the poetry of Donne as an older man, though both are marked by his wit and razor-sharp intellect.

The young Donne's poetry is the verse of a courtier playboy. Good examples of this stage of his development are "The Sun Rising" and "The Flea." After the ups and downs of political life (in Donne's case, downs at first), Donne turned to a religious career, eventually becoming Dean of St. Paul's Cathedral, the most influential pulpit in London. The poems and sermons of this period of Donne's life are marked by passionate, original, and searching thought regarding the Divinity and Christian faith. A good example of this, and one that well captures Donne's unmistakable tone, is "Holy Sonnet 14":

> Batter my heart, three-person'd God; for you
> As yet but knock; breathe, shine, and seek to mend;
> That I may rise, and stand, o'erthrow me, and bend
> Your force, to break, blow, burn, and make me new.
> I, like an usurp'd town, to another due,
> Labour to admit you, but O, to no end.
> Reason, your viceroy in me, me should defend,
> But is captived, and proves weak or untrue.
> Yet dearly I love you, and would be loved fain,
> But am betroth'd unto your enemy;
> Divorce me, untie, or break that knot again,
> Take me to you, imprison me, for I,
> Except you enthrall me, never shall be free,
> Nor ever chaste, except you ravish me.

All of Donne's poetry is remarkable for the quality of its language. Whether playful and sensual as in the earlier poems, or struggling with difficult questions of faith as in the latter poems, the language manages to remain direct, clear, and forthright without sacrificing beauty and originality of phrase. Thomas Carew's (1594?–1640) "An Elegy upon the Death of the Dean of St. Paul's, Dr. John Donne" celebrates just these qualities of Donne's verse. Viz.: "The Muses' garden, with pedantic weeds/ O'erspread, was purged by thee; the lazy seeds/ Of servile imitation thrown away,/ And fresh invention planted . . ."

John Milton

Paradise Lost (1667)

Paradise Lost is undoubtedly the most important of John Milton's works. Be able to recognize it; here's an excerpt (*V*, lines 772–784):

> Thrones, Dominations, Princedoms, Virtues, Powers,
> If these magnific Titles yet remain
> Not merely titular, since by Decree
> Another now hath to himself ingross't
> All Power, and us eclipst under the name
> Of King anointed, for whom all this haste
> Of midnight march, and hurried meeting here,
> This only to consult how we may best
> With what may be devis'd of honors new
> Receive him coming to receive from us
> Knee-tribute yet unpaid; prostration vile,
> Too much to one, but double how endur'd,
> To one and to his image now proclaim'd?

For a definition and other examples of blank verse, see our Glossary of terms on page 59.

Note that Milton writes in blank verse. Note also his merciless torture of English sentence structure. Subsequent English critics have faulted Milton on this aspect of his work, even half-humorously suggesting that Milton wrote in Latin using an English vocabulary. For just this reason, ETS likes to use Milton, especially *Paradise Lost*, on its grammar questions. When faced with one of these monsters, don't assume you're hallucinating—yes, the sentence really is 20 lines long, and yes, the subject really is the third word from the end.

It is important to remember, however, that *Paradise Lost* is not the only important work that Milton wrote. You should also familiarize yourself with the following works via our handy summaries:

Areopagitica (1644)

Areopagitica is Milton's best known prose piece, and it has been lauded and studied for its defense of free expression and its condemnation of censorship. Much of Milton's political prose, including his influential divorce tracts, is interested in separating the spheres of spiritual and temporal authority. In *Areopagitica*, Milton argues that free press is God's will because published books are the means by which man will hear God's Revelation. As such, the censor is blocking God's word in censoring creative artists. "…as good almost kill a man as kill a good book. Who kills a man kills a reasonable creature, God's image; but he who destroys a good book, kills reason itself, kills the image of God, as it were in the eye."

Comus (1634)

Comus is a "masque," a dramatic form in which all entertainment systems are go in music, singing, dancing, acting, and stage design. This dramatic form was often offered in performance as tribute to the patron, It flourished in Milton's time, and in fact, Milton gave this piece the name *A Mask, Presented at Ludlow*

Castle; the more common name *Comus* was later imposed by scholars. The plot concerns a lady lost in the woods who, upon falling asleep, is captured by the lecherous Comus and carried back to face a series of erotic harassments. The masque ends with these famous lines:

> Mortals, that would follow me,
> Love Virtue; she alone is free.
> She can teach ye how to climb
> Higher than the sphery chime;
> Or, if Virtue feeble were,
> Heaven itself would stoop to her.

Lycidas (1637)

Lycidas was written as a pastoral elegy for Milton's recently passed friend Edward King. The name "Lycidas" itself comes from Theocritus's *Idylls*; "Lycidas" also shows up in Herodotus. From the poem's opening lines, "Yet once more, O ye laurels, and once more," the invocation of nature is coupled with a symbol of poetic fame (the laurel), and throughout the poem, Lycidas becomes a point of contact between some shared pastoral past, classical tradition, and Christian tradition (with the "Pilot of the Galilean Lake" as St. Peter).

Lycidas is worth a read. It is fewer than 200 lines long (though, you've been warned, they're a LONG two hundred lines), but it can give you a strong sense of Milton's style. *Paradise Lost* it's not, but *Lycidas* has all the irregular rhythms and rhymes and heavily wrought allusiveness that make his poetry so difficult.

Famous lines include the following (in addition to those mentioned above): "Without the meed of some melodious tear." "But, oh! the heavy change, now thou art gone,/Now thou art gone and never must return!" "Fame is the spur that the clear spirit doth raise/(That last infirmity of noble mind)/To scorn delights and live laborious days"; "Look homeward, Angel, now, and melt with ruth:/ And, O ye dolphins, waft the hapless youth."

John Bunyan's *The Pilgrim's Progress* (1678–1684)

A truly easy work to spot, and that will be worth a point. Read a paragraph or two and you'll be fine. The story is an allegory of the believer's journey toward redemption. The protagonist, Christian, slogs through life, passing places like the Slough of Despond and Vanity Fair on his way to the Celestial City.

John Dryden (1631–1700)

The works of Dryden to know are *Absalom and Achitophel* and *Mac Flecknoe*. Look them over just enough to be able to recognize them. *Absalom and Achitophel* uses biblical characters to analogize a political crisis during the reign of Charles II. Absalom is the Duke of Monmouth, Achitophel is the Earl of Shaftesbury, and King David is Charles II. Essentially, the hedonistic Charles spent so much time with his mistress that he had plenty of offspring but no legitimate (Protestant) heir, which left his Catholic brother, James, successor to the throne. The details of the crisis are less important than recognizing the poem (by the names) and knowing that Dryden is the author. Note Dryden's use of heroic couplets. The poem is remarkable for Dryden's politic handling of an extremely sensitive situation.

Consider reading *Mac Flecknoe*—it's got an excellent points-to-pages ratio.

Mac Flecknoe is a withering satirical attack upon dramatist Thomas Shadwell, a contemporary of Dryden. The poem relates the succession of Shadwell (Mac Flecknoe) to the throne of dullness. The poem is told in ETS's favorite literary form, the mock epic, and along the way Dryden strews the poem with allusions to literary figures past and present. Because *Mac Flecknoe* is only 217 lines long and mentions so many names, reading it through is a sensible (though not essential) investment of your study time.

Whatever you do, don't get lost in Dryden literature. He was a prolific writer and much of his work, especially as a younger man, was in dramatic literature. Although his verse-plays are considered high-quality, none are stand-outs, and thus none are standard undergraduate study, and that means ETS doesn't ask questions about them.

Restoration Comedy (1660–1730)

Restoration comedies are ribald riffs on sex and society.

As a literary period, the Restoration can be thought of as extending from the restoration of Charles Stuart in 1660 to the French Revolution of 1789. The drama of the period was one of its most characteristic literary products. We've foreshortened the dates for Restoration drama in order to indicate the forms' heyday, but be aware that Sheridan's *The School for Scandal* was first produced in 1777. *School for Scandal* excepted, the best-known and most representative works of Restoration comedy were first staged within three decades of 1700.

For the test, you need to be able to identify the distinctive features of Restoration comedy. It will also be helpful to be able to place the correct author with the correct title, and you may even need to place a character in the correct play. You do not need to know plot summaries of specific plays.

Restoration comedies are comedies of language and manners, written with their own peculiar take on farce. They are almost always centered on the tension between the accepted social codes of behavior toward sex and marriage, and the rather more direct behavioral prerogatives of human lust and social ambition. The "war between the sexes" is another frequently occurring motif. ETS will select passages that reflect these themes. The plays typically open with a verse prologue to the audience (the plays are *not* in verse). These witty prologues generally provide an excellent introduction to the kind of cynical, punning, innuendo-laden language that you can expect from the plays. Provided below is a list of notable Restoration comedies, including the names of a few of the main characters. Note the way a character's name will typically reflect that character's outstanding foibles.

William Wycherley's *The Country Wife* (1675)

- Featuring Mr. Horner, Mr. Pinchwife, Sir Jasper Fidget, Mrs. Squeamish, and Mrs. Dainty Fidget

George Etherege's *The Man of Mode* (1676)

- Featuring Mr. Dorimant, Sir Fopling Flutter, and Mrs. Loveit

William Congreve's *The Way of the World* (1700)

- Featuring Millamant (a woman), Mirabell (a man), Mr. Fainall, Lady Wishfort, Foible (a woman), and Mincing (a woman)

Richard Sheridan's *The School for Scandal* (1777)

- Featuring Sir Peter Teazle, Maria, Lady Sneerwell, Sir Benjamin Backbite, and Charles Surface

Jonathan Swift's *Gulliver's Travels* (1726)

Be able to connect *Gulliver's Travels* with the following names:

- Lilliput (where everyone is six inches tall)

- Brobdingnag (where everyone is enormous)

- Laputa (a flying island)

- The Struldburgs (unhappy immortals who wish they could die)

- Houyhnhnms (intelligent, clean-living, right-thinking horses)

- Yahoos (idiotic, dirty, violent creatures who turn out to be people, or at least look like them)

Alexander Pope (1688–1744)

Pope wrote his verse almost exclusively in heroic couplets, and he consistently ends his lines on natural pauses. Glance over Pope's *An Essay on Criticism* and *The Dunciad*, but by far the most important work of Pope's for you to study is *The Rape of the Lock*. Here's an excerpt, from the invocation:

> What dire Offence from am'rous Causes springs,
> What mighty Contests rise from trivial Things,
> I sing-This verse to Caryl, Muse! is due;
> This, ev'n Belinda may vouchsafe to view:
> Slight is the Subject, but not so the Praise,
> If She inspire, and He approve, my Lays.

The Rape of the Lock concerns the real-life brouhaha surrounding an impertinent haircut given by one Lord Petre to Arabella Fermor (Arabella, called Belinda in the poem, is the work's central character). It is the most famous and most perfectly executed mock epic in English letters. All the conventions of the epic find their corollary in this poem. The epic invocation, the epic feast, the epic battle, the interference of the gods, and the epic simile are all given their upper-crust eighteenth-century English equivalent. For example, the epic feast is a dainty affair of coffee in little cups, the epic battle is played out at a card table, and the interfering gods are for the most part the spirits of dead demi-mondes. The satire is not at all a mean-spirited one; in fact, the participants were flattered to have their little flap elevated to the status of epic confrontation, even as that elevation poked fun at their own pretensions.

Like *The Rape of the Lock*, *The Dunciad* is a mock epic written in heroic couplets, but all similarity ends there. *The Dunciad* is a savage assault on bad poetry and writing by anyone who'd crossed Pope's path or otherwise offended him, particularly that of Colley Cibber, poet laureate of England. The poem concerns the coronation ceremony of Bayes as the poet laureate of Dulness, during which everyone in attendance falls asleep. The poem suggests that Dulness will ultimately prevail over all the arts and sciences.

Samuel Johnson (1709–1784) and James Boswell (1740–1795)

Johnson is simply too major a figure not to mention, but you needn't be too familiar with either his writing or that of his biographer Boswell. There will probably be one question, but only one, on either Mr. Johnson or Mr. Boswell.

Boswell wrote a gushing biography of Johnson.

Because the points-to-pages ratio with Johnson and Boswell is ridiculously low, here's what you should know: Success came late for Johnson, and he struggled with poverty into his forties but is considered the best English literary mind of the eighteeth century. Important works include "The Vanity of Human Wishes" (a poem), *The Lives of the English Poets* (biography), essays for the journal *The Rambler* (he edited it and pretty much wrote the whole thing), the first modern English Dictionary (which includes a sprinkling of tongue-in-cheek definitions, the most famous of which being: "*lexicographer*, a writer of dictionaries, a harmless drudge") and *Rasselas* (a melancholy novel about the Prince of Abyssinia's unsuccessful quest for a happy and fulfilling "choice of life"—a subject no doubt influenced by the fact that Johnson wrote it in a week in order to settle debts arising from his mother's funeral).

Our knowledge of Johnson's personality comes to us from his own works and the biography, *The Life of Johnson*, by his friend/disciple (but in no way peer) James Boswell. When a passage on the GRE Literature in English Subject Test discusses Johnson in a genial, sympathetic eighteenth-century style, you can be sure the author is Boswell. The portrait of Johnson that Boswell paints is of a supremely witty and erudite conversationalist with a deep melancholy streak. Johnson is shown to have both generosity of spirit and outbursts of irritability. The biography's most notable and innovative characteristic is that it doesn't merely describe Johnson or discuss his thought but shows us Johnson "in life." Boswell treats us to snatches of Johnson in conversation with the leading intellectual figures of the day captured in fly-on-the-wall fashion. (You might also add Boswell to your list of famous literary drunks.)

William Blake (1757–1827)

There are two distinct styles used by William Blake. The first is that of *Songs of Innocence* and *Songs of Experience*. Look over any of these short poems (be sure to look over "The Tyger") and note the childlike simplicity of Blake's meter and syntax.

"Tyger! Tyger! burning bright
In the forests of the night,
What immortal hand or eye
Could frame thy fearful
symmetry?"

"The Tyger"
William Blake, 1794

The other style Blake employs is that of works like *The Marriage of Heaven and Hell* and *Visions of the Daughters of Albion*. These are works of Blake, the no-holds-barred visionary mystic. (The elaborate personal theology he unfurls has most first-time readers baffled.) Anyway, ETS tends to favor selections in the *Songs of Experience* vein. It's worth mentioning that although Blake's modes of writing are stylistically quite distinct, they are fully consistent at their spiritual base. Indeed, the reconciliation of opposites is one of the cornerstones of Blake's philosophy.

The Gothic Novel (1764–1860)

Gothic novels (in the narrow sense the test will speak of) are those novels produced by the sensibility typified by gloomy half-deserted castles and crumbling ancestral manors with an evil twin locked in the attic jabbering homicidally to himself. The heroines of such novels have a penchant for fits of inopportune fainting, and there's always a room one ought not...shouldn't...*mustn't ever enter!* Oh, and I say, does it not seem as though that portrait's eyes follow one about the room most peculiarly?

The first date given above, 1764, is the year Horace Walpole published his *The Castle of Otranto*, the first true gothic novel. It was an instant success. The second date is more arbitrary; it indicates the end of the gothic novel's heyday, but in a real sense the gothic novel survives to the present day (although Stephen King will *probably not* be tested). For the GRE Literature in English Subject Test, you should know that Walpole's book was the first of this type and that Anne Radcliffe's even more popular *The Mysteries of Udolpho* took Walpole's aesthetic and added an important twist. In *The Castle of Otranto*, the events the book describes (for instance, statues bleeding) are truly supernatural. The Radcliffe formula presents events that appear supernatural but at the book's end are revealed to have perfectly real-world explanations.

This process of summing up and revealing the true causes of many seeming impossibilities at the work's end is called "gothic explique." It becomes an important feature of the Detective Story (a genre initiated by Edgar Allan Poe in his stories "The Muders on the Rue Morgue," and "The Purloined Letter").

Regarding Radcliffe's *The Mysteries of Udolpho*, you should know, as we've mentioned elsewhere, that Jane Austen's *Northanger Abbey* is in part a spoof of the gothic conventions laid out by Walpole and Radcliffe. Finally, one other early and popular gothic novel you should at least recognize as a part of the genre is M. G. "Monk" Lewis's *The Monk*.

"Fate sits on these dark battlements and frowns, And as the portal opens to receive me, A voice in hollow murmur through the courts Tells of a nameless deed."

Motto to Ann Radcliffe's *The Mysteries of Udolpho*

Jane Austen (1775–1817)

You should know that Jane Austen is noted for her understated ironic treatment of character. You should also know some of the main characters from each of her six major novels:

- *Sense and Sensibility* features Elinor and Marianne Dashwood, Lucy Steele, Edward Ferris, John Willoughby, and Colonel Brandon.

- *Pride and Prejudice* features Elizabeth Bennet, Fitzwilliam Darcy, Charles Bingley, and George Wickham.

- *Mansfield Park* features the Bertrams of Mansfield Park, Fanny Price, and Mrs. Norris.

- *Emma* features Emma Woodhouse ("handsome, clever and rich"), Mr. Knightley, Miss Bates, Frank Churchill, Harriet Smith, and Jane Fairfax.

- *Northanger Abbey* features Catherine Morland, the Allens, Henry Tilney, and John Thorpe. You should know that *Northanger Abbey* is in large part a parody of Anne Radcliffe's *The Mysteries of Udolpho*.

- *Persuasion* features Sir Walter, Elizabeth, and Anne Elliot, Frederick Wentworth, and Kellynch Hall (this last is a manor, not a person).

"It is a truth universally acknowledged, that a single man in possession of a good fortune must be in want of a wife."

Pride and Prejudice, Jane Austen, 1813

The Lake Poets: William Wordsworth, Samuel Taylor Coleridge, and Robert Southey; also Essayist Charles Lamb (ca. 1810)

William Wordsworth, Samuel Taylor Coleridge, and Robert Southey are called the Lake Poets because of their long residence in the Lake District of England. Only Wordsworth and Coleridge merit test study time.

We've already mentioned Wordsworth in conjunction with his Lucy poems (refer back to the A list at the beginning of this chapter). You also need to be familiar with his "Preface to *Lyrical Ballads*" and with *Lyrical Ballads* itself. Note Wordsworth's values of rustic people and rural settings, as well as nonacademic language. *Lyrical Ballads*, which Wordsworth and Coleridge published together, contains some of both poets' finest work and is, with Coleridge's *Biographia Literaria*, a seminal Romantic work.

As for Coleridge, Wordsworth's friend and collaborator, a question or two concerning him is likely to appear on the test. You need to be able to recognize his masterpiece, "Rime of the Ancient Mariner," and should also be familiar with his *Biographia Literaria*, which outlines his aesthetic principles. Essentially, Coleridge's thesis is that the imagination is the supreme faculty of the human intellect, and its cultivation is both the prerequisite and aim of poetry. Coleridge understands imagination to be more than the operation of mere fantasy; it is the process of keenly perceiving the phenomena of the world and self, and then re-expressing phenomena through the creative faculties of the poet's whole being, the mind and the soul, the rational and irrational.

Both Coleridge and Wordsworth, especially the latter, were valued correspondents of the delicately witty London essayist Charles Lamb. Lamb wrote a notable response to Wordsworth regarding *Lyrical Ballads*, which the poets had sent to Lamb for review. Lamb also liked to make much of the contrast between his love of the pleasures of urbanity and the Lake Poets' muddy-boots-and-daffodils joys.

The Victorian Essayists: Thomas Carlyle, John Ruskin, J. S. Mill, Matthew Arnold, and Cardinal Newman (ca. 1800–1900)

Many students are mildly panicked by the idea of having to differentiate between J. S. Mill and Cardinal Newman, or between Thomas Carlyle and John Ruskin. ETS will spring a few questions about these folks, and the good news is that the general level of ignorance regarding these essayists is such that the questions ETS does pose will be fairly easy. Knowing the subject matter of each of these writers' most famous works should be worth a few points.

Thomas Carlyle (1795–1881)

Carlyle was a prolific and often exasperating writer, whose opinions (he had them on everything) exerted considerable influence on the thought of his day. For the purposes of the test, you should familiarize yourself with his *Sartor Resartus*. It is an essentially philosophical work in the guise of fiction, similar to the approach later taken by Kierkegaard in *Either/Or*, or Nietzsche in *Thus Spake Zarathustra*. Carlyle was a student of German philosophy, particularly that of Immanuel Kant, and an early English advocate of Goethe.

The title, *Sartor Resartus*, means "the tailor reclothed." The work concerns the relationship of outward appearances and inward essences, and it also relates Carlyle's spiritual growth (Teufelsdröckh is the author's proxy). The names and phrases to associate with this work are Professor Teufelsdröckh, Weissnichtwo (the professor's hometown), the Everlasting Yea, the Everlasting No, and the Wanderer (which refers to Teufelsdröckh).

As heavy as all this may sound, Carlyle is an inventive, passionate, humorous, and sometimes downright weird writer, with a strong sense of the ridiculous. For example, in German, *Teufelsdröckh* translates as "Demondung," and *Weissnichtwo* as (loosely) "Who-knows-where." Glance over some of *Sartor Resartus*'s text to get a feel for Carlyle's berserk prose style.

John Henry, Cardinal Newman (1801–1890)

Newman converted from the Anglican faith to Roman Catholicism. His *Apologia Pro Vita Sua* details the reasoning behind his controversial switch. Newman also wrote an important and eloquent essay espousing the value of a liberal arts education entitled *The Idea of a University*. Newman's writing is remarkable for its rigorous clarity. He breaks ideas down point by point with an almost unassailable logic, yet without the slightest pedantry. This quality can be difficult to discern in the short excerpts you will be likely to see on the test, so simply know the subject matter of his two major works.

John Stuart Mill (1806–1873)

Almost from the cradle, Mill was a committed social theorist and reformer. His father, James Mill, the founder (with Jeremy Bentham) of Utilitarianism, educated J. S. at home with what seemed remarkable success. However, in his early twenties, J. S. suffered a period of profound depression, one that he attributed at least in part to an education that had favored logic at the expense of the fine arts. Mill's account of melancholia in his *Autobiography* is an often-studied text, and so one on which ETS might well pose a question.

Other works by Mill are as follows: *On Liberty*, a work which argues that in a democracy, the rights of individuals must be safeguarded against the "tyranny of the majority"; "What Is Poetry?", a work which defines "poetry" as the expression of the self to the self, as opposed to "eloquence," which is the expression of the self to another; and *The Subjection of Women*, a work that excoriates—on the moral, rational, and practical levels—the social fact of its title.

Matthew Arnold (1822–1888)

Arnold is, of course, a poet as well as an essayist, but with the possible exception of the poem "Dover Beach," it is as an essayist that Arnold will appear on the GRE Literature in English Subject Test. Arnold is best recognized by his content, as his style is not particularly distinctive. His works tend to call on prior ages, especially the ancient Greeks, as models of virtue and culture. Arnold is big on culture. He attacks "philistinism," which can be defined as tacky middle-class tastes, and he sings the praises of classical "sweetness and light." The phrase "sweetness and light" is used extensively in Arnold's *Culture and Anarchy*, but was originally coined by Jonathan Swift in his *Battle of the Books*.

"Such, I say, is the wonderful virtue of even the beginnings of perfection, of having conquered even the plain faults of our animality, that the religious organisation which has helped us to do it can seem to us something precious, salutary, and to be propagated, even when it wears such a brand of imperfection on its forehead as this."

Culture and Anarchy, Matthew Arnold, 1869

John Ruskin (1819–1900)

Predominantly an art critic, Ruskin isn't someone on whom you need spend much time, but there are two points to remember. First, Ruskin originated the critical term "the pathetic fallacy," which is the projection of the author's sentiment onto an inanimate object. Happy sunshine, gloomy fog (and cruel shoes?) are examples of the pathetic fallacy. Second, Ruskin's *The Stones of Venice* is a brilliant architectural study of Venice in which Ruskin "reads" the economic, social, and moral history of Venice through its permanent structures.

The Nineteenth-Century Americans (and What Happened to the Eighteenth-Century Americans)

We don't recommend spending a lot of time brushing up on eighteenth-century American literature. There is plenty of it, but little of such outstanding quality as to be standard classroom fare, so there is nothing for us to recommend without risking wasting your time.

In a quantitative sense there is far more nineteenth-century American literature, and there are also a few standard authors you can count on ETS querying and which we can point you toward.

Nathaniel Hawthorne (1804–1864)

A question or two concerning Hawthorne is certain. As with Jane Austen, you need to associate some names:

- *The Scarlet Letter* features Roger Chillingworth (the husband), the Reverend Arthur Dimmesdale (the lover), Hester Prynne (the bearer of the Scarlet A of adultery), and Pearl (the illegitimate offspring of Hester and Dimmesdale).

- *The Blithedale Romance* features Miles Coverdale, Hollingsworth, Zenobia, and Priscilla. Perhaps more important than recognizing these names is knowing that Blithedale Farm, where much of the novel's action takes place, is based on an actual utopian community called Brook Farm. Located near Boston, Brook Farm was founded by prominent Boston social and literary figures. Ralph Waldo Emerson, Nathaniel Hawthorne, Bronson Alcott, and Henry David Thoreau were all stockholders. As you might guess from these names, the dominant philosophy at Brook Farm was transcendentalism (a philosophical, religious, and cultural movement founded to contrast traditional European ideas). Later the community turned towards Fourierism before dissolving in 1847.

- *The House of Seven Gables* features the Pyncheons, especially Hepzibah Pyncheon. Other names are old Maule, Phoebe, Holgrave, and Clifford. The story's theme is that of the sins of the fathers visited upon later generations.

Herman Melville (1819–1891)

If you haven't read *Moby-Dick* recently, look over the text to get a handle on the peculiar style of that work, especially the Biblical-Shakespearean style of Ahab's monologues. The chapter called "The Candles" is a good place to look. Names you should associate with *Moby-Dick* are Ishmael (the narrator and sole survivor); Queequeg, Dashoo, and Tashtego (the savage harpooners); Starbuck (the first-mate); and the *Pequod* (the ship).

It pays to know a little of two of Melville's other works:

Billy Budd is the story of a handsome sailor (a stock seafaring character elevated to Christlike status in this tale) undone by his own goodness and the plottings of the repulsive Claggart.

"Bartleby the Scrivener" is a short story about the bizarrely alienated Bartleby, whose mantra, whenever asked to do *anything*, is the reply, "I'd prefer not to."

Walt Whitman (1819–1892)

A question of some kind about Whitman is a certainty. Because Whitman's style is so distinct and has been so influential, you should be able to recognize it. Look over his "Song of Myself." Note Whitman's long, rolling, exuberant lines and his use of repetition instead of rhyme to lend structure to his somewhat shaggy verse.

You might also be expected to know something of Whitman's biography. He grew up in Brooklyn. Much of his early career involved newspaper work. In Whitman's mid-thirties, after much wandering along the Atlantic seaboard, the South, and the Midwest, and with the ensuing life changes these wanderings engendered, Whitman's writing took a dramatic turn. His writing metamorphosed from the undistinguished, conventional, and even sappy stuff of his newspaper days into the radically original and uniquely American celebration of self, spirit, and democracy that is *Leaves of Grass*. The first edition of *Leaves of Grass* (1855) contained 12 poems. In subsequent editions (a total of nine editions were published under Whitman's supervision) Whitman added new poems, as well as enlarging and revising the poems of previous editions.

You should know that Whitman's thought, reflected in *Leaves of Grass*, was influenced by everything from German metaphysical philosophers (particularly Hegel) to Hindu religious texts such as the Upanishads. But it is most deeply indebted to the transcendental philosophy of Emerson. Given Whitman's ardor for the innate brotherhood of man and the spiritual virtues of democracy, the War between the States affected him profoundly. He spent much of the Civil War in Washington, D.C., as a volunteer nurse to both Union and Confederate wounded. His "When Lilacs Last in the Dooryard Bloom'd" and "O Captain, My Captain" are poems memorializing Abraham Lincoln.

Emily Dickinson (1830–1886)

As with Whitman, there is almost certainly going to be a question or two on Dickinson, and you will need to be able to spot the distinctive style of her verse. The best way to do this is to read several of her poems (which are seldom longer than 50 lines and often a mere four or five). Into her typically short, clipped lines, Dickinson manages to inject a radiant mystic intensity. Here's an example:

"Warmest climes but nurse the cruellest fangs: the tiger of Bengal crouches in spaced groves of ceaseless verdure. Skies the most effulgent but basket the deadliest thunders: gorgeous Cuba knows tornadoes that never swept tame northern lands. So, too, it is, that in these resplendent Japanese seas the mariner encounters the direst of all storms, the Typhoon. It will sometimes burst from out that cloudless sky, like an exploding bomb upon a dazed and sleepy town."

Moby-Dick
Chapter 119, "The Candles,"
Herman Melville, 1851

"I celebrate myself;
And what I assume you shall assume;
For every atom belonging to me, as good belongs to you."

"Song of Myself" *Leaves of Grass*, Walt Whitman, 1900

The difference between Despair
And Fear—is like the One
Between the instant of a Wreck—
And when the Wreck has been—

The Mind is smooth—no Motion—
Contented as the Eye
Upon the Forehead of a Bust—
That knows—it cannot see—

The dashes that end several of the lines above are an idiosyncrasy of Dickinson's style.

You should also know something of Dickinson's famously blank biography. She lived in the family home in Amherst, Massachusetts her entire life, seldom traveled, and did not marry. By any ordinary standard nothing happened to Dickinson, yet her more than 1000 poems are testimony to an extraordinarily intense inner life.

Virginia Woolf (1882–1941)

Woolf was incredibly prolific, and like T. S. Eliot (who is outlined in the following pages), she has had a profound impact on literature as both a novelist and a literary critic. Although representative of really only a single phase of her work, Woolf's two best-known novels remain *Mrs. Dalloway* (1925) and *To the Lighthouse* (1927).

Mrs. Dalloway narrates a single day in the life of Clarissa Dalloway as she readies her home for a party. It opens with the famous line, "Mrs. Dalloway said she would buy the flowers herself." The line is indicative of the way the novel eschews the traditional beginning-middle-end form and foregrounds the minor details of the lives of the characters. *Mrs. Dalloway* is written in an intimate stream-of-consciousness, less reliant on allusion than Joyce and the other Modernists and more interested in highlighting characters' interiority, especially by means of the free indirect style employed by Jane Austen and Henry James. Other major characters in the novel include Septimus Smith (a shellshocked veteran whose story offers a partial parallel to Clarissa's), Richard Dalloway, Sally Seton, and Peter Walsh.

To the Lighthouse describes the Ramsay family's two separate visits to this lighthouse. The style employed in the novel is similar to that of *Dalloway*, though *Lighthouse* is much more concerned with the effects of the passage of time. The book is split into three sections, the middle section of which, "Time Passes," is a kind of elliptical prose experiment meant to create the sense of the passage of time (Woolf herself thought of the book as H-shaped: two rooms separate by a long corridor). The novel is profoundly invested in epistemological questions, particularly as they are inflected by temporality and each character's own psychological experience of events. The interest of the book is well summed up in a line that appears in the third section of the book, "The Lighthouse": "nothing is merely one thing." Other major characters include Lily Briscoe, Charles Tansley, Augustus Carmichael, Paul Rayley, and Minta Doyle.

Equally important in the Woolf canon has been her nonfiction tract *A Room of One's Own* (1929), which is seen as one of the most important statements in twentieth-century feminist aesthetics. Woolf's general argument is summed up in the following famous quotation: "All I could do was to offer you an opinion upon one minor point—a woman must have money and a room of her own if she is to write fiction." In other words, women must be afforded the autonomy (financial and otherwise) that men enjoy if they are to write. Woolf uses an extended story of Shakespeare's (invented) sister Judith to demonstrate the various impediments that would block Judith from ever having the freedom to write as her brother William had.

James Joyce (1882–1941)

There are still many critics who would put Joyce on a direct line with Homer and Shakespeare as far as genius is concerned. For these critics, and for many others besides, Joyce's stream-of-consciousness masterpiece *Ulysses* (1922) is the great work of the twentieth century. As such, you should have at least a passing familiarity with *Ulysses* and the earlier novel *A Portrait of the Artist as a Young Man* (1916). In case you're not familiar, don't fret, Joyce is famously difficult, but his idiosyncrasies are easy to spot.

Joyce's most accessible work is his first book, the short-story collection *Dubliners* (1914). The most famous story from this collection is "The Dead," in which the main character Gabriel Conroy attends a party with his wife Gretta. A series of events, including Gretta's solemn reaction to one of the songs sung at the party, reveal a side of Gretta's past of which Gabriel had not previously been aware—a girlhood lover, Michael Furey, who died from illness. This "epiphany," as Joyce would call it, ruptures the almost pastoral construction of the rest of the story, as it ends with Gabriel's meditation on the snow: "His soul swooned slowly as he heard the snow falling faintly through the universe and faintly falling, like the descent of their last end, upon all the living and the dead."

Joyce followed *Dubliners* up with *A Portrait of the Artist as a Young Man*, a semi-autobiographical novel, featuring Stephen Dedalus. This novel takes free indirect discourse to the next level, opening with a kind of babyspeak and ending with pages from young Stephen's journal. A late dialogue in the novel contains the following famous line, taken by many to be Joyce's basic artistic credo: "The artist, like the God of creation, remains within or behind or beyond or above his handiwork, invisible, refined out of existence, indifferent, paring his fingernails."

Stephen's story is continued in *Ulysses*, in which Stephen figures as the Telemachus to a new character's, Leopold Bloom's, Odysseus. *Ulysses* follows the "travels" of Bloom throughout Dublin on an unremarkable day in 1904. The novel is structurally analogous to Homer's epic, and each of the "episodes" of the book is based on an episode in the epic. Although the novel is famous for its difficulty, one of its most famous lines is also one of its simplest: "yes I said yes I will Yes." This line is the conclusion of the "Penelope" episode, a long stream-of-consciousness from the perspective of Leopold's wife, Molly Bloom.

Finally, *Finnegans Wake* is Joyce's toughest novel of all, although saying it's tougher than *Ulysses* is like saying a trillion pounds is tougher to lift than a billion pounds. ETS in all likelihood will not test this novel, but in case they do, have a quick look at the language of the novel, itself basically English but incorporating as many as seventy different languages to create a kind of dreamspeak. The most famous passage, narrating the dialogue of two washerwomen, begins, "Well, you know or don't you kennet or haven't I told you every telling has a taling and that's the he and the she of it." Right.

William Faulkner (1897–1962)

William Faulkner is the main author of the High Modernist tradition in the United States. Although T. S. Eliot and Gertrude Stein (both outlined on the following pages) were both American by birth, each lived and worked abroad. Faulkner, by contrast, laid down deep roots in the United States, and nearly all of his work is focused on the American South. Faulkner wrote in the stream-of-consciousness style, and the major themes in his work include perspective, race, and the effects of history on life in the present. Faulkner's unique style is easily identifiable because of its regular perspectival shifts and employment of italics (often to indicate internal reflection). It's also a total freebie if they give you the name Yoknapatawpha County: Faulkner invented the place and set many of his stories and novels there.

The Sound and the Fury (1929) is perhaps Faulkner's best-known novel. It is split into four sections, each with a different narrator. The first section is notable for its use of a mentally disabled narrator named Benjy. The second section, narrated from the perspective of Quentin Compson (who appears again in *Absalom, Absalom!*), is written in a more recognizably Modernist style, conflating separate times and events. As will be further developed in *Absalom*, Quentin is obsessed by questions of Southernness and the downfall of the American South after the Civil War. Infatuated with his sister Caddy's purity (with some clearly incestuous leanings), Quentin is repulsed by her sexual promiscuity and extramarital pregnancy and ultimately commits suicide to escape the torment of his own thoughts. This is one interpretation of the reasons for his suicide. Another common interpretation is that the force and inappropriateness of Quentin's incestuous feelings alone which drive him to suicide. Either way, the result is the same, and Caddy names her daughter Quentin in honor of her deceased brother.

As I Lay Dying (1930) is Faulkner's most complex experiment in perspective. Addie Bundren has died, and to honor her dying wishes, the Bundren family attempts to transport her to Jefferson, where she wishes to be buried. Pretty simple story, but told by fifteen different narrators (including Addie from beyond the grave) in 59 chapters of varying length. Aside from the Bundrens, of whom there are many, other important characters include the Tulls and Reverend Whitfield, with whom Addie had an affair. The title is an allusion to Book XI of Homer's *Odyssey*.

Absalom, Absalom! (1936) concerns itself mainly with the life and death of Thomas Sutpen, a poor white who moves to Mississippi with the intention of becoming rich and powerful. Sutpen does so, with all the attendant riches of an antebellum Southern dynasty (read: plantation, slaves). As so much is ruptured for the American South after its defeat in the Civil War, though, Sutpen is unable to restore his home to its former glory, and the story becomes tangled in the literal and figurative pairings of Sutpen with his slaves. Quentin Compson (originally from *The Sound and the Fury*) is the primary narrator. He tells the story to his Harvard roommate Shreve in fragments, with some help from his father and his early memories of the story from his grandfather and Rosa Coldfield. As in many of Faulkner's novels, the variety among the narrators' perspectives puts the actual narrative events in some doubt, and many of Faulkner's most common themes are present: history, the state of the South, race, isolation.

Gertrude Stein (1874–1946)

While Gertrude Stein is nearly always listed among the names of the founders of Modernism, her work in recent years has fallen squarely into the more-read-about-than-read category. In some ways, she is best known as a literary-historical figure, holding court at her Paris apartment with her partner Alice B. Toklas for most of the first half of the twentieth century. Ernest Hemingway credited her with coining the term "lost generation" to describe the listless group of literary ex-pats in the 1920s. Stein's literary output is varied, but her best known work remains *Three Lives* (1909), three disconnected stories of women—"The Good Anna," "Melanctha," "The Gentle Lena"—in the fictional town of Bridgepointe. Her 1913 poem "Sacred Emily" features the famous line, "Rose is a rose is a rose is a rose." Stein's work is heavily influenced by Paul Cezanne's painting, in which every element of the canvas is considered equal to every other element in the canvas. The easiest ways to spot Stein's writing are through her use of repetition (cf., the whole "rose" thing) and from the fact that she writes almost exclusively in the present tense.

Stein's most accessible work is *The Autobiography of Alice B. Toklas* (1933), a biography told from the perspective of her lover. If you see a reference to Stein in the third person, don't be thrown off; it probably comes from the *Autobiography*. The book is as much a biography of Stein as it is an "autobiography" of Toklas, and much of the book concerns Stein's relationships with young artists (you may have heard of Picasso?) and her role in discovering and popularizing them. In fact, many are attracted to the book not as a portrait of Stein but as a portrait of the cultural milieu of Paris in the 1910s and 1920s, during which some pretty important stuff happened.

T. S. Eliot (1888–1965)

Eliot was the towering figure in pre-WWII American letters, and his influence extended well into the 1960s and beyond. Eliot is best known as a poet, and his poems "The Waste Land," "The Long Song of J. Alfred Prufrock," "Ash Wednesday," and "The Hollow Men" have been college-course staples since the 1950s. Eliot's poetry is marked by its heavy use of allusion to Biblical, classical, and literary sources ("The Waste Land" even has endnotes!); bleak sense of cultural emptiness and barrenness; and mash-up of poetry and prose styles.

"The Love Song of J. Alfred Prufrock" (1920): "Let us go then, you and I," begins this famous Eliot poem, one of the most anthologized in the English language. While not quite so difficult as much of Eliot's early work, the poem is still heavily wrought with allusions and disparate, seemingly disconnected, parts. In addition to the first line, this poem is full of famous lines, among them, ""In the room the women come and go/Talking of Michelangelo"; "And indeed there will be time/To wonder, 'Do I dare?' and, 'Do I dare?'"; "Do I dare/Disturb the universe?"; "I should have been a pair of ragged claws/Scuttling across the floors of silent seas."; and the great last stanza, "We have lingered in the chambers of the sea/By sea-girls wreathed with seaweed red and brown/Till human voices wake us, and we drown."

"The Waste Land" (1922): Alongside Joyce's *Ulysses*, "The Waste Land" is often considered one of the great works of the Anglophone Modernism. The poem is split up into five sections and supplemented by seven pages of notes. The poem's difficulty springs from its fragmentation (the parts don't always fit into an obvious whole), polyglot vocabulary (Latin, Greek, Italian in just the dedication), and dense cultural allusions. The first stanza alone opens with a vague allusion to Chaucer's *Canterbury Tales* (in that it references the cruelty of April's weather) and flips inexplicably to the memories of some speaker's girlhood. The idiosyncrasies of this poem will give you an advantage on this test, though, simply because the style is so identifiable.

"The Hollow Men" (1925): This poem is commonly seen as the last great poem of the early phase of Eliot's career and deals with many of the same post-WWI themes as "The Waste Land." Broadly speaking, the poem is concerned with the difficulty of the search for meaning (i.e., the "hollowness") in postwar Europe. "The Hollow Men" contains the famous and oft-quoted Eliot lines, "This is the way the world ends/This is the way the world ends/This is the way the world ends/Not with a bang but a whimper."

"Ash Wednesday" (1930): This poem is the first long poem Eliot published after his conversion to Anglicanism. "Ash Wednesday" also marks a stylistic turning point in Eliot's career, in which he began to rely more heavily on traditional forms of melody and prosody. The poem opens with the famous lines "Because I do not hope to turn again/Because I do not hope/Because I do not hope to turn."

"Tradition and the Individual Talent" (1919): Eliot was equally prolific and influential as a critic. His most famous work, "Tradition and the Individual Talent," acts as a kind of poetic manifesto for Eliot's pre-conversion work and offers a sustained argument in favor of "impersonal poetry." For Eliot, "tradition" is not simply a collection of cultural artifacts from the past; instead, "tradition" operates as a "simultaneous order" of timeless work, uniting past and present. The great artist attaches him- or herself to tradition rather than breaking with it. As such, Eliot does not believe in the inspired genius popularized by the Romantic poets, and argues for an artist that can use tradition to lift him or her above personal experience. Eliot further developed his theory of the impersonal poet throughout his career, as in "Hamlet and his Problems," which marks Eliot's introduction of the concept of the objective correlative. Impersonality became an important paradigm for High Modernist authors; note the similarity between "Tradition" and Joyce's statement in *A Portrait of the Artist as a Young Man* regarding the artist as being "like the God of creation."

SOME IMPORTANT FINAL WORDS ON
THE A, B, AND C LISTS

As we mentioned earlier, the A, B, and C lists are not meant to be comprehensive; you can see they aren't. As the beginnings of literary modernism, because as literature draws closer to our own day, the undergraduate curriculum becomes ever more nonstandard.

No list can take into account the particular strengths and weaknesses of the individual student. Our A, B, and C lists are meant as strong suggestions, as pointers toward where the inevitable gaps in your knowledge of literature in English may lie. Use them to complement your studies along with the practice test.

Take the practice test and read through the explanations *before* you begin any intensive study from the lists. The test and explanations, in tandem with the lists, will give you a strong, accurate picture of what work you need to do.

9

The Last List

WHAT ABOUT EVERYBODY ELSE?

You may have noticed that quite a few people seem to be missing from our review of what you should study for the test. What about Shelley, Byron, and Keats? What about the Brontës, Henry James? What about the majority of the twentieth century?

Relax. We said we weren't trying to be comprehensive, and we meant it. There's one more list to go. The last list.

THE LAST LIST

You've seen the A, B, and C lists. Why not a D list? The **D** list is for the **D**iagnostic, or what we usually call the practice test. The diagnostic is not just a practice test. It is an integral part of the study system this book presents. The A, B, and C lists were designed according to the points-to-pages ratio, with an eye toward authors and works that could be studied independently of the test. However, what ultimately matters is your ability to find the correct answers on the test. The practice test is the real deal, with passages and questions. The explanations tell you how to find specific answers to specific questions and they also tell you the details you need to know for this test. Unlike other books, this one doesn't just explain the correct answers; it also goes into detail about important *incorrect* choices as well. So, don't skip an explanation just because you got the question right.

Please bear in mind that we haven't included all the test material in explanations before the practice test. Remember that there's new information about important authors in the practice test explanations, so read them.

Following is a list of authors found in the explanations. If any of the names below are still uncomfortably unfamiliar to you, and you've already looked over the material we've recommended in the A, B, and C lists, use the list below to augment your studies by looking up an unfamiliar author in a literary anthology Also, be sure to use flashcards, following the tips we laid out starting on page 42

We also provide this list to refer to when you are unsure of when an author lived. Remember, a specific knowledge of dates is not essential for the test, and you should *not* waste time memorizing the dates in this list.

> Remember, the Norton anthologies are excellent, but they aren't the only good ones out there. We also recommend *The Oxford Companion to English Literature*, the *Cambridge Guide to Literature in English*, or you can always do an Internet search to find out more about an author or a literary work!

Aeschylus (525–456 BC)
Maya Angelou (1928–)
Jane Austen (1775–1817)
Honoré de Balzac (1799–1850)
John Berryman (1914–1972)
William Blake (1757–1827)
Jorge Luis Borges (1899–1986)
Anne Bradstreet (?1612–1672)
Anne Brontë (1820–1849)

Charlotte Brontë (1816–1855)
Emily Brontë (1818–1848)
Robert Browning (1812–1889)
Robert Burns (1759–1796)
Samuel Butler, author of
　　"Hudibras" (1613–1680)
Samuel Butler, author of *Erewhon*
　　and *The Way of All Flesh*
　　(1835–1902)

Lord Byron (1788–1824)
Albert Camus (1913–1960)
Thomas Carew (1594–1640)
Thomas Carlyle (1795–1881)
Thomas Chatterton (1752–1770)
Kate Chopin (1850–1904)
Samuel Taylor Coleridge
    (1772–1834)
William Congreve (1670–1729)
William Cowper (1731–1800)
Hart Crane (1899–1932)
R. H. Dana, Jr. (1815–1882)
Dante Alighieri (1265–1321)
Charles Dickens (1812–1870)
Emily Dickinson (1830–1886)
John Donne (1572–1631)
John Dos Passos (1896–1970)
Fyodor Dostoyevsky (1821–1881)
John Dryden (1631–1700)
W. E. B. Du Bois (1868–1963)
George Eliot (1819–1880)
T. S. Eliot (1888–1965)
Ralph Waldo Emerson (1803–1882)
George Etherege (?1634–1691)
William Faulkner (1892–1962)
Henry Fielding (1707–1754)
E. M. Forster (1879–1970)
Robert Frost (1874–1963)
George Gascoigne (1534–1577)
Elizabeth Gaskell (1810–1865)
Charlotte Perkins Gilman
    (1860–1935)
Allen Ginsburg (1926–1997)
Nathaniel Hawthorne (1804–1864)
Ernest Hemingway (1899–1961)
Gerard Manley Hopkins
    (1844–1889)
William Dean Howells (1837–
    1920)
Langston Hughes (1902–1967)
Henry James (1843–1916)
Samuel Johnson (1709–1784)
James Joyce (1882–1941)
John Keats (1795–1821)

Charles Lamb (1775–1834)
Walter Savage Landor (1775–1864)
William Langland (?1330–?1386)
Hugh Latimer (?1492–1555)
D. H. Lawrence (1885–1930)
T. E. Lawrence (1888–1935)
Wyndham Lewis (1882–1957)
Malcolm Lowry (1909–1957)
John Lyly (?1554–1606)
Christopher Marlowe (1564–1593)
Herman Melville (1819–1891)
J. S. Mill (1806–1873)
Edna St. Vincent Millay (1892–
    1950)
John Milton (1608–1674)
Flannery O'Connor (1925–1964)
Samuel Pepys (1633–1703)
Edgar Allan Poe (1809–1849)
Alexander Pope (1688–1744)
Ezra Pound (1885–1972)
Marcel Proust (1871–1922)
Rainer Maria Rilke (1875–1926)
Arthur Rimbaud (1854–1891)
John Ruskin (1819–1900)
William Shakespeare (1564–1616)
George B. Shaw (1856–1950)
P. B. Shelley (1792–1822)
Sir Philip Sidney (1554–1586)
John Skelton (?1460–1529)
Sophocles (496–406 BC)
Edmund Spenser (?1552–1599)
Charles Algernon Swinburne
    (1837–1909)
Alfred Tennyson (1809–1892)
Dylan Thomas (1914–1953)
Mark Twain (1835–1910)
John Webster (?1578–?1632)
Edith Wharton (1862–1937)
Walt Whitman (1816–1892)
Oscar Wilde (1854–1900)
Virginia Woolf (1882–1941)
William Wordsworth (1770–1850)
W. B. Yeats (1865–1939)

So, now you can turn the page and take our practice test. Remember to read the explanations for *all* the questions, even the ones you get right. Only by reading them will you learn the type of details that might be tested on the GRE Literature in English Subject Test. Reading the explanations will also give you a good review of books that might be tested but don't offer a high enough points-to-pages ratio, or that we aren't sure enough will be on the test to have included in the A, B, and C lists. We'll also review some general techniques, principles, and terms that you have already read about in this book.

PART ◆ IV

The Princeton Review
Practice Test

The best way to study for the GRE Literature in English Subject Test is to take The Princeton Review practice test and read all of our explanations. The test was designed to be as much like the real Literature in English Subject Test as possible *and* to reinforce what we've taught in the preceding chapters.

When you sit down to take the practice test, try to take it under conditions as much like the real test conditions as possible. Take it in a room where you won't be disturbed, and have someone else time you. (When timing oneself, it's too tempting to think: "Oh, I'll just take a little break and then restart the time." There are no breaks during the real test.) Don't check whether you've answered a question correctly until you've completed the practice test. You need to get used to the anxiety of not knowing how well you're doing; there is no way to check your performance during the real test.

While taking the test, be sure to use the techniques we've taught you. Use POE to guess aggressively. Manage your time effectively. By the time the test is over, you should have a very good idea of what taking the Literature in English Subject Test is all about. After you've read through the explanations and reviewed our study lists, you should have an excellent idea of what further reading you need to do in order to score more points.

Good luck!

LITERATURE IN ENGLISH SUBJECT TEST

Time—170 Minutes

230 Questions

<u>Directions:</u>   Each of the questions or incomplete statements below is followed by five suggested answers or completions. Select the one that is best in each case and then completely fill in the corresponding oval on the answer sheet.

Questions 1–5

What dire offense from amorous causes springs,
What mighty contests rise from trivial things,
I sing—This verse to Caryll, Muse! is due:
Line   This, even Belinda may vouchsafe to view:
(5)   Slight is the subject, but not so the praise,
If she inspire, and he approve my lays.
   Say, what strange motive, Goddess! could compel
A well-bred lord to assault a gentle belle?
Oh, say what stranger cause, yet unexplored,
(10)   Could make a gentle belle reject a lord?

1. The first six lines of the passage above contain

   (A) a simile
   (B) an extended metaphor
   (C) an epic invocation
   (D) a risqué pun
   (E) a reference to an obscure Greek god

2. The passage is drawn from

   (A) a larger mock-heroic work
   (B) a classical epic
   (C) a series of verse vignettes
   (D) the verse preface to a comic novel
   (E) the prologue to a masque

3. The "dire offense" referred to in line 1 is

   (A) disobedience to the gods
   (B) an adulterous infidelity
   (C) the "theft" of a lock of hair
   (D) a murder
   (E) sexual relations with a swan

4. In the passage above, lines 1–6 are written in

   (A) end-stopped couplets
   (B) enjambed couplets
   (C) iambic hexameter
   (D) terza rima
   (E) blank verse

5. Which of the following choices is the closest to the meaning in context of "vouchsafe" (line 4)?

   (A) safeguard
   (B) deign
   (C) protect
   (D) praise
   (E) attest

GO ON TO THE NEXT PAGE.

Questions 6–8 refer to the passages that follow.

6. Which is by Yeats?

7. Which is by Arnold?

8. Which is by Coleridge?

(A) And here, in the beginning, permit me to say a few words in regard to a some-what peculiar principle which, whether rightfully or wrongfully, has always had its influence in my own critical estimate of the poem. I hold that a long poem does not exist. I maintain that the phrase, "a long poem," is simply a flat contra-diction in terms.

(B) The *imagination* then, I consider either as primary, or secondary. The primary *imagination* I hold to be the living Power and prime Agent of all human Per-ception, and as a repetition in the finite mind of the eternal act of creation in the infinite I AM. The secondary Imagination I consider as an echo of the former, co-existing with the conscious will, yet still as identical with the primary in the *kind* of its agency, and differing only in *degree*, and in the *mode* of its operation.

(C) Culture looks beyond machinery, culture hates hatred; culture has one great passion, the passion for sweetness and light. It has one even yet greater!—the passion for making them *prevail*. It is not satisfied till we *all* come to a perfect man; it knows that the sweetness and light of the few must be imperfect until the raw and unkindled masses of humanity are touched with sweetness and light.

(D) A good and lofty work of art may be incomprehensible, but not to simple, un-perverted peasant labourers (all that is highest is understood by them)—it may be, and often is, unintelligible to erudite, perverted people destitute of religion. And this continually occurs in our society, in which the highest feelings are simply not understood. For instance, I know people who consider themselves most refined, and who say that they do not understand the poetry of love to one's neighbor, of self-sacrifice, or of chastity. . . .

(E) Symbolism, as seen in the writers of our day, would have no value if it were not seen also, under one "disguise or another, in every great imaginative writer," writes Mr. Arthur Symons in *The Symbolist Movement in Literature*, a subtle book which I cannot praise as I would, because it has been dedicated to me; and he goes on to show how many profound writers have in the last few years sought for a philosophy of poetry in the doctrine of symbolism, and how even in countries where it is almost scandalous to seek for any philosophy of poetry, new writers are following them in their search.

GO ON TO THE NEXT PAGE.

Character: Now we have come to the plain at the end of the earth,
the Scythian tract, and an untrodden wilderness.
Line And you Hephaistos, must turn your mind to the orders
(5) the father gave you,—to discipline and pin down
this outlaw here upon the lofty ragged rocks
in unbreakable bonds of chains adamantine.
It was your flower, the gleam of civilising fire,
he stole and handed it over to mortals.

9. In line 9, "he" refers to

   (A) Hercules
   (B) Zeus
   (C) Prometheus
   (D) Achilles
   (E) Tantalus

10. Which of the following is an example of poetic inversion?

   (A) "Scythian tract" (line 3)
   (B) "untrodden wilderness" (line 3)
   (C) "lofty ragged rocks" (line 6)
   (D) "chains adamantine" (line 7)
   (E) "he stole and handed it" (line 9)

11. In classical Greek mythology, Hephaistos created, or was directly responsible for, which of the following?

   (A) The shield of Achilles
   (B) The Parthenon
   (C) The Trojan War
   (D) The labyrinth of King Minos
   (E) The Trojan horse

12. It is a strange drama, a tragi-comic Oedipus O'Rex that succeeds almost despite itself. Christy Mahon has killed his father, or so we believe, and is toasted handsomely for it until his father shows up very much alive, an event which dims Christy's new-won fame considerably. They go at it again, Christy "kills" his father again (though with far less general approval), and Old Mahon returns again—groping onto the stage on his hands and knees—whereupon father and son become, at least for the moment, reconciled.

The drama described above is

   (A) Synge's *The Playboy of the Western World*
   (B) Yeats's *The Countess Cathleen*
   (C) O'Casey's *The Plough and the Stars*
   (D) Wilde's *Salomé*
   (E) Shaw's *Mrs. Warren's Profession*

GO ON TO THE NEXT PAGE.

The discussion of Melville's *Moby Dick* that follows takes place among five speakers, each of whom offers a different critical perspective.

13. Which speaker's views most show the influence of post-structuralist theory?

14. Which speaker's views most show the influence of psychoanalytic theory?

15. Which speaker's views most show the influence of structuralist theory?

(A) Ahab must surely be seen as the moral stake that pins down the novel's center—a tortured center, I'll grant you. It's through Ahab that Melville's great concern is conveyed. That concern is *not* the problem of evil. No—I think it's quite clear that the issue throughout is faith, or rather bad faith. What final wrong or right can there be without a faith in God? None. But how can one have faith in an arbitrary uncaring God? Worse, why should one? Ahab lives these questions as does no other character in American fiction.

(B) What antiquated claptrap! "Bad faith," "evil," "tortured (moral) center." And then all this supposition about Melville! Please, stay with the text—the whole of it. What meaning the novel possesses is produced by the narrative field the text creates, not *sui generis* of course, but in reference to pre-existing story architectures. In that sense then, we can perhaps say that Ahab and the *Pequod* are in some sense central. Indeed, at sea, out of view of land, the horizon forms a vast encompassing circle. It's these motifs really, of the center in search of the perimeter, that produce sense, meaningfully and textually.

(C) Splendid, as long as in the name of the text one annihilates the majority of it— as long as one posits and privileges some historicist architectural authority (talk about antiquated!) and discounts the multiplicity of readings, and readings of readings, available. What I find in *Moby Dick* above all is a violent slippage of signs, an ecstatic and transgressive heteroglossia that abuts the language of the King James Bible with that of ordinary seamen, and rubs the cadences of willful evil with those of innocence, fear, and obedience. If you want to search for meanings in the text look there, in the scuppers of language where one vocabulary washes over the next.

(D) This multiplicity is all well and good, but don't you ever wish you could say *something*? In my opinion, your position taken to its logical conclusion devolves into a kind of wildly democratic reader-response criticism if not into simple nihilism. Some readings *are* more privileged than others, and rightly so. Melville had some sort of intention when he wrote, an intention deeper, I dare say, than simply rubbing one language against another. Why create characters? Why bother with a story? And I simply don't understand this fetish for denying the author's existence.

(E) Oh, but that's not so hard to understand, is it? Critic-denies-author strikes me as yet another deflection of the oedipal impulse to murder one's father, the *author*ity. And of course the author's intentions should be privileged, but let's be clear that with "intentions," we include those subconscious motives within Melville that compelled him to write. To take just one rather blatant example, Ahab's missing leg seems a powerful rendering of castration-anxiety. Intentional? Yes. Conscious? Unlikely.

GO ON TO THE NEXT PAGE.

16. "Listen to them—the children of the night. What music they make!" Seeing, I suppose, some expression in my face strange to him, he added:—
"Ah, sir, you dwellers in the city cannot enter into the feelings of the hunter." Then he rose and said:—
"But you must be tired. Your bedroom is all ready, and tomorrow you shall sleep as late as you will. I have to be away till the afternoon; so sleep well and dream well!" With a courteous bow, he opened for me himself the door to the octagonal room, and I entered my bedroom . . . .

The narrator of the passage above is

(A) Bram Stoker's Jonathan Harker
(B) Edgar Allan Poe's Arthur Gordon Pym
(C) James Fenimore Cooper's Natty Bumppo
(D) Charles Dickens's David Copperfield
(E) Saul Bellow's Augie March

17. The tale-within-the-tale has long been a favorite device of storytellers, perhaps because it allows a narrator, such as _____, a plausible and convenient mechanism by which to develop characters in their own voice, provide narrative variety, and, in the relation of teller to tale, establish a meaningful and often ironic counterpoint. A less sophisticated but no less important aspect of the tale-within-the-tale is the inevitable suspense that arises when one narrative is interrupted for another, as _____ knew so well.

Which of the following best completes the blanks in the passage above?

(A) John Milton in *Lycidas* . . . Mephistopheles
(B) Robert Browning in "Caliban upon Setebos". . . Raskolnikov
(C) Coleridge in *The Rime of the Ancient Mariner*. . . Mr. Lockwood
(D) Chaucer in *The Canterbury Tales* . . . Scheherazade
(E) John Dryden in *Absalom and Achitophel* . . . Sancho Panza

Questions 18–19

The human species, according to the best theory I can form of it, is composed of two distinct races, the men who borrow, and the men who lend. To these
Line two original diversities may be reduced all those
(5) impertinent classifications of Gothic and Celtic tribes, white men, black men, red men. All the dwellers upon earth, "Parthians, and Medes, and Elamites," flock hither, and do naturally fall in with one or other of these primary distinctions. The infinite superiority of
(10) the former, which I choose to designate as the *great race*, is discernible in their figure, port, and a certain instinctive sovereignty. The latter are born degraded. "He shall serve his brethren." There is something [.
. . . .]
(15) contrasting with the open, trusting, generous manners of the other.
Observe who have been the greatest borrowers of all ages—Alcibiades—Falstaff—Sir Richard Steele— our late incomparable Brinsley—what a family like-
(20) ness in all four!

18. The passage as a whole is best described as

(A) mock-heroic
(B) playful
(C) parodic
(D) instructive
(E) nonsensical

19. Which of the following is the text extracted from the passage and replaced by brackets in lines 13 and 14?

(A) genuinely wholesome and frank in the first's manner
(B) in the air of one of this caste, lean and suspicious
(C) genuinely wholesome and frank in the latter's manner
(D) in the air of a borrower, weak and untrustworthy
(E) too flattering and insincere in the borrower's comport

GO ON TO THE NEXT PAGE.

20. I had different ways of occupying myself while I lay
    awake. I would think of a trout stream I had fished
    along when I was a boy and fish its whole length very
    carefully in my mind, fishing very carefully under all
    the logs, all the turns of the bank, the deep holes and
    the clear shallow stretches, sometimes catching trout
    and sometimes losing them.

    The speaker of the passage above is

    (A) Twain's Huck Finn
    (B) Fitzgerald's Nick Carraway
    (C) Melville's Billy Budd
    (D) Salinger's Seymour Glass
    (E) Hemingway's Nick Adams

Questions 21–23 refer to selections below.

21. Which is written in rhyme royal?

22. Which contains a pair of tercets?

23. Which is written in heroic couplets?

(A) That is no country for old men. The young
    In one another's arms, birds in the trees
    —Those dying generations—at their song,
    The salmon-falls, the mackerel-crowded seas,
    Fish, flesh, or fowl, commend all summer
        long
    Whatever is begotten, born, and dies.
    Caught in that sensual music all neglect
    Monuments of unaging intellect.

(B) I thought of Chatterton, the marvelous Boy
    The sleepless Soul that perished in his pride;
    Of Him who walked in glory and in joy
    Following his plow, along the mountain-side:
    By our own spirits are we deified:
    We Poets in our youth begin in gladness;
    But thereof come in the end despondency and
        madness.

(C) My heart-aches, and a drowsy numbness pains
    My sense, as though of hemlock I had drunk,
    Or emptied some dull opiate to the drains
    One minute past, and Lethe-wards had sunk:
    'Tis not through envy of thy happy lot,
    But being too happy in thine happiness—
    That thou, light-winged Dryad of the trees,
    In some melodious plot
    Of beechen green, and shadows numberless,
    Singest of summer in full-throated ease.

(D) There dwelt a man in fair Westmoreland,
        Johnie Armstrong men did him call,
    He had neither lands nor rents coming in,
        Yet he kept eight score men in his hall.

(E) A little learning is a dangerous thing;
    Drink deep, or taste not the Pierian spring.
    There shallow draughts intoxicate the brain
    And drinking largely sobers us again.

GO ON TO THE NEXT PAGE.

24. "Turn on the light," he said.
    "Bigger! What's happened?"
    "Turn on the light!"
    She said nothing and did not move. He groped
    forward, sweeping the air with his open palm for the
    cord; he found it and jerked on the light. Then he
    whirled and looked about him, expecting to see some-
    one lurking in the corners of the room.
    "What's happened?" She came forward and touched
    his clothes. "You're wet."
    "It's all off," he said.
    "I don't have to do it?" She asked eagerly.
    Yes; she was thinking only of herself now. He was
    alone.

    This passage is taken from

    (A) Maya Angelou's *Heart of a Woman*
    (B) James Baldwin's *Giovanni's Room*
    (C) Zora Neale Hurston's *Their Eyes Were
        Watching God*
    (D) Ralph Ellison's *Invisible Man*
    (E) Richard Wright's *Native Son*

GO ON TO THE NEXT PAGE.

25. Which is by Charlotte Brontë?

26. Which is by Edith Wharton?

27. Which is by Kate Chopin?

28. Which is by Virginia Woolf?

(A) The sunshade continued to approach slowly. Beneath its pink-lined shelter were his wife, Mrs. Pontellier, and young Robert Lebrun. When they reached the cottage, the two seated themselves with some appearance of fatigue upon the upper step of the porch. . . . "What folly! to bathe at such an hour in such heat!" exclaimed Mr. Pontellier. . . .

"You are burnt beyond recognition," he added, looking at his wife as one looks at a valuable piece of personal property which has suffered some damage.

(B) And was Mr. Rochester now ugly in my eyes? No, reader. Gratitude, and many associations, all pleasurable and genial, made his face the object I best liked to see; his presence in a room was more cheering than the brightest fire.

(C) Selden paused in surprise. In the afternoon rush of the Grand Central Station his eyes had been refreshed by the sight of Miss Lily Bart.

. . . What was Miss Bart doing in town at that season? If she had appeared to be catching a train, he might have inferred that he had come on her in the act of transition between one and another of the country-houses which disputed her presence after the close of the Newport season; but her desultory air perplexed him.

(D) Mr. Thornton sate on and on. He felt that his company gave pleasure to Mr. Hale; and was touched by the half-spoken wishful entreaty that he would remain a little longer—the plaintive "Don't go yet," which his poor friend put forth from time to time. He wondered why Margaret did not return; but it was with no view of seeing her that he lingered.

(E) She was not old yet. She had just broken into her fifty-second year. . . . Clarissa (crossing to the dressing-table) plunged into the very heart of the moment, transfixed it, there—the moment of this June morning on which was the pressure of all the other mornings, seeing the glass dressing-table, and all the bottles afresh, collecting the whole of her at one point (as she looked into the glass), seeing the delicate pink face of the woman who was that very night to give a party. . .

GO ON TO THE NEXT PAGE.

                    She had
A heart—how shall I say?—too soon made glad,
Too easily impressed; she liked whate'er
Line She looked on, and her looks went everywhere.
(5)   Sir, 'twas all one! My favor at her breast,
      The dropping of the daylight in the West,
      The bough of cherries some officious fool
      Broke in the orchard for her, the white mule
      She rode with round the terrace—all and each
(10) Would draw from her alike the approving speech,
      Or blush, at least. She thanked men—good! but thanked
      Somehow—I know not how—as if she ranked
      My gift of a nine-hundred-years-old name
      With anybody's gift. Who'd stoop to blame
(15) This sort of trifling? Even had you skill
      In speech—which I have not—to make your will
      known to such an one, and say, "Just this
      Or that in you disgusts me; here you miss,
      Or there exceed the mark"—and if she let
(20) Herself be lessoned so, nor plainly set
      Her wits to yours, forsooth, and made excuse,
      —E'en then would be some stooping; and I choose
      Never to stoop.

29. In context, the lines "—and if she let/Herself be les-
    soned so, nor plainly set/Her wits to yours, forsooth,
    and made excuse" most nearly mean

    (A) and if she listened but made false excuses
    (B) and if she understood and forgave
    (C) and if she even ever so slightly mocked the
         speaker
    (D) and if she accepted the speaker's reproofs
    (E) and if she reluctantly acquiesced

30. The passage as a whole suggests that the speaker

    (A) was ultimately forced to tolerate his wife's flirta-
         tiousness
    (B) deeply resented what he took to be his wife's
         affronts to his dignity
    (C) felt only mildly perturbed by his wife's many
         pleasures
    (D) became increasingly disgusted by his openly
         adulterous wife
    (E) suffered a crisis of faith because of his wife's
         behavior

31. It seems at first to be nothing more, nor less, than an
    expertly rendered portrait of the middle-class man-
    ners of a particular time and place. But from the mo-
    ment Gabriel sees his wife upon the stairs listening to
    the singing, to the final lines, in which he watches the
    snow fall at the window, the story both narrows and
    broadens. It telescopes to a fine bright point focused
    upon Gabriel's realization of his own inner exile and
    opens into an evocation of every human loneliness
    and loss, an evocation as huge and quietly profound
    as "the snow falling faintly through the universe. . . ."

    The passage above discusses

    (A) Conrad's "Youth"
    (B) McCullers's *The Ballad of the Sad Cafe*
    (C) Joyce's "The Dead"
    (D) Lawrence's "The Odour of Chrysanthemums"
    (E) James's *The Aspern Papers*

32. In *Paradiso,* Dante's guide is

    (A) Beatrice
    (B) Charon
    (C) Virgil
    (D) Leda
    (E) Aristotle

GO ON TO THE NEXT PAGE.

Questions 33–36

      Busy old fool, unruly sun,
        Why dost thou thus,
    Through windows and through curtains call on us?
Line Must to thy motions lovers' seasons run?
(5)   Saucy pedantic wretch, go chide
      Late school boys and sour prentices
    Go tell court huntsmen that the king will ride,
     Call country ants to harvest offices;
    Love, all alike, no season knows, nor clime,
(10) Nor hours, days, months, which are the rags of time.

33. In line 8, the word "offices" means

    (A) duties
    (B) rooms
    (C) honors
    (D) parties
    (E) fields

34. If in the next stanza the sun were to speak—rebuking the poet for his impudence—this would be an example of

    (A) hyperbole
    (B) prosopopoeia
    (C) symbolism
    (D) metaphor
    (E) synecdoche

35. Which of the following best paraphrases the poem's theme?

    (A) All's fair in love and war.
    (B) Love is timeless.
    (C) The way of all flesh is dust.
    (D) Lovers inhabit another world.
    (E) Make hay while the sun shines.

36. The passage is by

    (A) Donne
    (B) Dryden
    (C) Marvell
    (D) Shakespeare
    (E) Marlowe

Questions 37–40

      Nature's most secret steps
    He like her shadow has pursued, where'er
    The red volcano overcanopies
Line Its fields of snow and pinnacles of ice
(5) With burning smoke, or where bitumen lakes
    On black bare pointed islets ever beat
    With sluggish surge, or where the secret caves
    Rugged and dark, winding among the springs
    Of fire and poison, inaccessible
(10) To avarice or pride, their starry domes
    Of diamond and of gold expand above
    Numberless and immeasurable halls,
    Frequent with crystal column, and clear shrines
    Of pearl, and thrones radiant with chyrsolite.

37. The subject of the main clause of the sentence above is

    (A) "Nature's" (line 1)
    (B) "steps" (line 1)
    (C) "He" (line 2)
    (D) "volcano" (line 3)
    (E) "caves" (line 7)

38. In the context of the passage "expand" (line 11) is

    (A) a transitive verb that takes "domes" (line 10) as its object
    (B) a transitive verb that takes "halls" (line 12) as its object
    (C) a transitive verb that takes "shrines" (line 13) as its object
    (D) an intransitive verb with "domes" (line 10) as its subject
    (E) an intransitive verb with "halls" (line 12) as its subject

39. "Burning smoke" (line 5) is syntactically parallel to

    (A) "secret steps" (line 1)
    (B) "sluggish surge" (line 7)
    (C) "bitumen lakes" (line 5)
    (D) "Numberless and immeasurable" (line 12)
    (E) "clear shrines" (line 13)

GO ON TO THE NEXT PAGE.

40. The author of the passage is

    (A) Milton
    (B) Shelley
    (C) Spenser
    (D) Browning
    (E) Blake

Questions 41–42

The water of the Gulf stretched out before her,
gleaming with the million lights of the sun. The voice of
the sea is seductive, never ceasing, whispering, clamor-
Line ing, murmuring, inviting the soul to wander in abysses of
(5) solitude. All along the white beach, up and down, there
was no living thing in sight. A bird with a broken wing
was beating the air above, reeling, fluttering, circling
disabled down, down to the water.

41. The passage alludes to which of the following figures?

    (A) Medusa
    (B) Penelope
    (C) Aphrodite
    (D) Icarus
    (E) Perseus

42. The figure alluded to would best serve as an allegory
    for

    (A) the suffering caused by a sudden loss of
        innocence
    (B) the healing effect of pure beauty upon the
        human soul
    (C) the fatal effect of curiosity, disobedience, and
        excessive ambition
    (D) the tactic of combating evil by reflecting it upon
        itself
    (E) the "perfect wife," ever faithful, patient, and
        clever

Questions 43–44

As to the poetical Character itself, (I mean that sort
of which, if I am anything, I am a Member; that sort
distinguished from the Wordsworthian or egotistical
Line sublime; which is a thing per se and stands alone) it is
(5) not itself—it has no self—it is every thing and nothing—
It has no character—it enjoys light and shade; it lives in
gusto, be it foul or fair, high or low, rich or poor, mean or
elevated—It has as much delight in conceiving an Iago
as an Imogen. What shocks the virtuous philosopher,
(10) delights the camelion Poet.

43. In the passage, Iago and Imogen (lines 8–9) repre-
    sent, respectively

    (A) the wicked and the good
    (B) an excellently rendered character and one poorly
        rendered
    (C) the grotesque and the ideally formed
    (D) a product of Shakespeare's imagination and the
        product of a mediocre playwright's
        imagination
    (E) a strong personality and a weak personality

44. Which of the following statements is most consistent
    with the position expressed in the passage above?

    (A) I am not ashamed to admit I am a poet, despite
        the fact that poets are either egotists or inca-
        pable of decisive action.
    (B) A poet's moral sense is more precise, complex,
        and rigorous than that of a philosopher's.
    (C) There is a type of poet that relishes life's varie-
        gated experiences without regard to tradi-
        tional value judgments.
    (D) I do not care for society's petty rules, and scorn
        propriety.
    (E) Poetry is all encompassing. Nothing is outside
        of poetry's scrutiny, from glorious acts of
        heroism to the banality of a tepid cup of weak
        tea.

GO ON TO THE NEXT PAGE.

45. The Grecian women (both Spartan and Athenian alike), tired of their husbands' perpetual absence, ally to offer the Greek men an ultimatum: no sex until the wars cease. The premise is simple, the text is bawdy even by modern standards, and, well-performed, the play remains both shocking and funny. When first performed, however, behind the humor lay a serious concern. The catastrophic invasion of Sicily had left the Athenians with a real desire for peace.

The play referred to above is

(A) *Clouds*
(B) *Frogs*
(C) *Lysistrata*
(D) *Medea*
(E) *Knights*

46. He lived amidst th' untrodden ways
        To Rydal Lake that lead;
A bard whom there were none to praise
        And very few to read.

The passage alludes to a poem by

(A) Marlowe
(B) Herrick
(C) Coleridge
(D) Wordsworth
(E) Shakespeare

47. The rivalry of Andromache and Hermione has been dramatized by both

(A) Sophocles and Beckett
(B) Goethe and Strindberg
(C) Euripides and Racine
(D) Aeschylus and Sartre
(E) Aristophanes and O'Neill

48. *7 forgyf us ure gyltas swa swa we forgyfa urum gyltendum.*

Which of the following is the closest translation for meaning of the Anglo-Saxon sentence above?

(A) And forgive us our sins as we forgive sinners against us.
(B) Give us seven gold coins, and we give to you golden peace.
(C) These seven forged gold coins are forged of gilt.
(D) The seven fighters are guilty as your guilty looks prove.
(E) Forget us if guilty we are, and forget our guiltiness.

GO ON TO THE NEXT PAGE.

High priest of Homer, not elect in vain
Deep trumpets blow before thee, shawms behind
Mix music with the rolling wheels that wind
Line   Slow through the laboring triumph of the train:
(5)   Fierce history, molten in thy forging brain,
Takes form and fire and fashion from thy mind,
Tormented and transmuted out of kind:
But howsoe'er thou shift thy strenuous strain,
Like Tailor smooth, like Fisher swollen, and now
(10)   Grim Yarrington scarce bloodier marked than thou,
Then bluff as Mayne's or broadmouthed Barry's glee,
Proud still with hoar predominance of brow
And beard like foam swept off the broad blown sea,
Where'er thou go, men's reverence goes with thee.

49. The subject of the poem above is

(A) Swinburne
(B) Crabbe
(C) Nashe
(D) Chapman
(E) Shakespeare

50. The octave of the poem above is that of

(A) an Italian sonnet
(B) a sestina
(C) a Spenserian sonnet
(D) an English sonnet
(E) a villanelle

51. The subject of this poem is also the subject of a poem by

(A) Dryden
(B) Webster
(C) Shakespeare
(D) Wordsworth
(E) Keats

52. "I have known them to become quite offensive, the monkey's usually the difficulty," he gossips. "Huna-mans or hanumans they call them: funny name, isn't it, like houyhnhnms! It's Hindu I believe, it's an Ape-god. They are the mascots of the river-crossing. In the eyes of all these people they're sacred."

The passage above makes an allusion to

(A) the sprites and fairies of the forest of Arden
(B) the myth of Sisyphus
(C) the Book of Revelations
(D) an imaginary race of talking horses
(E) the *Nibelungenlied*

GO ON TO THE NEXT PAGE.

Questions 53–55

Mock on, Mock on, Voltaire, Rousseau;
Mock on, Mock on, 'tis all in vain.
You throw the sand against the wind,
And the wind blows it back again.

Line
(5) And every sand becomes a Gem
Reflected in the beams divine;
Blown back, they blind the mocking Eye,
but still in Israel's paths they shine.

The Atoms of Democritus
(10) And Newton's Particles of light
Are sands upon the Red sea shore,
Where Israel's tents do shine so bright.

53. In the context of the poem above, Voltaire and Rousseau

(A) typify the inconsequentiality of earthly strivings in the presence of the divine
(B) typify Enlightenment thinkers who rely too much upon rationality
(C) represent figures of heroic but ultimately futile achievement
(D) represent leading proponents of Luther's Protestant Reformation
(E) are personal enemies of the poet

54. Which of the following is closest to the poem's principle theme?

(A) Absolute power corrupts absolutely.
(B) There are more things in heaven and earth, Horatio, than are dreamt of in your philosophy.
(C) To err is human, to forgive divine.
(D) All for one and one for all.
(E) If I have seen farther than others it is because I've stood upon the shoulders of giants.

55. The author of the poem above is also the author of

(A) "Intimations of Immortality"
(B) *Absalom and Achitophel*
(C) "An Essay on Criticism"
(D) *Volpone*
(E) "The Tyger"

Questions 56–57

Not that always where the language is intricate the thought is subtle, or the image always great where the line is bulky; the equality of words to things is very often
Line neglected, and trivial sentiments and vulgar ideas disap-
(5) point the attention, to which they are recommended by sonorous epithets and swelling figures.

56. In the passage above, Samuel Johnson—writing of Shakespeare—believes that Shakespeare

(A) is sometimes so coarse as to be without appeal
(B) sometimes treats subjects which are not properly literary
(C) sometimes fails properly to relate style to content
(D) is more highly esteemed than is reasonable
(E) treats ordinary material in such a way as to render it sublime

57. The use (and perhaps overuse) of "sonorous epithets and swelling figures" is a prominent characteristic of

(A) euphuism
(B) skeltonics
(C) strong-stress verse
(D) Restoration comedy
(E) transcendentalism

GO ON TO THE NEXT PAGE.

Questions 58–60

His steps are not upon thy paths—thy fields
Are not a spoil for him,—thou dost arise
And shake him from thee; the vile strength he wields
Line For earth's destruction thou dost all despise,
(5)   Spurning him from thy bosom to the skies
And send'st him, shivering in thy playful spray
And howling, to his Gods, where haply lies
His petty hope in some near port or bay,
And dashest him again to earth:—there let him lay.

58. In the passage above, "thee" refers to

(A) the reader
(B) human kind
(C) the ocean
(D) the people of Athens
(E) Mount Olympus

59. The verse form employed is that of

(A) one of the first five stanzas of chant royal
(B) a complete caudate sonnet
(C) a terza rima stanza
(D) a heroic stanza
(E) a Spenserian stanza

60. A departure from the accepted grammar of the author's day (and our own) occurs in his use of

(A) "spoil" in line 2
(B) "shake" in line 3
(C) "spurning" in line 5
(D) "petty" in line 8
(E) "lay" in line 9

61. Though some may know her only as a poet, the author of the inaugural ode "On the Pulse of Morning," _____, first came to national and international literary attention as an autobiographer. Before that she had been, among other things, a playwright, a dancer, a cook, a mother, briefly both a madam and a prostitute, a civil rights leader, and even the first black woman street-car conductor in San Francisco.

The name that correctly completes line 3 is

(A) Maya Angelou
(B) Gwendolyn Brooks
(C) Nikki Giovanni
(D) Zora Neale Hurston
(E) Lorraine Hansberry

Questions 62–63

She had apparently read widely, and although she was a faithful Puritan wife, she could not always accept in entire docility the sterner aspects of the New
Line England variety of Calvinism . . . Her *Contempla-*
(5)   *tions*, for example, although overformal by modern standards, is a brave attempt to express poetically some sense of the physical beauty of Massachusetts; her lines in praise of _____, have defiant vigor and wit:

(10)   Now say, have women worth? Or have they none?
Or had they some, but with our Queen is't gone?
Nay Masculines, you have thus taxt us long,
But she, though dead, will vindicate our wrong.
Let such as say our Sex is void of Reason,
(15)   Know tis a Slander now, but once was Treason.

Many a minor English poet of her day, more celebrated than _____, wrote nothing that is better than her best, even though her best conforms to the Puritan's utilitarian view of art and to his distrust of
(20)   the frankly sensuous.

62. Which of the following correctly completes the first blank (line 8) in the passage above

(A) Mary, Queen of Scots
(B) Queen Victoria
(C) Queen Isabella
(D) Queen Anne
(E) Queen Elizabeth

63. Which of the following correctly completes the second blank (line 17) in the passage above?

(A) Margery Kempe
(B) Mary Rowlandson
(C) Anne Bradstreet
(D) Sarah Orne Jewett
(E) Mary Wollstonecraft

GO ON TO THE NEXT PAGE.

What a do was there made in London at a certein man because he sayd, and ded at that time on a iust cause. Burgesses quod he, nay butterflies. Lorde what
Line a do there was for yat worde. And yet would God they
(5) were no worse then butterflies. Butterflies do but theyre nature, the butterflye is not couetouse, is not gredye of other mens goodes, is not ful of enuy and hatered, is not malicious, is not cruel, is not mercilesse. The butter-flye gloriethe not in hyr owne dedes, nor prefereth the
(10) tradicions of men before Gods worde; it committeth no idolatry nor worshyppeth false goddes. But London can not abyde to be rebuked suche is the nature of man. If they be prycked, they wyll kycke.

64. Which of the following best describes the author's meaning?

   (A) The people of London should not have been compared to butterflies.
   (B) By some measures, a comparison between Lon-doners and butterflies favors the butterflies.
   (C) Butterflies are morally superior to men.
   (D) He wishes that men were butterflies.
   (E) The nature of mankind is wickedness.

65. The passage was written in the

   (A) ninth century
   (B) eleventh century
   (C) thirteenth century
   (D) sixteenth century
   (E) nineteenth century

66. Then rear your standards; let your sounding drums
Direct our soldiers to Damascus' walls.
Now, _____, the mighty Soldan comes,
And leads with him the great Arabian king,
To dim thy baseness and obscurity,
Famous for nothing but for theft and spoil;
To raze and scatter thy inglorious crew
Of Scythians and slavish Persians.

Which one of the following will correctly complete the passage?

   (A) Gilgamesh
   (B) Volpone
   (C) Mercutio
   (D) Tamburlaine
   (E) Siegfried

67. In a posthumously published volume of collected essays entitled *Mystery and Manners* (1969) she ad-vocated "violent means" to get her vision across: with a "hostile audience," the writer must make her "vision apparent by shock—to the hard of hearing you shout, and for the almost blind you draw large and startling figures." Christ-haunted prophets, religious hucksters, and visionary farm hands, many of the characters in _____ stories and novels inhabit a South that she associated with the urgency of faith: "The South," she explained in a letter (1957), "still believes that man has fallen and that he is only perfectible by God's grace, not by his own unaided efforts." Her characters are therefore often caught in the grip of a violent spiritual struggle in which they are ultimately saved or lost.

Which of the following correctly completes the pas-sage above?

   (A) Welty's
   (B) O'Connor's
   (C) Cather's
   (D) Gordimer's
   (E) Sarton's

GO ON TO THE NEXT PAGE.

Molly then taking a thigh-bone in her hand fell in among the flying ranks, and dealing her blows with great liberality on either side, overthrew the carcass
Line of many a mighty hero and heroine.
(5)   Recount, O Muse, the names of those who fell on this fatal day. First, Jemmy Tweedly felt on his hinder head the direful bone. Him the pleasant banks of sweetly winding Stour had nourished, where he first learnt the vocal art with which wandering up and
(10) down at wakes and fairs, he cheered the rural nymphs and swains, when upon the green they interweave the sprightly dance, while he himself stood fiddling and jumping to his own music. How little now avails his fiddle? He thumps the verdant floor with his carcass.
(15) Next old Echepole, the sow-gelder, received a blow in his forehead. . . .
     But now fortune, fearing she had acted out of character and had inclined too long to the same side, especially as it was the right side, hastily turned
(20) about: for now Goody Brown, whom Zekiel Brown caresses in his arms; nor he alone, but half the parish besides, so famous was she in the fields of Venus; nor indeed less in those of Mars. The trophies of both these her husband always bore about on his head and
(25) face; for if ever human head did by its horns display the amorous glories of a wife, Zekiel's did; nor did his well-scratched face less denote her talents (or rather talons) of a different kind.

68. The passage depicts Goody Brown as

(A) a wife, loving and devoted to a half-wit husband
(B) a beautiful and strong-willed woman of whom her husband is proud
(C) known for her insight into both romantic psychology and military strategy
(D) prudish, moralizing, and shrewish
(E) both unfaithful and physically abusive of her husband

69. The selection is from

(A) *Tess of the D'Urbervilles*
(B) *Emma*
(C) *Tom Jones*
(D) *David Copperfield*
(E) *Daniel Deronda*

70. The passage

(A) parodies the style of *The Iliad*
(B) parodies the classicist tendencies of writers like Richardson
(C) parodies the epic simile
(D) uses epic style to add dramatic weight to the scene
(E) uses the conventional epic style of the author's time.

71. The "horns" (line 25) are

(A) a familiar trope for the cuckold
(B) a symbol of sexual desire
(C) an example of synecdoche
(D) a metaphor for stupidity
(E) a comic reference to the martial apparel of Hector

72. Mars and Venus are the Roman equivalents, or near equivalents, to

(A) Zeus and Hera
(B) Apollo and Athena
(C) Hermes and Artemis
(D) Ares and Aphrodite
(E) Cupid and Psyche

73. Which of the following works treats its subject with devices parallel to those of the passage?

(A) Pope's *The Rape of the Lock*
(B) Spenser's *The Faerie Queene*
(C) Shakespeare's *The Phoenix and the Turtle*
(D) Tennyson's "Ulysses"
(E) Bunyan's *Pilgrim's Progress*

GO ON TO THE NEXT PAGE.

Thus doing, your name shall flourish in the print-
ers' shops; thus doing, you shall be of kin to many a
poetical preface; thus doing, you shall be most fair,
Line most rich, most wise, most all; you shall dwell upon
(5) superlatives. Thus doing, though you be *libertino pa-
tre natus*, you shall suddenly grow *Herculea proles,
Si quid mea carmina possunt.*
Thus doing, your soul shall be placed with
Dante's Beatrix, or Virgil's Anchises. But if (fie of
(10) such a but) you be born so near the dull making
cataract of Nilus that you cannot hear the planet-
like music of Poetry, if you have so earth-creeping a
mind that it cannot lift itself up to look to the sky of
Poetry, or rather, by a certain rustical disdain, will
(15) become such a Mome as to be a Momus of Poetry;
then, though I will not wish unto you the ass's ears
of Midas, nor to be driven by a poet's verses (as
Bubonax was) to hang himself, nor to be rhymed to
death, as is said to be done in Ireland; yet thus much
(20) curse I must send you, in the behalf of all poets,
that while you live, you live in love, and never get
favour for lacking skill of a Sonnet, and, when you
die, your memory die from the earth for want of an
Epitaph.

74. Which of the following could replace "earth-creeping" (line 12) with the least loss of the author's
meaning?

(A) distracted
(B) pedestrian
(C) humorless
(D) vacuous
(E) evil

75. Which of the following most closely restates the
sense of "that while you live, you live in love and
never get favour for lacking skill of a Sonnet"?

(A) May you be deeply in love but suffer unrequited,
because unable to fashion adequate verse, you
cannot gain your beloved's notice.
(B) May you love life all your life but lack the ability to convey your feelings with poetry.
(C) While you live, may you never understand what
it is to love a sonnet.
(D) May you live only as long as it takes to write an
unskilled sonnet.
(E) May you be always in love but fail as a lover,
because in a metaphorical sense, you lack
even the rudimentary skill of fashioning a
sonnet in proper meter and rhyme.

76. The "ass's ears of Midas" (lines 16–17) refers to a
story that also involves

(A) a demi-god whose liver is perpetually torn by
vultures
(B) a man condemned to push a rock up a hill *ad
infinitum*
(C) a musical contest between a lyrist and a piper
(D) a forbidden box which when opened releases
evil into the world
(E) a riddle posed by the Sphinx

77. Which of the following best describes the tone of the
passage?

(A) It parodies the scholarly writing of the period
through the use of needlessly complicated
syntax and diction as well as obscure and
erudite references.
(B) It moves from a light-hearted mocking tone of
praise to one that by the passage's end is in
deadly earnest.
(C) It presents itself as objective at first but then
frankly exposes the author's bias with a tone
first of displeasure, and finally, of open contempt.
(D) It is from beginning to end a tongue-in-cheek
burlesque that relies on dubious aphorisms
and deliberately misinterpreted or garbled
quotes and stories in order to poke fun at the
author's own pretensions.
(E) It humorously uses ironically hyperbolic praise
and scorn to offset the author's genuine passion for his subject.

78. In lines 11 and 12 "the planet-like music of Poetry"

(A) synaesthetically suggests poetry sounds as
lovely as planets are huge
(B) refers to a model of the universe in which the
movements of the stars and planets around
the earth create a celestial music
(C) implies a comic misinterpretation of the theories
of Kepler and Copernicus
(D) makes a humorously inept comparison between
the majestic silence of the planets in space
and the musical sound of poetry
(E) refers to the pulsing rhythmic sound some planets make as they spin upon their axes

GO ON TO THE NEXT PAGE.

Questions 79–85. Identify the author or work from which the following passages were drawn using the style and content of the passage to make your decision.

79. If it was a question of an *Imperium*, he said to himself, and if one wished, as a Roman, to recover a little the sense of that, the place to do so was on London Bridge, or even, on a fine afternoon in May, at Hyde Park Corner. It was not indeed to either of those places that these grounds of his predilection, after all sufficiently vague, had, at the moment we are concerned with him, guided his steps; he had strayed simply enough into Bond Street, where his imagination, working at comparatively short range, caused him now and then to stop before a window in which objects massive and lumpish, in silver and gold, in the forms to which precious stones contribute, or in leather, steel, brass, applied to a hundred uses and abuses, were as tumbled together as if, in the insolence of the Empire, they had been the loot of far-off victories.

   (A) T. S. Eliot
   (B) Ernest Hemingway
   (C) John Dos Passos
   (D) Henry James
   (E) E. M. Forster

80. What happens to a dream deferred?
   Does it dry up
   like a raisin in the sun?
   Or fester like a sore—
   and then run? Does it stink like rotten meat?
   Or crust and sugar over—
   like a syrupy sweet?
   Maybe it just sags
   like a heavy load.

   Or does it explode?

   (A) Langston Hughes
   (B) Countee Cullen
   (C) W. E. B. Du Bois
   (D) Paul Laurence Dunbar
   (E) Amiri Baraka

81. Now as I was young and easy under the apple boughs
   About the lilting house and happy as the grass was green,
        The night above the dingle starry,
           Time let me hail and climb
        Golden in the heydays of his eyes,
   And honored among wagons I was prince of the apple towns
   And once below a time I lordly had the trees and leaves
        Trail with daisies and barley
        Down the rivers of the windfall light.

   (A) Ted Hughes
   (B) William Carlos Williams
   (C) Ezra Pound
   (D) Dylan Thomas
   (E) Sylvia Plath

82. Novels are now so fully accepted by every one pretending to cultivated taste . . . that it is refreshing to have them frankly denounced, and to be invited to revise one's ideas and feelings in regard to them. . . . For my own part I will confess that I believe fiction in the past to have been largely injurious, as I believe the stage play to be still almost wholly injurious, through its falsehood, its folly, its wantonness, and its aimlessness. It may be safely assumed that most of the novel-reading which people fancy an intellectual pastime is the emptiest dissipation, hardly more related to thought . . . than opium eating; in either case the brain is drugged, and left weaker and crazier for the debauch.

   (A) William Dean Howells
   (B) Herman Melville
   (C) Mark Twain
   (D) Henry James
   (E) Jack London

83. So they're gone, she thought, sighing with relief and disappointment. Her sympathy seemed to be cast back on her, like a bramble across her face. She felt curiously divided, as if one part of her were drawn out there—it was a still day, hazy; the Lighthouse looked this morning at an immense distance; the other had fixed itself doggedly, solidly, here on the lawn. She saw her canvas as if it had floated up and placed itself white and uncompromising directly before her.

   (A) Djuna Barnes
   (B) Virginia Woolf
   (C) William Faulkner
   (D) F. Scott Fitzgerald
   (E) Gertrude Stein

84. *September 2, 1666*

   Lords day. Some of our maids sitting up late last night to get things ready against our feast today, Jane called us up, about 3 in the morning, to tell us of a great fire they saw in the City. So I rose, and slipped on my nightgown and went to her window, and thought it to be on the back side of Mark Lane at the furthest. . . . By and by Jane comes and tells me that she hears that above 300 houses have been burned down tonight by the fire we saw, and that it was now burning down all Fish Street by London Bridge.

   (A) Samuel Pepys
   (B) John Bunyan
   (C) Mary Wollstonecraft
   (D) Sir Thomas More
   (E) Sir Thomas Mallory

85. Charles Lamb I sincerely believe to be in some considerable degree *insane*. A more pitiful, rickety, gasping, staggering, stammering Tom Fool I do not know. He is witty by denying truisms, and abjuring good manners. His speech wriggles hither and thither with an incessant painful fluctuation; not an opinion in it or a fact or even a phrase that you can thank him for: more like a convulsion fit than natural systole and diastole.—Besides he is now a confirmed shameless drunkard: *asks* vehemently for gin-and-water in strangers' houses; tipples until he is utterly mad, and is only not thrown out of doors because he is too much despised for taking such trouble with him! Poor Lamb! Poor England where such a despicable abortion is named genius!

   (A) John Ruskin
   (B) Matthew Arnold
   (C) Thomas Carlyle
   (D) Oscar Wilde
   (E) Walter Pater

GO ON TO THE NEXT PAGE.

Questions 86–88

                    Her heavenly form
         Angelic, but more soft, and feminine,
         Her graceful innocence, her every air
Line   Of gesture or least action overawed
  (5)   His malice, and with rapine sweet bereaved
         His fierceness of the fierce intent it brought:
         That space the evil one abstracted stood
         From his own evil, and for the time remained
         Stupidly good, of enmity disarmed,
 (10)   Of guile, of hate, of envy, of revenge.
         But the hot Hell that always in him burns
         Though in mid Heaven, soon ended his delight,
         And tortures him now more, the more he sees
         Of pleasure not for him ordained: then soon
 (15)   Fierce hate he recollects.

86. Which of the following best describes the construc-
    tion of the first clause of the first sentence?

    (A) Subject—Verb—Direct object
    (B) Subject—Verb—Direct object—Indirect object
    (C) Subject—Direct object—Verb
    (D) Direct object—Verb—Subject
    (E) Direct object—Indirect object—Verb—Subject

87. Which of the following is closest to the meaning in
    context of "abstracted" (line 7)?

    (A) abashed
    (B) perplexed
    (C) dismayed
    (D) intrigued
    (E) removed

88. Which of the following passages also appears in the
    poem?

    (A) Now whenas sacred light began to dawn
        In Eden on the humid flow'rs, that breath'd
        their morning incense, when all things that
            breathe
        From th' Earth's great altar send up silent praise
        To the Creator, and his nostrils fill
        With grateful smell, forth came the human pair.

    (B) Yes, I remember when the changeful earth,
        And twice five summers on my mind had
            stamped
        The faces of the moving year, even then
        I held unconscious intercourse with beauty
        Old as creation, drinking in a pure
        Organic pleasure from the silver wreaths
        Of curling mist, or from the level plain
        Of waters colored by impending clouds.

    (C) I have walked and prayed for this young child an
            hour
        And heard the sea-wind scream upon the tower,
        And under arches of the bridge, and scream
        In the elms above the flooded stream;
        Imagining in excited reverie
        That the future years had come,
        Dancing to the frenzied drum,
        Out of the murderous innocence of the sea.

    (D) And noon is suddenly dark, is lustrous, is silent
            and dark
        Men are unseen, beneath the shading hats;
        Only, from out the foliage of the secret loins
        Red flamelets here and there reveal
        A man, a woman there.

    (E) Thus far both armies to Belinda yield;
        Now to the Baron fate inclines the field.
        His warlike amazon her host invades,
        The imperial consort of the crown of Spades.
        The Club's black tyrant first her victim died,
        Spite of his haughty mien and barbarous pride.

GO ON TO THE NEXT PAGE.

89. Which of the following is NOT characteristic of a work observing the neoclassical principles of dramatic form?

(A) decorum
(B) unity of time
(C) unity of place
(D) unity of action
(E) ironic subplot

90. ...what we do determine oft we break.
Purpose is but the slave to memory,
Of violent birth, but poor validity;
Which now, like fruit unripe sticks on the tree,
But fall unshaken, when they mellow be.
Most necessary tis that we forget
To pay ourselves what to ourselves is debt;
What to ourselves in passion we propose,
The passion ending, doth the purpose lose.

Which of the following best summarizes the meaning of the lines (from *Hamlet*) above?

(A) The truth of a statement is determined more by the genuineness of the passion with which it was uttered, than by the factual accuracy of the statement itself.
(B) Regardless of what it is one endeavors to do, the outcome of that endeavor cannot be known beforehand.
(C) Lies may at first serve their purpose, but are ultimately unravelled and exposed by the contradictions they create.
(D) Emotion might prompt one to make a promise, but as the emotion which stirred the pledge wanes, the will to uphold the pledge often wanes as well.
(E) It is not necessary to honor one's debts to one-self, because when promises of that kind are broken no one's trust has been violated.

Questions 91–94 refer to the selections below.

91. Which begins *Notes from the Underground*?

92. Which begins *Remembrance of Things Past*?

93. Which begins *The Notebooks of Malte Laurids Brigge*?

94. Which begins *The Stranger*?

(A) Madame Vauquer, formerly Mademoiselle de Conflans, is now an old woman. For the past forty years she has a kept a private lodging house in a Paris street running between the Latin Quarter and the Faubourg Saint Marceau.

(B) For a long time I used to go to bed early. Sometimes, when I had put out my candle, my eyes would close so quickly that I had not even time to say to myself: "I'm falling asleep." And half an hour later the thought that it was time to go to sleep would awaken me.

(C) Today, mama died. Or maybe yesterday, I don't know. I received a telegram from the home: "Mother deceased. Burial tomorrow. Deepest regrets." Which means nothing. Maybe it was yesterday.

(D) I am a sick man. ....I am a spiteful man. I am an unattractive man. I believe my liver is diseased. However I know nothing at all about my disease, and do not know for certain what ails me.

(E) So this is where people come to live; I would have thought it is a city to die in. I have been out. I saw: hospitals. I saw a man who staggered and fell. A crowd formed around him and I was spared the rest.

GO ON TO THE NEXT PAGE.

95. Either of these two figures might justly be called the American protagonist *par excellence*, yet they are opposites, polar opposites. Where one is rigid, strict and utterly purposeful, the other is relaxed, curiously gentle, and aimless. But it is the God obsessed New England Protestant who rebels against God and nature, who becomes a raging and tragic fool, while the rebellious, foolish, sardonic atheist proves, in simplicity, to be both wise and somehow holy.

The characters discussed above are

(A) Natty Bumppo and Holden Caulfield
(B) Quentin Compson and Benjy Compson
(C) Arthur Dimmesdale and Hester Prynne
(D) Captain Ahab and Huckleberry Finn
(E) Jake Barnes and Daisy Miller

96. The foolish knight errant and his muddle-headed squire: one immediately thinks of *Don Quixote,* forgetting that English letters once sent out just such a pair in order to travesty—in a comically rhymed and mercilessly stumbling tetrameter—the Presbyterians, Independents, and indeed the entire Parliamentarian cause in England's great domestic conflict of the seventeenth century.

The work referred to above is

(A) *The Rape of the Lock*
(B) *Absalom and Achitophel*
(C) *Dunciad*
(D) *Hudibras*
(E) *Mac Flecknoe*

97. He built the novel around a notice he chanced across in the newspaper: a young man of humble origins and formerly a seminary student had been executed for the attempted murder of a woman he loved.

The novel referred to above is

(A) Stendhal's *The Red and The Black*
(B) Mann's *Buddenbrooks*
(C) Balzac's *Lost Illusions*
(D) Flaubert's *Sentimental Education*
(E) Hamsun's *Growth of the Soil*

98. But at my back I always hear
Time's wingéd chariot hurrying near;
And yonder all before us lie
Deserts of vast eternity

The lines above are from

(A) "To His Coy Mistress"
(B) "The Emperor of Ice-Cream"
(C) "In Memoriam A.H.H."
(D) "Elegy Written in a Country Church Yard"
(E) "To an Athlete Dying Young"

99. The play, if not as wholly abandoned to violence and perversity as Webster's *Duchess of Malfi* (the composition of which it influenced), is surely a dark and bloody creation. By the drama's end Horatio is murdered, Lorenzo and Balthazar are both killed, lovely Bel-imperia is dead by her own hand, and mad Hieronimo is a suicide as well, though not before gruesomely mutilating himself on stage.

The theatrical work described above is

(A) Jonson's *Volpone*
(B) Sheridan's *The School for Scandal*
(C) Congreve's *The Way of the World*
(D) Dryden's *The Conquest of Granada*
(E) Kyd's *The Spanish Tragedy*

GO ON TO THE NEXT PAGE.

Most famous Worthy of the world, by whome
That warre was kindled, which did Troy inflame,
And stately towres of Ilion whilome
Line   Brought unto balefull ruine, was by name
(5)   Sir Paris far renowmd through noble fame,
Who through great prowess and bold hardinesse
From Lacedaemon fetcht the fairest Dame,
That ever Greece did boast, or knight possesse,
Whom Venus to him gave for meed of worthinesse

100. The woman referred to in line 7 is

(A) Aphrodite
(B) Penelope
(C) Hero
(D) Guinevere
(E) Helen

101. The grammatical subject of the sentence that comprises the stanza above is

(A) Lacedaemon (line 7)
(B) Paris (line 5)
(C) Dame (line 7)
(D) Worthy (line 1)
(E) Venus (line 9)

102. In context, the word "fairest" (line 7) means

(A) most just
(B) most lightly complexioned
(C) most comely
(D) most faithful
(E) most appropriate

103. The larger work the stanza is taken from is

(A) *Sir Gawain and the Green Knight*
(B) *The Faerie Queene*
(C) *Hero and Leander*
(D) Chapman's *Iliad*
(E) *Morte D'Arthur*

104. The last line of the stanza is called

(A) an encomium
(B) an anapestic
(C) an alexandrine
(D) a pyrrhic
(E) an envoy

. . . but has she any right to agitate calm, consistent
Lady Bertram? Is it not like giving pug three faces and
setting him to guard the gates of hell? Ought not her
Line   ladyship to remain on the sofa saying, "This is a dreadful
(5)   and sadly exhausting business about Julia and Maria, but
where is Fanny gone? I have dropped another stitch?"
      I used to think this, through misunderstanding
_____'s method—exactly as Scott misunderstood
it when he congratulated her for painting on a square of
(10) ivory. She is a miniaturist, but never two-dimensional.
All her characters are round, or capable of rotundity.

105. The author of the passage above is

(A) E. M. Forster
(B) T. S. Eliot
(C) Matthew Arnold
(D) D. H. Lawrence
(E) W. B. Yeats

106. The author's name that correctly fills in the blank (line 8) is

(A) Iris Murdoch
(B) Virginia Woolf
(C) Jane Austen
(D) Charlotte Brontë
(E) Elizabeth Gaskell

107. Which is the mythological entity alluded to in lines 2–3?

(A) Cerberus
(B) Charon
(C) Hydra
(D) Hades
(E) Chimera

GO ON TO THE NEXT PAGE.

108. Like Kafka, _____ came to international attention through his short stories, and like Kafka,
his characteristic stories are less concerned with the
Line   portraiture of individual actors than with the philo-
(5)   sophical exploration of modernist anxieties concerning the self and meaning. Where Kafka writes of
limitless bureaucracy, incomprehensible rules, and
futile compulsions, _____ writes of labyrinths,
actual and metaphysical, of infinite libraries, of
(10)   dreams that dream the dreamer, of duplicate worlds
and duplicate selves, of inescapable and fascinating
solipsisms. Either writer's work might be seen as an
extended meditation on a single sentence: "*I seem to
have become lost.*"

Which of the following author's names correctly fills
the blanks (lines 1 and 8) in the discussion above?

(A) George Orwell
(B) Vladimir Nabokov
(C) Bernard Malamud
(D) Jorge Luis Borges
(E) Andre Gide

109. Was ever woman in this humor wooed?
Was ever woman in this humor won?
I'll have her, but I will not keep her long.
What! I, that killed her husband and his father,
To take her in her heart's extremest hate,
With curses in her mouth, tears in her eyes,
The bleeding witness of my hatred by,
having God, her conscience, and these bars against
me,
And I no friends to back my suit withal
But the plain Devil and dissembling looks,
And yet to win her, all the world to nothing!
Ha!

The lines above are spoken by

(A) Iago
(B) Hamlet
(C) Mercutio
(D) Julius Caesar
(E) Richard III

110. And I applied my mind to seek and to search out by
wisdom all that is done under heaven; it is an unhappy business that God has given to the sons of men
to be busy with. I have seen everything that is done
under the sun; and behold, all is vanity and a striving
after the wind.

This passage from the Revised Standard Version of
the King James Bible is found in which book?

(A) Ecclesiastes
(B) Obadiah
(C) Malachi
(D) Luke
(E) Hebrews

GO ON TO THE NEXT PAGE.

Questions 111–112

There's a certain Slant of light,
Winter Afternoons—
That oppresses, like the Heft
Of Cathedral Tunes—
Line
(5) Heavenly Hurt, it gives us—
We can find no scar,
But internal difference,
Where the meanings, are—

None may teach it—Any—
(10) 'Tis the Seal Despair—
An imperial affliction
Sent us of the Air—

When it comes, the Landscape listens—
Shadows—hold their breath—
(15) When it goes, 'tis like the Distance
On the look of Death—

111. In line 15 "it" grammatically refers to

(A) cathedral tunes
(B) affliction
(C) slant
(D) despair
(E) air

112. The author of the poem is also the author of which of
the following lines?

(A) "Two roads diverged in a yellow wood"
(B) "Because I could not stop for death"
(C) "And after many a summer dies the swan"
(D) "I have seen the best minds of my generation
destroyed by madness, starving, hysterical,
naked"
(E) "When lilacs last in the dooryard bloom'd"

113. An axe angles
from my neighbor's ashcan;
It is hell's handiwork,
the wood not hickory,
The flow of the grain
not faithfully followed.

The lines above are from a poem that

(A) exhibits a form characteristic of Old English
verse
(B) is in free verse
(C) is in blank verse
(D) parodies beat poetry
(E) parodies symbolist poetry

114. Fare thee well, great heart!
Ill-weav'd ambition, how much art thou shrunk!
When that this body did contain a spirit,
A kingdom for it was too small a bound,
but now two paces of the vilest earth is room enough.

These lines eulogize

(A) Tamburlaine
(B) Faustus
(C) Lear
(D) Lady Macbeth
(E) Hotspur

GO ON TO THE NEXT PAGE.

'Tis an old mistress you'll meet here tonight,
Whose charms you once have looked on with delight.
But now, of late, such dirty drabs have known ye,
Line A muse o' th' better sort's ashamed to own ye.
(5) Nature well-drawn and wit must now give place
To gaudy nonsense and to dull grimace;
Nor is it strange that you should like so much
That kind of wit, for most of yours is such.
But I'm afraid that while to France we go,
(10) To bring you home fine dresses, dance, and show,
The stage, like you, will but more foppish grow.
Of foreign wares why should we fetch the scum,
When we can be so richly served at home?
For, heav'n be thanked, 'tis not so wise an age
(15) But your own follies may supply the stage.
Though often plowed, there's no great fear the soil
Should barren grow by the too-frequent toil,
While at your doors are to be daily found
Such loads of dunghill to manure the ground.

115. This passage comes from

(A) a verse essay condemning Sentimental comedy
(B) a seventeenth-century collection of popular Puritan lay-sermons
(C) the prologue of a Jacobean masque
(D) the prologue of a Restoration comedy
(E) a satirical denunciation of French theater-goers and fashion

116. Which of the following is closest to the meaning, in context, of "own" (line 4)?

(A) possess
(B) wed
(C) recognize
(D) hold
(E) rule

117. "Drabs" (line 3) refer to

(A) prostitutes
(B) commoners
(C) dullards
(D) unfashionably dressed people
(E) sinners

118. Lines 12–19 discuss

(A) the corrupting effect of foreign influence
(B) those social ills the theater must attempt to amend
(C) the richness of plots traditionally available to poets and playwrights
(D) the disturbing truth that the violent incidents portrayed on stage occur, in England as in France, outside the theater as well as in it
(E) the audience's own vices and misdeeds as an appropriate and abundant source of comedy

GO ON TO THE NEXT PAGE.

Get up! get up for shame! The blooming morn
Upon her wings presents the god unshorn.
   See how Aurora throws her fair
Line   Fresh-quilted colors through the air:
(5)   Get up, sweet slug-a-bed, and see

          _____

Each flower has wept and bowed toward the east
Above an hour since, yet you not dressed;
   Nay, not so much as out of bed?

119. Which of the following correctly fills line 6 above?

    (A) Can such delights be in the street?
    (B) Before that we have left to dream,
    (C) Time shall throw a dart at thee.
    (D) In small proportions we just beauties see.
    (E) The dew bespangling herb and tree.

120. "Aurora" (line 3) refers to

    (A) a song-bird
    (B) the mythical goddess of dawn
    (C) a servant
    (D) a rainbow
    (E) a gypsy dancer

121. The passage is the beginning of

    (A) Donne's "The Sun Rising"
    (B) Lyly's "Oh, For a Bowl of Fat Canary"
    (C) Herrick's "Corinna's Going A-Maying"
    (D) Milton's *Paradise Regained*
    (E) Spenser's *Prothalamion*

     _____ is a well-to-do young bourgeois, a
morbidly sensitive dilettante fond of translating Os-
sian (he fancies himself a poet as well, or at least a
Line poetic soul), who falls madly in love with the happily
(5)   married Lotte. His elaborate attentions flatter her, but
she is too conventional (and too content with Albert,
her husband) to conduct an affair. Despairing, he
writes a last diary entry (the novel is told almost
entirely in diary form) and shoots himself with pistols
(10) borrowed from Albert.
     Although today's reader might find the novel's
alternatively weeping, raging, sighing, fawning protagonist somewhat foolish, on publication the novel
was a sensational success and struck such a nerve
(15) with its contemporary readers that it inspired several
"copy-cat" suicides.

122. The blank (line 1) is correctly filled by

    (A) Candide
    (B) Frederic
    (C) Lucien
    (D) Werther
    (E) Axel

123. The work referred to in the passage is most representative of which of the following genres?

    (A) Satire
    (B) *Sturm und Drang*
    (C) The existential novel
    (D) *Bildungsroman*
    (E) Expressionism

124. The fictional treatment of an actual socialist-utopian
community (Brook Farm) is the subject of

    (A) Twain's *Letters from Earth*
    (B) Hawthorne's *The Blithedale Romance*
    (C) Crane's *Maggie: A Girl of the Streets*
    (D) Orwell's *Homage to Catalonia*
    (E) Cather's *My Ántonia*

GO ON TO THE NEXT PAGE.

What a wonderful elusive personality he has become to us, this genius who penetrated to the quick hundreds of divers souls, yet of whom we know so
Line little as a man. To try and understand anyone, let
(5) alone a figure of his prepossessing stature from such absurdist details as knowing that he left his second-best bed to his wife, Anne Hathaway, is an impossibility. Better to remain content with our one great certainty, that though he died _____, "He was
(10) not of an age, but for all time!"

125. The subject of the passage above is

   (A) William Shakespeare
   (B) John Dryden
   (C) Andrew Marvell
   (D) Geoffrey Chaucer
   (E) Christopher Marlowe

126. The blank (line 9) is correctly replaced with

   (A) in the fourteenth century
   (B) in 1579
   (C) in the year of our Lord 1616
   (D) young
   (E) almost unknown

127. The quotation that ends the passage is from a verse eulogy by the subject's friend and rival

   (A) Thomas Shadwell
   (B) Samuel Johnson
   (C) Ben Jonson
   (D) Christopher Marlowe
   (E) Thomas Kyd

128. Which of the following mottoes best reflects the theme of the passage's last sentence?

   (A) *veni, vidi, vici*
   (B) *honi soit qui mal y pense*
   (C) *ars longa, vita brevis*
   (D) *cogito ergo sum*
   (E) *carpe diem*

Utopia was once my name,
That is, a place where no one goes.
Plato's Republic now I claim
Line To match, or beat at its own game;
(5) For that was just a myth in prose,
But what he wrote of, I became,
Of men, wealth, laws a solid frame,
A place where every wise man goes:
Eutopia is now my name.

129. The author of the work above was also

   (A) Dean of St. Paul's Cathedral
   (B) executed because of religious and political differences between himself and Henry VIII
   (C) a noted metaphysical poet
   (D) an adventurer, poet, and confidante to Queen Elizabeth
   (E) able to write only between recurring bouts of suicidal madness

130. Strictly translated *Utopia* means

   (A) no-place
   (B) excellent place
   (C) place of perfect morals
   (D) fantastical place
   (E) bad place

131. Which of the following novels is a parody of a 'Utopian' society?

   (A) Jonathan Swift's *A Tale of the Tub*
   (B) Lewis Carroll's *Alice in Wonderland*
   (C) George Orwell's *Keep the Aspidistra Flying*
   (D) Samuel Butler's *Erewhon*
   (E) Aldous Huxley's *Eyeless in Gaza*

GO ON TO THE NEXT PAGE.

Questions 132–135

    In a somer sesoun whanne softe was the sonne
    I shop me into a shroud as I a shep were;
    In abite as an Ermyte, vnholy of werkis,
Line wente wyde in Þis world wondris to here.
 (5) But on a may morwenygn on maluerne hilles
    Me befel a ferly, of fairie me Þoushte:
    I was wery for wandrit & wente me to reste
    Vndir a brood bank be a bourn side,
    And as I lay & lenide & lokide on Þe watris
(10) I slomeride into a slepyng, it swishede so merye.
    Þanne gan I mete a merueillous sweuene,
    Þat I was in a wildernesse, wiste I neuere where.

132. Which of the following best captures the meaning of
lines 7–10 above?

  (A) I was forewarned, and went to the rest [of them]
under a broad oak, and as I lay and leaned
and looked on the matters I stumbled into a
trap, it seemed so to me.

  (B) I was very forward and went to the rest [of
them] under a broad bank by a stream and as
I lay and leaned and lounged on the cushion I
slipped asleep, it was so soft.

  (C) I was wary, forewarned, and wanted to hide
myself under a broad oak on the shadowy
side, and as I lay and listened and looked on
the matters I fell into a sleeplike trance, it
frightened me so.

  (D) I was weary from wandering and went to rest
at the broad bank by a brookside, and as I
lay and leaned and looked on the waters it
sounded so merry I slumbered into a sleep.

  (E) I was weary from wandering and went to the rest
[of them] under a broad oak at a stream side,
and as I lay and leaned and looked on the
matters I slipped asleep.

133. The source of the passage is

  (A) Froissart's *Chronicle*
  (B) *Beowulf*
  (C) Webster's *Duchess of Malfi*
  (D) the "Song of Songs"
  (E) Langland's *Piers Plowman*

134. The passage is an example of

  (A) Old English epic verse
  (B) a folk ballad
  (C) an anonymous early English translation of the
        Old Testament
  (D) Jacobean dramatic verse
  (E) Middle English alliterative verse

135. The author of the passage is most nearly contemporary to

  (A) William Shakespeare
  (B) John Bunyan
  (C) Edmund Spenser
  (D) Geoffrey Chaucer
  (E) Caedmon

GO ON TO THE NEXT PAGE.

Both _____ and "Count No 'count" seemed,
at age 29, to be destined for failure. Ultimately of
course both writers would come to be regarded as
Line among the great writers of their respective nations,
(5) each bringing an enormous fictional universe to life
from wholly native soil. In fact each author's vision
has stamped itself so powerfully upon its subject
that by no means is it hyperbolic to say the one created Paris, and the other, the American deep south.
(10) After reading in the *Comedie Humaine* it is no
longer possible to walk in the Faubourg St. Germain
without finding the light curiously 19th century,
without Rastignac's too-knowing smile playing
suddenly on one's lips; nor can one visit a decaying
(15) ante-bellum mansion without straying into Yoknapatawpha county.

136. The blank in line 1 is correctly completed by

  (A) Balzac
  (B) Flaubert
  (C) Maupassant
  (D) Sand
  (E) Proust

137. The American author discussed in the passage is

  (A) Truman Capote
  (B) Tennessee Williams
  (C) William Styron
  (D) William Faulkner
  (E) Mark Twain

FIRST CHARACTER: You hate mankind?

SECOND CHARACTER: Heartily, inveterately.

FIRST CHARACTER: Your husband?

Line SECOND CHARACTER: Most transcendently; aye,
(5)   though I say it, meritoriously.

FIRST CHARACTER: Give me your hand upon it.

SECOND CHARACTER: There.

FIRST CHARACTER: I join with you; what I have said
    has been to try you.

(10) SECOND CHARACTER: Is it possible? Dost thou hate those
    vipers men?

FIRST CHARACTER: I have done hating 'em and am
    now come to despise 'em . . . and yet I am thinking
    sometimes to carry my aversion further . . . by mar-
(15)   rying. If I could but find one that loved me very well
    and would be thoroughly sensible of ill usage, I think
    I should do myself the violence of undergoing the
    ceremony.

SECOND CHARACTER: You would not make him a cuckold?

(20) FIRST CHARACTER: No, but I'd make him believe I did, and
    that's as bad.

SECOND CHARACTER: Why had not you as good do it?

FIRST CHARACTER: Oh, if he should ever discover it, he
    would then know the worst, and be out of his pain;
(25)   but I would have him ever to continue upon the rack
    of fear and jealousy.

138. In context the word "try" (line 9) means

  (A) weigh
  (B) test
  (C) aggravate
  (D) deceive
  (E) attempt

GO ON TO THE NEXT PAGE.

139. In context the word "sensible" (line 16) most nearly means

    (A) reasonable
    (B) tolerant
    (C) oblivious
    (D) aware
    (E) immune

140. The dialogue is from

    (A) Genet's *The Maids*
    (B) Brecht's *The Good Woman of Sezchuan*
    (C) Congreve's *The Way of the World*
    (D) Wycherly's *The Country Wife*
    (E) Shakespeare's *Much Ado About Nothing*

141. "It" in line 22 refers to

    (A) murder
    (B) marriage
    (C) shrewishness
    (D) theft
    (E) adultery

Questions 142–146

Perchance he for whom this bell tolls may be so ill as that he knows not it tolls for him; and perchance I may think myself so much better than I am,
Line as that they who are about me and see my state may
(5) have caused it to toll for me, and I know not that. The church is catholic, universal, so are all her actions; all that she does belongs to all. . . . .All mankind is of one author and is one volume; when one man dies, one chapter is not torn out of the book but translated
(10) into a better language; and every chapter must be so translated. God employs several translators; some pieces are translated by age, some by sickness, some by war, some by justice; but God's hand is in every translation, and his hand shall bind up all our scat-
(15) tered leaves again for that library where every book shall lie open to one another. As therefore the bell that rings to a sermon calls not upon the preacher only, but upon the congregation to come, so this bell calls us all.

142. The author of the passage above is

    (A) John Donne
    (B) Ralph Waldo Emerson
    (C) Henry Thoreau
    (D) Francis Bacon
    (E) Thomas Hobbes

143. The bell referred to throughout the passage is

    (A) the Liberty Bell
    (B) a bell that rings vespers
    (C) a bell that rings a death knell
    (D) a lighthouse bell that warns ships of nearby shoals
    (E) the bell at Concord Congregation church

144. In the passage "translation" (line 14) represents in part

    (A) unjust death
    (B) religious conversion
    (C) unexpected death
    (D) the inevitable release of the soul from the body
    (E) the hand of God in all things

GO ON TO THE NEXT PAGE.

145. Lines 7–16 contain a figure closest to which of the following tropes of the classical epic?

    (A) the epic question
    (B) the *in medias res* beginning
    (C) the epic simile
    (D) the epic invocation
    (E) the epic list

146. Which of the following lines is found later in the same work from which the passage above was taken?

    (A) "The world is charged with the grandeur of God, it will flame out, like shining from shook foil"
    (B) "No man is an island, entire of itself; every man is a piece of the continent, a part of the main"
    (C) "Look on my Works ye Mighty and despair!"
    (D) "Death is a dialogue between the spirit and the dust"
    (E) "O harp and altar, of the fury fused, (How could mere toil align thy choiring strings!)"

Questions 147–151 refer to the excerpts from *The Canterbury Tales* below.

147. Which describes Perteltote?

148. Which describes the Miller?

149. Which describes the person at the center of the quarrel in the Knight's Tale?

150. Which describes the Wife of Bath?

151. Which describes Nicholas of the Miller's tale?

    (A) With him ther was dwellinge a poure scoler,
        Hadde lerned art, but al his fantasye
        Was turned for to lerne astrologye . . .
        And therto he was sleigh and ful privee,
        And lyk a mayden meke for to see.

    (B) And in a tour, in angwish and in wo
        Dwellen this Palamoun and his felawe Arcite,
        For evermore; ther may no gold hem quyte.
        This passeth yeer by yeer, and day by day,
        Til it fil oness, in a morwe May,
        That Emelye, that fairer was to sene
        Than is the lilie upon his stalke grene,
        And fressher than the May with floures newe . . .
        Er it were day, as was hir wone to do,
        She was arisen and al redy dight.

    (C) He was a janglere and a goliardeys;
        And that was most of sinne and harlotryes.
        Wel coude he stelen corn, and tollen thryes;
        And yet he hadde a thombe of gold, pardee.

    (D) Curteys she was, discreet, and debonaire,
        And compaignable, and bar hiself so faire,
        Sin thilke day that she was seven night old,
        That trewely she hath the herte in hold
        Of Chauntecleer.

    (E) Hir coverchiefs ful fyne were of ground:
        I dorste swere they weyeden ten pound
        That on a Sonday were upon here heed. . . .
        She was a worthy womman al hir lyve;
        Housboundes at chirche-dore she hadde fyve,
        But therof nedeth nat to speke as nouthe.

GO ON TO THE NEXT PAGE.

I pardon that man's life. What was thy cause?
Adultery?
Thou shalt not die. Die for adultery? No,
Line The wren goes to't and the small gilded fly
(5) does lecher in my sight.
Let copulation thrive; . . .
To't, luxury, pell-mell, for I lack soldiers.
Behold yond simp'ring dame,
Whose face between her forks presages snow;
(10) That minces virtue and does shake the head
To hear of pleasures name—
The fitchew nor the soiled horse goes to't
With a more riotous appetite.
Down from the waist they are Centaurs,
(15) Though women all above;
But to the girdle do the gods inherit,
Beneath is all the fiends': there's hell, there's darkness,
There is the sulphurous pit, burning, scalding,
Stench, consumption. Fie, fie, fie! pah, pah!

152. Which of the following is the correct attribution of
the lines above?

(A) Lear, in his madness, raves to the blinded
Gloucester on the subjects of sensuality and
carnality.
(B) Othello, consumed with jealousy, speaks ill of
Desdemona as Emilia listens.
(C) Mercutio, appalled that Romeo has fallen in love
with a Capulet, gives him counsel on women,
marriage, and adultery.
(D) Benedict explains his feelings about adultery to
Beatrice, and then pokes exaggerated fun at
womankind's lustiness.
(E) Petruchio, rebuffed again by Katherina, voices
his discontent in a comic monologue against
women.

153. The best paraphrase (for meaning) of "But to the
girdle do the gods inherit" (line 16) is

(A) only a woman's clothing is valued by the gods
(B) a woman's lower half is owned by the gods
(C) a woman's soul goes no deeper than her
garments
(D) a woman's spiritual good is found only from the
waist up
(E) the narrow path is the path to God

It is a truth universally acknowledged that a
single man in possession of a good fortune must be
in want of a wife.
Line However little known the feelings or views of
(5) such a man may be on his first entering a neigh-
bourhood, this truth is so well fixed in the minds
of the surrounding families that he is considered as
the rightful property of some one or other of their
daughters.
(10) "My dear Mr. Bennet," said his lady to him one
day, "have you heard that Netherfield Park is let at
last?"
Mr. Bennet replied that he had not.
"But it is," returned she; "for Mrs. Long has just
(15) been here, and she told me all about it."
Mr. Bennet made no answer.
"Do not you want to know who has taken it?"
cried his wife impatiently.

154. The author of the passage above is also the author of

(A) *Northanger Abbey*
(B) *Tom Jones*
(C) *Sartor Resartus*
(D) *Humphry Clinker*
(E) *Jane Eyre*

155. The passage above suggests the author's own much
noted

(A) broad, farcical sense of humor.
(B) candid, unflinching realism
(C) subtle satiric sense, often comic, sometimes
biting
(D) cynical and melancholy detachment
(E) passionate enthusiasm for all things romantic

156. In line 3, the phrase "in want" acts as which part of
speech?

(A) verb
(B) adjective
(C) adverb
(D) pronoun
(E) noun

GO ON TO THE NEXT PAGE.

For genius like Shakespeare's is not born among
laboring, uneducated, servile people. It was not born
in England among the Saxons and the Britons. It is
Line not born today among the working classes. How,
(5) then, could it have been born among women whose
work began, according to Professor Trevelyan, almost
before they were out of the nursery. . . . Yet genius
of a sort must have existed among women as it must
have existed among the working classes. Now and
(10) again an Emily Brontë or a Robert Burns blazes out
and proves its presence. But certainly it never got
itself on to paper. When, however, one reads of a
witch being ducked, of a woman possessed by devils,
of a wise woman selling herbs, or even of a very
(15) remarkable man who had a mother, then I think we
are on the track of a lost novelist, a suppressed poet,
of some mute and inglorious Jane Austen, some Emily Brontë who dashed her brains out on the moor or
mopped and mowed about the highways crazed with
(20) the torture her gift had put her to.

157. The author of the passage above is

(A) Aphra Behn
(B) Eudora Welty
(C) Virginia Woolf
(D) George Eliot
(E) Clifford Odets

158. "some mute and inglorious Jane Austen" (line 17)
echoes a line from

(A) Ezra Pound's "Hugh Selwyn Mauberley"
(B) John Milton's *Samson Agonistes*
(C) Samuel Taylor Coleridge's "Kubla Khan"
(D) Byron's *Don Juan*
(E) Thomas Gray's "Elegy Written in a Country
    Church Yard"

159. Which of the following pseudonyms was used by an
author mentioned in the passage?

(A) George Sand
(B) Ellis Bell
(C) Shamela Andrews
(D) Elia
(E) Thomas Rowley

160. The passage is

(A) an argument for the existence of female and
    working-class writers of great stature.
(B) an assertion, contrary to Professor Trevelyan's
    opinion, that the women in a great writer's
    life (e.g., the mother) are of hitherto unrecog-
    nized importance.
(C) an argument for the existence of women with
    potential but frustrated artistic genius that
    offers conjectural evidence of some of the
    places that frustrated genius may have found
    outlet.
(D) a plea for the economic and social equality of
    women.
(E) a protest against the social factors that have op-
    pressed women and the working classes alike.

GO ON TO THE NEXT PAGE.

Questions 161–164 refer to the excerpts below.

161. In which is the speaker Jaques?

162. In which is the speaker Odysseus?

163. In which is the speaker Caliban?

164. In which is the speaker Satan?

(A)   At first the infant,
Mewling and puking in the nurse's arms.
Then the whining schoolboy, with his satchel
And shining morning face, creeping like snail
Unwillingly to School. And then the lover,
Sighing like furnace, with a woeful ballad
Made to his mistress' eyebrow. . . .
               Last scene of all,
that ends this strange eventful history,
Is second childishness, and mere oblivion,
Sans teeth, sans eyes, sans taste, sans every thing.

(B) Setebos, Setebos, and Setebos!
Thinketh, He dwelleth i' the cold o' the moon.
Thinketh He made it, with the sun to match,
But not the stars; the stars come otherwise;
Only made clouds, winds, meteors, such as that:
Also this isle, what lives and grows thereon,
And snakey sea which rounds and ends the same.

(C) And then went down to the ship,
Set keel to breakers, forth on the godly sea, and
We set up mast and sail on that swart ship,
Bore sheep aboard her, and our bodies also
Heavy with weeping, and winds from sternward
Bore us out onward with bellying canvas.

(D) O sacred, wise, and wisdom-giving plant,
Mother of science! now I feel thy power
Within me clear, not only to discern
Things in their causes, but to trace the ways
Of highest agents, deemed however wise.
Queen of this universe! do not believe
Those rigid threats of death. Ye shall not die;
How should ye? By the fruit? it gives you life
To knowledge.

(E)   Dream after dream ensues;
And still they dream that they shall still succeed.
And still are disappointed. Rings the world
With the vain stir. I sum up half mankind
And add two-thirds of the remaining half,
And find the total of their hopes and fears
Dreams, empty dreams.

GO ON TO THE NEXT PAGE.

Questions 165–168

From fairest creatures we desire increase,
That thereby beauty's rose might never die,
But as the riper should by time decease,
Line His tender heir might bear his memory:
(5) But thou, contracted to thine own bright eyes,
Feed'st thy light's flame with self-substantial fuel,
Making a famine where abundance lies,
Thyself thy foe, to thy sweet self too cruel.
Thou that are now the world's fresh ornament,
(10) And only herald to the gaudy spring,
Within thine own bud buriest the content,
And, tender chorl, mak'st waste in niggarding:
        Pity the world, or else this glutton be,
        To eat the world's due, by the grave and thee.

165. Which of the following is the best paraphrase of line 5?

(A) You are wedded only to yourself.
(B) Your eyes are as bright as fire.
(C) You conceal yourself within your eyes.
(D) Your eyes are windows into your soul.
(E) Now, look into yourself!

166. Which of the following is the best paraphrase of line 12?

(A) Sweet youth, you waste everything.
(B) Young curmudgeon, your losses come through hoarding.
(C) Delicate flower, it would be a waste to pick you.
(D) Fresh meat is wasted when left uncooked.
(E) Good food turns quickly to waste when eaten hastily.

167. The closest synonym for "increase" (line 1) is

(A) enlargement
(B) gain
(C) offspring
(D) interest
(E) benefit

168. Which of the following is closest in meaning to the last two lines of the passage?

(A) But since he died and poets better prove,
    Theirs for their style I'll read, his for his love.
(B) But day doth daily draw my sorrows longer,
    And night doth nightly make grief's length seem stronger.
(C) Then may I dare to boast how I do love thee,
    Till then, not show my head where thou mayst prove me.
(D) Thy unus'd beauty must be tomb'd with thee,
    Which used lives th' executor to be.
(E) Ah, but those tears are pearl which the love sheeds,
    And they are rich, and ransom all ill deeds.

GO ON TO THE NEXT PAGE.

Questions 169–172 refer to the answer choices below.

169. Which of the following refers to Beckett's *Happy Days*?

170. Which of the following refers to Sartre's *No Exit*?

171. Which of the following refers to Genet's *The Balcony*?

172. Which of the following refers to Chekov's *Three Sisters*?

(A) The drama takes place in the large, comfortable living room of a well-to-do family's country estate. Newspapers are read. Servants come and go. But an air of quiet frustration and a sense that life is passing by hangs over all that occurs. The principal characters' main concern is not so much for the life they lead, as the life they are not leading elsewhere.

(B) In the opening scene, the play's principal character is found up to her waist in a rubbish pile.

(C) The theme of the play is simple: Hell is other people.

(D) The drama concerns a family's ravages upon itself. They love each other and hate each other in nearly equal (and enormous) portions. No one is pure. The father is a vain, self-deluded alcoholic, the children diseased (either mentally or physically), and the mother wanders through much of the latter half of the play in a morphine-induced haze.

(E) The drama takes place in the chambers of a bordello as a revolution or an uprising occurs on the streets outside. Within, the characters amuse themselves by enacting upon each other grotesque parodies of power and humiliation.

Questions 173–181. Identify the author or the work in each of the following passages, basing your decision upon the content and style of each passage.

173. Coketown, to which Messrs. Bounderby and Gradgrind now walked, was a triumph of fact; it had no greater taint of fancy in it than Mrs. Gradgrind herself. Let strike the keynote, Coketown, before pursuing our tune.

It was a town of red brick, or of brick that would have been red if the smoke and ashes had allowed it. . . . It was a town of machinery and tall chimneys, out of which interminable serpents of smoke trailed themselves forever and ever, and never got uncoiled.

(A) Charles Dickens's *Hard Times*
(B) Tobias Smollett's *Humphry Clinker*
(C) George Eliot's *Daniel Deronda*
(D) Thomas Hardy's *The Mayor of Casterbridge*
(E) Upton Sinclair's *The Jungle*

174. We had now got hardened to Cape weather, the vessel was under reduced sail, and everything secured on deck and below, so that we had little to do but to steer and to stand our watch. Our clothes were all wet through, and the only change was from wet to more wet. There is no fire in the forecastle, and we cannot dry clothes at the galley. It was in vain to think of reading or working below, for we were too tired, the hatchways were closed down, and everything was wet and uncomfortable, black and dirty, heaving and pitching.

(A) Daniel Defoe's *Robinson Crusoe*
(B) Herman Melville's *Pierre*
(C) Jack London's *The Sea-Wolf*
(D) Robert L. Stevenson's *Kidnapped*
(E) Richard H. Dana, Jr.'s *Two Years Before the Mast*

GO ON TO THE NEXT PAGE.

175. Such exaltation of thought, while it let adrift the spirit, and gave it licence in strange airs, lost it the old patient rule over the body. The body was too coarse to feel the utmost of our sorrows and of our joys. Therefore, we abandoned it as rubbish: we left if below us to march forward, a breathing simulacrum, on its own unaided level, subject to influences from which in normal times our instincts would have shrunk. The men were young and sturdy; and hot flesh and blood unconsciously claimed a right in them and tormented their bellies with strange longings. Our privations and dangers fanned this virile heat, in a climate as racking as can be conceived. We had no shut places to be alone in, no thick clothes to hide our nature. Man in all things lived candidly with man.

(A) Joseph Conrad's *Almayer's Folly*
(B) William Morris's *The Earthly Paradise*
(C) T. E. Lawrence's *The Seven Pillars of Wisdom*
(D) e. e. cummings's *The Enormous Room*
(E) Robert Graves's *Goodbye to All That*

176. I am a man, and alive. I am man alive, and as long as I can, I intend to go on being alive.
For this reason I am a novelist. And being a novelist, I consider myself superior to the saint, the scientist, the philosopher, and the poet, who are all great masters of different bits of man alive, but never get the whole hog.
   The novel is the one bright book of life. Books are not life. They are only tremulations on the ether. But the novel as a tremulation can make the whole man alive tremble. Which is more than poetry, philosophy, science, or any other book-tremulation can do.

(A) John Dos Passos
(B) Henry James
(C) Wallace Stevens
(D) Jack Kerouac
(E) D. H. Lawrence

177. "This Rector of Broxton is little better than a pagan!" I hear one of my readers exclaim. "How much more edifying it would have been if you had made him give Arthur some truly spiritual advice. You might have put into his mouth the most beautiful things—quite as good as reading a sermon."
   Certainly I could, if I held it the highest vocation of the novelist to represent things as they never have been and never will be. . . . But it happens, on the contrary, that my strongest effort is to avoid any such arbitrary picture, and to give a faithful account of man and things as they have mirrored themselves in my mind.

(A) George Eliot
(B) Sarah Orne Jewett
(C) Edith Wharton
(D) Jane Austen
(E) Willa Cather

178. Ineluctable modality of the visible: at least that if no more, thought through my eyes. Signatures of all things I am here to read, seaspawn and seawrack, the nearing tide, that rusty boot. Snotgreen, bluesilver, rust: coloured signs. Limits of the diaphane. But he adds: in bodies. Then he was aware of them bodies before of them coloured. How? By knocking his sconce against them, sure, Go easy. Bald he was and a millionaire, *maestro di color che sanno*. Limit of the diaphane in. Why in? Diaphane, adiaphane. If you can put your five fingers through it, it is a gate, if not a door. Shut your eyes and see.

(A) Virginia Woolf
(B) Thomas Hardy
(C) James Joyce
(D) Thomas Carlyle
(E) William Faulkner

GO ON TO THE NEXT PAGE.

179. The Consul walked on a little farther, still unsteadily; he thought he had his bearings again, then stopped:

¡BRAVA ATRACCIÓN!

10 c. máquina infernal

he read, half struck by some coincidence in this. Wild attraction. The huge looping-the-loop machine, empty, but going full blast over his head in this dead section of the fair, suggested some huge evil spirit, screaming in its lonely hell, its limbs writhing, smiting the air like flails of paddle wheels. Obscured by a tree, he hadn't seen it before. The machine stopped also . . .

"—Mistair. Money money money." "Mistair! Where har you go?"

The wretched children had spotted him again; and his penalty for avoiding them was to be drawn inexorably, though with as much dignity as possible, into boarding the monster.

(A) Graham Greene's *Brighton Rock*
(B) Thomas Pynchon's *V*
(C) E. M. Forster's *A Passage to India*
(D) Colin Wilson's *The Outsider*
(E) Malcolm Lowry's *Under the Volcano*

180. Life, friends, is boring. We must not say so.
After all, the sky flashes, the great sea yearns,
we ourselves flash and yearn,
and moreover my mother told me as a boy
(repeatedly) 'Ever to confess you're bored
means you have no

Inner Resources.' I conclude now I have no
inner resources, because I am heavy bored.
Peoples bore me,
literature bores me, especially great literature,
Henry bores me, with his plights and gripes
as bad as Achilles,

who loves people and valiant art, which bores me.
And the tranquil hills & gin, look like a drag
and somehow a dog
has taken itself & its tail considerably away
into mountains or sea or sky, leaving
behind: me, wag.

(A) Samuel Beckett
(B) John Berryman
(C) Robert Lowell
(D) Charles Olson
(E) Richard Wilbur

181. From the winter of 1821, when I first read Bentham, and especially from the commencement of the *Westminster Review*, I had what might truly be called an object in life; to be a reformer of the world. My conception of my own happiness was entirely identified with this object. . . . But the time came when I awakened from this as from a dream. It was autumn of 1826. I was in a dull state of nerves, such as everybody is occasionally liable to; . . . one of those moods when what is pleasure at other times becomes insipid or indifferent. . . . the lines in Coleridge's *Dejection*—I was not then acquainted with them—exactly describe my case:
A grief without a pain, void, dark and drear,
A drowsy, stifled, unimpassioned grief,
Which finds no natural outlet or relief
In word, or sigh, or tear.

(A) William Wordsworth
(B) Oscar Wilde
(C) Cardinal Newman
(D) Thomas Carlyle
(E) J.S. Mill

---

182. You must not wonder, though you think it strange,
To see me hold my louring head so low,
And that mine eyes take no delight to range
About the gleams which on your face do grow.
The mouse which once hath broken out of trap
Is seldom 'ticéd with the trustless bait,
But lies aloof for fear of more mishap,
And feedeth still in doubt of deep deceit.
The scorchéd fly, which once hath 'scaped the flame,
Will hardly come to play again with fire,
Whereby I learn that grievous is the game
Which follows fancy dazzled by desire:
    So that I wink or else hold down my head
    Because your blazing eyes my bale have bred.

The sonnet above suggests that

(A) a woman's beauty is more dangerous to a man than a mouse-trap is to a mouse.
(B) the poet, scorned or wronged by his beloved, now avoids looking at his former love for fear of renewed pain.
(C) the poet is angry at having been wronged and now seeks revenge.
(D) the poet playfully regrets having caused his beloved pain.
(E) the pain felt at loss of love is the deepest pain one can feel.

GO ON TO THE NEXT PAGE.

183. In mathematics, music, or chess, the child prodigy is almost the rule, each generation seems to produce one or two; in literature the prodigies fall one to an era or less. American letters can't yet claim a truly world-class literary prodigy, (*pace* Capote), but the English and the French have theirs undeniably. Both were little criminals, the one a (wondrous!) forger and liar, and the other a violently debauched *enfant terrible* capable it seemed of any outrage. But write "Bristowe Tragedie" or "The Drunken Boat" at sixteen and all will—eventually—be forgiven.

The works mentioned in the passage are by

(A) Marlowe and Villon
(B) Clare and Radiguet
(C) Keats and Stendhal
(D) Shelley and Verlaine
(E) Chatterton and Rimbaud

184. I couldn't forgive him or like him, but I saw that what he had done was, to him, entirely justified. It was all very careless and confused. They were careless people, Tom and Daisy—they smashed things and creatures and then retreated back into their money or their vast carelessness, or whatever it was that kept them together, and let other people clean up the mess they had made. . . .

The author of the passage above is also the creator of

(A) Amory Blaine
(B) Jake Barnes
(C) Flem Snopes
(D) Tom Joad
(E) Sally Bowles

Questions 185–186 refer to the answer choices below.

Lay your sleeping head, my love,
Human on my faithless arm;
Time and fevers burn away
Line Individual beauty from
(5) Thoughtful children, and the grave
Proves the child ephemeral:
But in my arms till break of day
Let the living creature lie,
Mortal, guilty, but to me
(10) The entirely beautiful.

185. Which of the following is syntactically parallel to "burn away" (line 3)?

(A) Lay (line 1)
(B) children (line 5)
(C) proves (line 6)
(D) ephemeral (line 6)
(E) entirely (line 10)

186. The author of the passage above is

(A) A.E. Housman
(B) W.H. Auden
(C) Algernon Charles Swinburne
(D) Gerard Manley Hopkins
(E) Wallace Stevens

GO ON TO THE NEXT PAGE.

187. Brilliant, versatile, prolific, and passionate, he has written novels, essays, stories, and plays, almost all controversial. The publication of his first book saw him hailed as a spokesman for blacks in America, a role he took on uneasily. Openly homosexual in the hostile climate of America in the 50s and 60s, he demonstrated an unwavering artistic and moral courage. He protested injustice wherever he saw it and from whatever direction it came, never afraid to break ranks and go against "party-lines." He would say that his only party was truth, and however hostile he at times became, his outrage was not so much that of a black man, or a homosexual, as that of an artist, of a deeply thinking, deeply feeling, human being.

The author discussed above is

(A) W. E. B. Du Bois
(B) Malcolm X
(C) Richard Wright
(D) James Baldwin
(E) LeRoi Jones

188. "I don't see Melanctha why you should talk like you would kill yourself just because you're blue. I'd never kill myself Melanctha just 'cause I was blue. I'd maybe kill somebody else Melanctha 'cause I was blue, but I'd never kill myself. If I ever killed myself Melanctha it'd be by accident, and if I ever killed myself by accident Melanctha, I'd be awful sorry."

The passage above is from

(A) West's *The Day of the Locust*
(B) Stein's *Three Lives*
(C) Hawkes's *The Lime Twig*
(D) Faulkner's *As I Lay Dying*
(E) Gaddis's *The Recognitions*

Questions 189–190

But pardon, gentles all,
The flat unraised spirits that hath dar'd
On this unworthy scaffold to bring forth
Line So great an object. Can this cockpit hold
(5) The vasty fields of France? Or may we cram'
Within this wooden O the very casques
That did affright the air at Agincourt?
O, pardon! Since a crooked figure may
Attest in little place a million,
(10) And let us, ciphers to this great accompt
On your imaginary forces work. . . .
Piece out our imperfection with your thoughts;
Into a thousand parts divide one man,
And make imaginary puissance;
(15) Think, when we talk of horses, that you see them
Printing their proud hoofs i' th' receiving earth
For tis' your thoughts that now must deck our kings,
Carry them here and there, jumping o'er times,
Turning th' accomplishment of many years
(20) Into an hour-glass.

189. The passage above is from

(A) *Two Gentlemen of Verona*
(B) *Much Ado About Nothing*
(C) *Henry V*
(D) *Richard II*
(E) *Tamburlaine*

190. Which of the following best describes the passage?

(A) The speaker poses ironic rhetorical questions about the need for imagination in theatrical endeavors in order to establish the comic tone of the piece about to be performed.
(B) The speaker avows the drama's intention to uphold the neoclassical unities.
(C) The speaker seeks to whet the audience's appetite for the grand staging it is about to witness.
(D) The speaker acknowledges the audience's actual physical surroundings, admits the physical limitations of staging, and asks for the audience's willing suspension of disbelief.
(E) The speaker, with comic bluntness, apologizes for the absurdity of dramatizing the spectacle of war upon the stage.

GO ON TO THE NEXT PAGE.

But thou art gone, and thy strict laws will be
Too hard for libertines in poetry.
They will repeal the goodly exiled train
Line Of gods and goddesses, which in thy just reign
(5)   Were banished nobler poems; now with these
The silenced tales in the *Metamorphoses*
Shall stuff their lines and swell the windy page,
Till verse, refined by thee in this last age,
Turn ballad-rhyme, or those old idols be
(10) Adored again with new apostasy.

191. In line 1, "thy" refers to

   (A) Ovid
   (B) Milton
   (C) Seneca
   (D) Donne
   (E) Shelley

192. The passage makes explicit reference to the work of

   (A) Ovid
   (B) Seneca
   (C) Keats
   (D) Cicero
   (E) Byron

193. In line 5, "banished" modifies

   (A) libertines (line 2)
   (B) They (line 3)
   (C) train (line 3)
   (D) gods and goddesses (line 4)
   (E) poems (line 5)

GO ON TO THE NEXT PAGE.

Questions 194–197 refer to the following passages.

194. Which refers to Telemachus?

195. Which refers to George Etherege?

196. Which refers to Alexander?

197. Which refers to Orpheus?

The underscore (_____) denotes the omission of a proper name.

(A) Let gentle _____ in triumph tread the stage,
    Make Dorimant betray, and Loveit rage;

(B) Twas at the royal feast, for Persia won
    by Philip's warlike son

(C) _____ could lead the savage race;
    and trees uprooted left their place
    Sequacious of the lyre

(D) And thou, who didst the stars and sunbeams know,
    Self-schooled, self-scanned, self-honored, self secure,
    Didst tread on earth unguessed at—better so!

(E) This is my son, mine own _____,
    To whom I leave the scepter and the isle,
    Well-loved of me

---

198. Dear Bosie,—After long and fruitless waiting I have
     determined to write to you myself, as much for your
     sake as for mine, as I would not like to think that I
     had passed through two long years of imprisonment
     without ever having received a single line from you,
     or any news or message even, except such as gave me
     pain.
     Our ill-fated and most lamentable friendship has end-
     ed in ruin and public infamy for me, yet the memory
     of our ancient affection is often with me.

     (The passage above was composed in Reading Gaol.)

     "Bosie" refers to

     (A) George Gordon, Lord Byron
     (B) Lord Alfred Douglas
     (C) Lytton Strachey
     (D) Edmund Wilson
     (E) Paul Verlaine

GO ON TO THE NEXT PAGE.

Questions 199–200

Thus, for instance, in *Alton Locke*:

> They rowed her in across the rolling foam—
> The cruel, crawling foam.

The foam is not cruel, neither does it crawl. The state of mind which attributes to it these characters of a living creature is one in which reason is unhinged by grief.

199. The passage is meant to provide an example of

   (A) the intentional fallacy
   (B) the affective fallacy
   (C) bathos
   (D) metaphor
   (E) the pathetic fallacy

200. The author of the passage is

   (A) John Ruskin
   (B) Walter Pater
   (C) Cardinal Newman
   (D) Matthew Arnold
   (E) F. R. Leavis

Questions 201–202

My attachments are all local, purely local. I have no passion (or have had none since I was in love, and then it was the spurious engendering of poetry and
Line books) to groves and valleys. The rooms where I was
(5) born, the furniture which has been before my eyes all my life, a bookcase which has followed me about (like a faithful dog, only exceeding him in knowl-edge) wherever I have moved, old chairs, old tables, streets, squares, where I have sunned myself, my old
(10) school—these are my mistresses. Have I not enough, without your mountains? I do not envy you. I should pity you, did I not know that the mind will make friends of anything.

201. The passage was part of a letter sent to

   (A) Mark Twain
   (B) William Wordsworth
   (C) Thomas Carew
   (D) Sir John Suckling
   (E) Lawrence Sterne

202. The author of the passage is

   (A) Robert Herrick
   (B) John Ruskin
   (C) Lawrence Sterne
   (D) Jonathan Swift
   (E) Charles Lamb

GO ON TO THE NEXT PAGE.

Questions 203–206. Match each passage below to the work from which it was drawn.

203. "I now know thee, thou clear spirit, and I now know that thy right worship is defiance. To neither love nor reverence wilt thou be kind; and e'en for hate thou canst but kill; and all are killed. No fearless fool now fronts thee. I own thy speechless, placeless power; but to the last gasp of my earthquake life will dispute its unconditional, unintegral mastery in me."

204. "Ah, ha!" said at length the infuriated jester. "Ah, ha! I begin to see who these people *are* now!" Here, pretending to scrutinize the king more closely, he held the flambeau to the flaxen coat which enveloped him, and which instantly burst into a sheet of vivid flame. In less than half a minute the whole eight orangoutangs were blazing fiercely, amid the shrieks of the multitude who gazed at them horror-stricken, and without the power to render them the slightest assistance.

205. Peter Quint had come into view like a sentinel before a prison. The next thing I saw was that, from outside, he had reached the window, and then I knew that, close to the glass and glaring through it, he offered once more to the room his white face of damnation. It represents but grossly what took place within me at the sight to say that on the second my decision was made; yet I believe that no woman so overwhelmed ever in so short a time recovered her grasp of the *act*. It came to me in the very horror of the immediate presence that the act would be, seeing and facing what I saw and faced, to keep the boy himself unaware.

206. The nurse, holding the basket at arm's length as if it were a bedpan, opened the door to a big dry hot room with greenish distempered wall where in the air tinctured with smells of alcohol and iodoform hung writhing a faint sourish squalling from other baskets along the wall. As she set her basket down she glanced into it with pursed-up lips. The newborn baby squirmed in the cottonwool feebly like a knot of earthworms.

(A) Henry James's *The Turn Of The Screw*
(B) Herman Melville's *Moby Dick*
(C) John Dos Passos's *Manhattan Transfer*
(D) Edgar Allan Poe's "Hop-Frog"
(E) Charlotte Perkins Gilman's "The Yellow Wallpaper"

GO ON TO THE NEXT PAGE.

207. And when the morning arose, then the angels has-
tened Lot, saying, "Arise, take thy wife, and thy two
daughters, which are here; lest thou be consumed in
the iniquity of the city."

The passage above refers to the story of

(A) Joseph and his brothers
(B) Abraham and Isaac
(C) Samson
(D) Sodom and Gomorrah
(E) Daniel and the lion's den

208. "Where, my kind doctor, did you gather those herbs,
with such a dark flabby leaf?"
"Even in the graveyard here at hand," answered the
physician continuing his employment. "They are new
to me. I found them growing on a grave, which bore
no tombstone, nor other memorial of the dead man,
save these ugly weeds, that have taken upon themselves to keep him in remembrance. They grew out of
his heart, and typify, it may be, some hideous secret
that was buried with him, and which he had done better to confess during his lifetime."

The speakers in the passage above are

(A) Dimmesdale and Chillingworth
(B) Silas Marner and Eppie
(C) Heathcliff and Lockwood
(D) Frank Churchill and Mr. Woodhouse
(E) Lydgate and Mr. Casaubon

Questions 209–212 refer to excerpts below.

209. Which are the final lines of Coleridge's *Rime of the
Ancient Mariner*?

210. Which are the first lines of Shelley's verse tribute to
Keats?

211. Which are the final lines of Eliot's *The Waste Land*?

212. Which are the final lines of Keats's "Ode on a Grecian Urn"?

(A) Datta. Dayahvam. Damyataya.
     Shantih shantih shantih

(B) A sadder and a wiser man,
     He rose the morrow morn.

(C) "Beauty is truth, truth beauty," —that is all
     Ye know on earth, and all ye need to know.

(D) I weep for Adonais—he is dead!

(E) Turning and turning in the widening gyre
     The falcon cannot hear the falconer

GO ON TO THE NEXT PAGE.

213. But original deficience cannot be supplied. The want of human interest is always felt. _____ is one of the books which the reader admires and lays
Line down, and forgets to take up again. None ever wished
(5) it longer than it is. Its perusal is a duty rather than a pleasure. We read _____ for instruction, retire harassed and over-burdened, and look elsewhere for recreation; we desert our master and seek for companions.

The blanks (lines 2 and 6) in the passage above (by Johnson) are correctly filled with

(A) *Dr. Faustus* . . . Marlowe
(B) *Hamlet* . . . Shakespeare
(C) *Absalom and Achitophel* . . . Dryden
(D) *An Essay on Criticism* . . . Pope
(E) *Paradise Lost* . . . Milton

214. The young, Harvard-educated radical—at odds with the accommodationist negro spokesman, Booker T. Washington—called for full political, social, and economic equality for negroes just at the time when caste barriers were being erected practically everywhere in the South.

The author discussed above is

(A) W. E. B. Du Bois
(B) Claude McKay
(C) James Baldwin
(D) Charles Waddell Chesnutt
(E) Jean Toomer

215. That I must die I knew without your edict. But if I am to die before my time, I count that a gain; for who, living as I do in the midst of many woes, would not call death a friend?

    It saddens me little, therefore, to come to my end. If I had let my mother's son lie in death an unburied corpse, that would have saddened me, but for myself I do not grieve. And if my acts are foolish in your eyes, it may be that a foolish judge condemns my folly.

The lines above are spoken by

(A) Jason to Medea
(B) Antigone to Creon
(C) Oedipus to Tiresias
(D) Clytemnestra to Agamemnon
(E) Lysistrata to Lampito

216. *Than cam the Byffhop of Caunturbyry, whych was a noble clerke and an holy man, and thus he feyde unto fir Mordred:*
"Sir what woll ye do? Woll ye firste difpleafe God and fytthyn shame youre felff and all knyghthode? For ys nat kynge Arthur youre uncle, and no farther but youre modirs brothir, and uppon her he hymfelffe begate you, uppon hys own fyfter? Therefore how may ye wed youre owne fadirs wyff?"

The passage above is from

(A) *Beowulf*
(B) *The Canterbury Tales*
(C) *Le Morte D'Arthur*
(D) *Sir Gawain and the Green Knight*
(E) *Piers Ploughman*

217. In *Justine*, Durrell describes a "A sky of hot nude pearl. . . ." Which of the following employs the most similar figure of language?

(A) our boat danced on the waves . . .
(B) or stain her honour, or her new brocade . . .
(C) farewell, false love, the oracle of lies . . .
(D) was this the face that launched a thousand ships . . .
(E) her laughter sparkled, it dazzled . . .

218. Come with me and be my love,
And we will all the pleasures prove
Of peace and plenty, bed and board
That chance employment may afford

This stanza, the first of C. Day Lewis's poem "Song," directly quotes the opening couplet of a poem by

(A) William Shakespeare
(B) Christopher Marlowe
(C) John Donne
(D) Robert Herrick
(E) Samuel Johnson

GO ON TO THE NEXT PAGE.

Questions 219–221 all refer to the following choices.

(A) Whom Jove the Bull desired and bore away

(B) A shudder in the loins engenders there
The broken wall, the burning roof and tower
And Agamemnon dead.

(C) Although a subtler sphinx renew
Riddles of death Thebes never knew.

(D) Our Adonais has drunk poison—oh!
What deaf and viperous murderer could crown
Life's early cup with such a draught of woe?

(E) And leaving bays profound and rocks abrupt,
Redder than Coral round Calypso's cave?

219. Which refers to *The Odyssey*?

220. Which refers to the cursed House of Atreus?

221. Which refers to Oedipus?

---

222. To avoid happy endings, which some scandalized
producers would inevitably cobble together themselves, he himself wrote an alternate ending for the
play, in which Nora returns to her husband and her
children.

The drama referred to in the passage above is

(A) Ibsen's *A Doll's House*
(B) Strindberg's *The Ghost Sonata*
(C) Chekov's *The Cherry Orchard*
(D) Brecht's *Mother Courage*
(E) O'Neill's *Long Day's Journey into Night*

223. Hans Castorp is a searcher after the Holy
Grail. . . . Perhaps you will read the book again from
this point of view. And perhaps you will find out
what the Grail is: the knowledge and the wisdom, the
consecration, the highest reward, for which not only
the foolish hero but the book itself is seeking. You
will find it in the chapter called "Snow" where Hans
Castorp . . . dreams his dream of humanity. If he does
not find the Grail yet he divines it, in his deathly
dream, before he is snatched downwards from his
heights into the European catastrophe. It is the idea of
the human being, the conception of a future humanity
that has passed through and survived the profoundest
knowledge of disease and death.

In the passage above

(A) Erich Maria Remarque discusses *All Quiet on
the Western Front*
(B) Céline discusses *Journey to the End of the Night*
(C) Vladimir Nabokov discusses *Pale Fire*
(D) Thomas Mann discusses *The Magic Mountain*
(E) Kafka discusses *The Castle*

GO ON TO THE NEXT PAGE.

Questions 224–225 refer to the following passage.

A foolish consistency is the hobgoblin of little minds, adored by little statesmen and philosophers and divines. With consistency a great soul has simply nothing to do. He may as well concern himself with his shadow on the wall.

224. The passage is from

(A) Melville's *Journal of a Visit to London and the Continent*
(B) Poe's "The Philosophy of Furniture"
(C) Emerson's *Self-Reliance*
(D) Longfellow's *Letters*
(E) Hawthorne's *Mosses from an Old Manse*

225. The meaning of the passage is in most accord with which one of the following?

(A) Do I contradict myself?
Very well then . . . I contradict myself
I am large . . . I contain multitudes.

(B) What is a lordling's pomp? A cumbrous load,
Disguising oft the wretch of human kind,
Studied in arts of hell, in wickedness refin'd.

(C) All human things are subject to decay
And, when fate summons, monarchs must obey.

(D) For tho' from out our bourne of Time and Place
The flood may bear me far,
I hope to see my Pilot face to face
When I have crost the bar.

(E) For sweetest things turn sourest by their deeds;
Lilies that fester smell far worse than weeds.

Questions 226–227 refer to the passage below.

I do not of course claim to have invented *sprung rhythms* but only *sprung rhythm*; I mean that single lines and single instances of it are not uncommon in English
Line and I have pointed them out in lecturing. . . In Nursery
(5) Rhymes, Weather Saws, and Refrains they are very common—but what I do in the *Deutschland* etc. is to enfranchise them as a regular and permanent principle . . .

226. The author of the passage is

(A) James Joyce
(B) Johann Wolfgang von Goëthe
(C) Gertrude Stein
(D) Matthew Arnold
(E) Gerard Manley Hopkins

227. Sprung rhythm is

(A) a verse form in which the last line of a stanza is "sprung," that is, it radically and deliberately departed from the rhythm which preceded it.
(B) a method of poetic composition based on an alliterative line.
(C) the effect produced by successive poetic lines containing internal rhymes.
(D) a type of scansion that counts only the stressed syllables in a line of poetry.
(E) a scansion that groups recurring patterns of stressed and unstressed syllables into the "feet" which compose a poetic line.

GO ON TO THE NEXT PAGE.

Flood-tide below me! I see you face to face!
Clouds of the west—sun there half an hour high—I
    see you also face to face.
Line Crowds of men and women attired in the usual
(5)   costumes, how curious you are to me!
On the ferry-boats the hundreds and hundreds that cross,
returning home, are more curious to me than
you suppose,
And you that shall cross from shore to shore years hence
(10) are more to me and more in my meditations,
than you might suppose.

228. The "ferry-boats" (line 6) carry passengers across the

    (A) Thames river in London
    (B) Mersey river in Liverpool
    (C) East river between Brooklyn and Manhattan
    (D) English channel between France and England
    (E) Mississippi river in St. Louis

229. Lines 6–10 contain

    (A) references to *The Odyssey* and *The Iliad*.
    (B) expressions of interest in the people of both the
        poet's own time and those of the future.
    (C) descriptions of naval maneuvers.
    (D) reflections on the bizarre quality of the people
        the poet sees as well as those to come.
    (E) allusions to the Genesis tale of the Flood.

230. The author is

    (A) Walk Whitman
    (B) Lord Byron
    (C) Mark Twain
    (D) Henry Wadsworth Longfellow
    (E) William Wordsworth

STOP
IF YOU FINISH BEFORE TIME IS CALLED, YOU MAY CHECK YOUR WORK ON THIS TEST.

NO TEST MATERIAL ON THIS PAGE.

HOW TO SCORE THE PRINCETON REVIEW
GRE LITERATURE IN ENGLISH SUBJECT TEST

When you take the real exam, the proctors will collect your test booklet and bubble sheet and send your answer sheet to New Jersey where a computer (yes, a big old-fashioned one that has been around since the 1960s) looks at the pattern of filled-in ovals on your answer sheet and gives you a score. We couldn't include even a small computer with this book, so we are providing this more primitive way of scoring your exam.

DETERMINING YOUR SCORE

STEP 1 Add up the total number of questions you got right (total right):

_____
(total right)

STEP 2 Add up the number of questions you got wrong (total wrong)—do *not* count blanks:

_____ $\div 4 =$ _____
(total wrong)   (error penalty)

STEP 3 Now, divide the number of incorrect answers by 4 and round to the nearest whole number (error penalty):

_____   –   _____
(total right)   (error penalty)

STEP 4 Subtract error penalty from the total right. This will give you your corrected raw score:

_____
(raw score)

STEP 5 To find your scaled point score, look up your corrected raw score on the conversion table on the next page.

_____
(final score)

TABLE FOR TOTAL SCORES
GRE LITERATURE IN ENGLISH SUBJECT TEST

Corrected Raw Score	Total Scaled Score	Percentile	Corrected Raw Score	Total Scaled Score	Percentile
217+	800	99	101–106	480	29
210–216	770	99	96–100	470	26
200–209	750	99	90–95	450	21
195–199	730	99	85–89	440	17
190–194	710	98	80–84	430	14
184–189	690	97	74–79	420	12
178–183	670	95	69–73	410	10
173–177	660	92	62–68	390	7
167–172	650	89	57–61	380	5
161–166	630	83	51–56	370	4
156–160	620	81	44–50	360	3
149–154	610	76	39–43	350	3
142–148	600	73	33–38	340	2
137–141	580	65	27–32	320	2
132–136	570	58	22–26	300	1
127–131	550	50	17–21	270	0
121–126	530	45	11–16	250	0
116–120	510	41	6–10	230	0
111–115	500	38	0–5	220	0
107–114	490	33			

PART **V**

Answers and Explanations

Answers:

1. C	47. C	93. E	139. D	185. C
2. A	48. A	94. C	140. C	186. B
3. C	49. D	95. D	141. E	187. D
4. A	50. A	96. D	142. A	188. B
5. B	51. E	97. A	143. C	189. C
6. E	52. D	98. A	144. D	190. D
7. C	53. B	99. E	145. C	191. D
8. B	54. B	100. E	146. B	192. A
9. C	55. E	101. D	147. D	193. B
10. D	56. C	102. C	148. C	194. E
11. A	57. A	103. B	149. B	195. A
12. A	58. C	104. C	150. E	196. B
13. C	59. E	105. A	151. A	197. C
14. E	60. E	106. C	152. A	198. B
15. B	61. A	107. A	153. D	199. E
16. A	62. E	108. D	154. A	200. A
17. D	63. C	109. E	155. C	201. B
18. B	64. B	110. A	156. B	202. E
19. B	65. D	111. C	157. C	203. B
20. E	66. D	112. B	158. E	204. D
21. B	67. B	113. A	159. B	205. A
22. C	68. E	114. E	160. C	206. C
23. E	69. C	115. D	161. A	207. D
24. E	70. A	116. C	162. C	208. A
25. B	71. A	117. A	163. B	209. B
26. C	72. D	118. E	164. D	210. D
27. A	73. A	119. E	165. A	211. A
28. E	74. B	120. B	166. B	212. C
29. D	75. A	121. C	167. C	213. E
30. B	76. C	122. D	168. D	214. A
31. C	77. E	123. B	169. B	215. B
32. A	78. B	124. B	170. C	216. C
33. A	79. D	125. A	171. E	217. E
34. B	80. A	126. C	172. A	218. B
35. D	81. D	127. C	173. A	219. E
36. A	82. A	128. C	174. E	220. B
37. C	83. B	129. B	175. C	221. C
38. A	84. A	130. A	176. E	222. A
39. B	85. C	131. D	177. A	223. D
40. B	86. A	132. D	178. C	224. C
41. D	87. E	133. E	179. E	225. A
42. C	88. A	134. E	180. B	226. E
43. A	89. E	135. D	181. E	227. D
44. C	90. D	136. A	182. B	228. C
45. C	91. D	137. D	183. E	229. B
46. D	92. B	138. B	184. A	230. A

1. **C** The line, "I sing—This verse to Caryll, Muse! is due" is an epic invocation, which means a call to a divinity who will inspire and bless the verse. The muses were the goddesses of the arts and of learning for the Greeks and Romans. Their number and characteristics varied over time, but note a few of the more important muses and their associated arts: Calliope, epic poetry; Erato, lyric poetry; Melpomene, tragedy; Thalia, comedy. Pope does not specify to which muse his address is made in the poem. John Caryll was a friend of Pope's who suggested that Pope write the poem.

2. **A** The passage is taken from the opening of Pope's *The Rape of the Lock*. The poem is a mock epic, and probably the purest example of that genre in English. It uses traditional epic devices (derived from classical sources such as Homer) for the ironic treatment of non-heroic material. *The Rape of the Lock* is based on an actual occurrence in which a gentleman, Lord Petre, took a lock of hair from a gentlewoman, Arabella Fermor (called Belinda in the poem), of whom he was enamored. This minor transgression caused an uproar between the two parties' families. By treating this subject in an epic manner, Pope ironically foregrounds the participants' own exaggerated concern. As always, you should pay particular attention to names. The names Caryll and Belinda (particularly Belinda, which occurs frequently throughout the poem) should immediately cause the following words to flash across your mind's eye: Pope's *The Rape of the Lock*, a mock-heroic work.

3. **C** The explanation for question 2 provides all the information you need to answer this question correctly. The rather silly-sounding answer choice (E) refers to the myth of Leda and the Swan, which you should be familiar with when taking the test. It's discussed further in the explanation to question 32.

4. **A** All five answer choices are terms you should be familiar with for the test. The passage is written in heroic couplets, that is, pairs of iambic pentameter lines rhyming, *aabbcc*, etc. An "end-stopped line" is one in which the end of a line occurs at a natural pause and where the meaning of the line is in some sense complete.

An "enjambed line" is the opposite of an end-stopped line: the meaning runs on to the next line (or lines) and there is no natural pause. In the passage, the line "Say, what strange motive, Goddess! could compel" is enjambed. The rest of the passage's lines are end-stopped. Enjambment is a technique poets have used frequently in all periods of English literature. One poet's mastery of enjambment (in heroic couplets) bears particular scrutiny. See question 29, which refers to Robert Browning's "My Last Duchess." That poem (and Browning's "monologue" poems in general) makes use of enjambment to give the speaker's voice a natural quality even as the poem obeys the formal rules of traditional metered verse. Such a display of technical virtuosity in a work of art is called a *tour de force*.

5. **B** The key here is context. If you didn't refer back to the passage you might easily have picked one of the incorrect choices. To a modern reader, the most familiar use of "vouchsafe" is probably "to assure or guarantee." In Pope's day, the primary usage of vouchsafe (a usage that extended well into the nineteenth century) is "to grant—as with condescension—permit, deign." Vouchsafe can also mean "to bestow graciously," but that definition is not found among the answer choices.

Questions 6–8

The correct answers are as follows: **6 is (E), 7 is (C), 8 is (B)**.

This may have seemed a difficult set of questions. Here's how you should have approached them. First (and always), consider how the test is written. The test writer does not expect you to have memorized the critical writings of Arnold, Yeats, or Coleridge, but you are expected to know something about these writers. Each correct answer contains a clue or clues to direct you to its author.

You should know that Yeats's poetry is characterized by symbolism and that he would be likely to discuss it. You might also reason that the symbolist movement was a late nineteenth-century phenomenon of French origin and therefore post-dates Coleridge.

The clue to Matthew Arnold is the phrase "sweetness and light," which is associated with Arnold although it was actually coined by Swift in his *Battle of the Books*. It refers to the quality and beneficial values of classical literature (particularly "Hellenism"). Arnold was a devout classicist and very much a believer in sweetness and light. The passage is drawn from his seminal *Culture and Anarchy*. Briefly, the central thesis of this work is that culture (the arts) ideally nourishes, promotes, and calls forth the best in humankind.

The clue to Coleridge is the word "imagination." You should know that Coleridge was a romantic, and that for the romantics, imagination was linked to the divine in humans and was an inexhaustible source of goodness. Coleridge subdivided the concept of imagination into "primary imagination" and "secondary imagination." "Primary imagination" occurs spontaneously, a similar concept to that of artistic inspiration. "Secondary imagination" is somewhat less profound because it occurs only when one is conscious of the act of imagining something.

Note that these questions don't ask you to identify passages among several romantics or symbolists, etc. That would be too difficult. Remember, there are very few authors and works you need to truly know in depth, but a great many authors and works you need simply to know about.

FYI: Answer choice (A) is by Poe. Answer choice (D) is by Tolstoy. Both selections arguably illustrate the fact that a great artist is not necessarily a great critic.

9. **C** The passage is from the opening of Aeschylus's tragedy *Prometheus Bound*. In Greek mythology, Prometheus is a Titan who befriends and helps to civilize man (in some versions of the myth, he creates man from clay). One of the gifts Prometheus bestows upon mankind is fire. In Aeschylus's version, he has stolen fire from the god of fire and craftsmanship, Hephaistos (spelling varies). This enrages Zeus, who has Prometheus bound to a cliff and tormented. Each day a vulture rends and eats Prometheus's liver. Prometheus suffers, but as an immortal he cannot die. His liver regenerates, only to be consumed again the next day. P. B. Shelley uses this version of the story in his *Prometheus Unbound*. In another version of the story, Zeus offers a very different punishment. He has a woman created, Pandora, and sends her to Prometheus's brother. Pandora brings with her a jar that, when opened, releases evil into the world.

10. **D** Poetic inversion is the practice of inverting the customary order of words (in this case, of noun and adjective).

11. **A** In Homer's *Iliad*, Achilles's armor (created by Hephaistos) is worn into battle by his friend Patroclus, who is killed and stripped by the Trojan Hector. Achilles's mother, the nymph Thetis, orders a new set of armor from Hephaistos, which is delivered to Achilles the next day. The centerpiece of the new set of armor is a magnificent shield (which Homer describes *at length*).

Here's why the other answer choices are incorrect:

(B) Athenians built the Parthenon.

(C) The Trojan War was caused when Paris ran away with Menelaus's wife, Helen; but this act and the ensuing war were in another sense created by the gods, primarily Zeus. (See Chapter 7 for more on the Trojan War and its characters.) It all becomes quite tangled, but *The Iliad*, the characters involved, and the stories surrounding them are an important source in English literature and, more pertinently, a frequent source of questions on the test.

(D) The labyrinth of King Minos refers to the maze on the island of Crete that housed the half-bull, half-man Minotaur. It was created by Daedalus. That name should ring a bell regarding modern literature. Stephen Daedalus is the name of James Joyce's fictional self in *A Portrait of the Artist As a Young Man*, and also a character in his *Ulysses*.

(E) The Trojan horse was built by Epeius, a Greek craftsman. The horse is referred to in Homer's *The Odyssey* and Virgil's *Aeneid*. Again, for more on the classical sources you should brush up on the material in Chapter 7.

12. **A** If Irish drama isn't your cup of tea, this might be a good question to leave for your second pass. However, if you can eliminate even one choice—guess. The passage describes Irish playwright J. M. Synge's *The Playboy of the Western World*, which premiered in 1907. The play's themes and its morally unflattering portrayal of the Irish working class drew protest and angry criticism even as Synge's language was praised for its poetic richness.

Here's an explanation of the other answer choices:

(B) Yeats's international reputation is based primarily on his poetry, but one shouldn't overlook his contribution to Irish theater. He helped found the Irish National Theater Company, and he was one of the directors of the Abbey Theater in Dublin. *The Countess Cathleen*, Yeats's first published play (1892), dramatizes an Irish fable concerning people who sell their souls in order to obtain food during a famine. Yeats is an important author to know for the test. You are almost certain to see a question or two that involves his work.

(C) O'Casey's *The Plough and the Stars* has Irish nationalism (and poverty) as its theme. The play sparked considerable outrage at its 1926 premiere in Dublin for presenting an unidealized vision of the Irish "folk."

(D) Wilde's *Salomé* is the story of "bring me the head of John the Baptist" and the "Dance of Seven Veils."

(E) In *Mrs. Warren's Profession*, the profession is prostitution. It was a scandalous play in its time. In fact, with the exception of the Yeats, the plays in the answer choices all created a scandal.

Questions 13–15

The correct answers are as follows: **13 is (C), 14 is (E), 15 is (B)**.

The trick here, again, is to think in terms of how the test is written. No single paragraph can adequately summarize a school of literary criticism. Furthermore, there is more cross-pollination of thought between schools than ETS might like. Many of the most important critics are not easily categorized. What the writers at ETS will do is offer choices that use the broadest figures of a particular school's style and approach. For example, a Marxist approach will discuss class relations and historical materialism.

Answer choice (A), in discussing a center, might have been a tempting choice for the structuralist, but it doesn't go far enough. The largest concern of critic (A) is the relation of the work (*Moby-Dick*) to the moral universe. When moral issues predominate, the critical type is best classified as humanist. Matthew Arnold is a leading nineteenth-century exponent of classical humanism. A later and more dogmatic champion of the humanist agenda (that is, of seeing art as having primarily a moral/educational function) is Irving Babbitt.

Answer choice (B) is structuralist. Note that our somewhat obnoxious critic (B) insists on "staying with the text," an admonition made (in slightly differing senses) by several twentieth-century schools of criticism, not just the structuralists. The key to this choice is the phrase "story architectures," and the use of terms like "center" and "perimeter" in an almost literal geometric sense. This clearly makes (B) a structuralist-influenced approach. Note that this is specifically *literary* structuralism.

Choice (C) is post-structuralist. In common use, the term post-structuralist refers to either the deconstructionist school of criticism or to those critics who, although not deconstructionists per se, have been markedly influenced by deconstructionist critic Jacques Derrida's critique of structuralist linguistics. Answer choice (C) has several phrases that tip its hand as a deconstructionist passage. The most important thing to look for is the acceptance of multiple readings. For the deconstructionists, a text cannot be held to just one interpretation. Words are signs that point toward meaning (the signified), but the meaning pointed to is always only found in more words, which in turn point toward other words, hence a never-ending slippery chain of signifiers that *is* meaning, and yet eludes a stable interpretation. Key deconstructionist phrases are "sign," "signifier," "multiplicity," "slippage," and "differance."

The term "heteroglossia" is a nod to Russian critic Mikhail Bakhtin. Bakhtin was marginalized and his work was little known in the West until the mid 1970s. His work has since become increasingly studied and influential. One of Bakhtin's central theses is that the novel as a form is characterized by the play of the microlanguages that exist within a language. For Bakhtin, the novel is where the language of the farmer can "do battle" with the language of the scholar, or where the language of irony can discourse with the language of sincerity.

Finally, in choice (C), note that as (B) is a structuralist, (C) critiques (B); post-structuralism is in large part a critique of structuralism.

Choice (D) is of no particular school, simply someone who doesn't care for critic (C)'s point of view.

Choice (E) is Freudian. There is much more to psychoanalytic theory now than Freud, but for the purposes of the literature test, Freud will suffice. The oedipal complex is one of Freud's most widely known discoveries, and as long as you noticed its presence in critic (E)'s jabbering, this choice probably didn't give you much trouble.

16. **A** The passage doesn't give you much to go on, but we hope you recognized the line "children of the night . . ." as coming from Bram Stoker's *Dracula*. Jonathan Harker is the character whose diaries and letters narrate much of the book.

Not recognizing these things, you might have eliminated those author–character pairs in the answer choices you did know. Arthur Gordon Pym (B) is from *The Narrative of Arthur Gordon Pym*, Poe's only novel. It concerns the adventures of a young man who stows away aboard a ship.

Natty Bumppo (C) is the main character of James Fenimore Cooper's *Leather-Stocking Tales*. Bumppo is at various times also called "Deerslayer," "Hawkeye," and "Leatherstocking." He is a nature lover and a crack shot who always does the righteous thing.

David Copperfield (D) is the main character of Dickens's *David Copperfield*, but you knew that. Dickens's works are voluminous enough that you won't be expected to know them all, but *Copperfield* is one of the more important, and if your test does have a Dickens question, this is one of the works it is likely to be drawn from. You should know that *Copperfield* is partly autobiographical. The characters Mr. and Mrs. Micawber and Uriah Heep are from *David Copperfield*.

Augie March (E) is the narrator of Saul Bellow's *The Adventures of Augie March*, a coming-of-age novel set in depression-era Chicago.

17. **D** This question calls on your knowledge of the works and characters given in the answer choices. In this question, each answer choice contains a great deal of information: an author, a title, and a character. For eliminating answer choices, the more information the better, so don't let an unfamiliar item or two scare you off. Your task is to find the answer choice that pairs a work containing tales-within-tales . . . and the narrator of a frame-tale. A "frame-tale" refers to the larger story that contains the other stories within it. For example, in *The Canterbury Tales*, the narrator relates the pilgrims' journey to Canterbury. This is the frame-tale within which the pilgrims tell their individual tales.

In this question, chances are that the second blank was the easier of the two for you to determine, especially if you are familiar with Scheherazade, the narrator of *The Thousand and One Arabian Nights*. She uses the suspense of interrupted stories to keep from being beheaded by the Sultan. If you are not familiar with Scheherazade, eliminate any of the characters in the answer choices you do recognize; none of them use interrupted stories in order to provide suspense to any significant degree. As always, use the names that you do recognize. Names, names, names. That is what at least 50 percent of this test is about. Here's a brief gloss of the **second half** of each incorrect answer choice.

(A) Mephistopheles is the satanic tempter of the Faust myth, dramatized by Christopher Marlowe and by the late eighteenth- and early nineteenth-century German, Goethe, as well as by Thomas Mann.

(B) Raskolnikov is the eventually repentant murderer (he kills his noxious landlady with an ax) in Dostoyevsky's *Crime and Punishment*.

(C) Mr. Lockwood is the first narrator of Emily Brontë's *Wuthering Heights*.

(E) Sancho Panza is the fat, ignorant, lovable, faithful squire of *Don Quixote*, the main character of the eponymous novel by Miguel de Cervantes.

Now, once you've eliminated what you could using the second half of the answer choices, go to the first half. A good clue to use from the passage is the phrase "long been a favorite device." Which of the works in the answer choices is the oldest?—Chaucer's. Secondly, the relevant part of the passage emphasizes irony; Chaucer is considered a master ironist (and you should know this). A more or less strained argument could be made for the other choices, which do perhaps involve some degree of nested storytelling, but the best fit is clearly Chaucer's *The Canterbury Tales*.

Here's a brief discussion of the **first half** of the incorrect choices:

(A) Milton's *Lycidas* is a pastoral elegy, a genre you should know a little about (discussed in Chapter 8).

(B) Browning's "Caliban upon Setebos" refers to one of the author's celebrated dramatic monologues. Caliban you should recognize as Prospero's semi-human servant in *The Tempest*. Setebos is the deity Caliban and his witch mother, Sycorax, worship.

(C) *The Rime of the Ancient Mariner* is yet another dramatic poem. Coleridge's mariner tells a man on the way to a wedding the story of how, by senselessly killing an albatross, he brought a world of bad luck down upon himself and his companions and must now, in penance, travel the world relating his tale.

(E) Dryden's *Absalom and Achitophel* is a long allegorical poem that uses biblical figures to represent the players in a political upheaval of Dryden's time. The issue under dispute was the perennial English problem of the relations of power among Catholicism, Protestantism, the King, and Parliament. In the poem, King David represents Charles II, whose position Dryden supports delicately in the poem, while trying to appear unbiased.

18. **B** The selection is from an essay by Charles Lamb. Lamb was a celebrated London wit, and a friend to Wordsworth and Coleridge among others. In much of his writing he used the pen name Elia.

The passage is gently playful. It is not mock-heroic; it doesn't parody anything in particular; and it's neither instructive nor nonsensical.

19. **B** Here your task was to understand that the deleted phrase referred to lenders, and must contrast with "open, trusting, generous manners of the other." (D) and (E) can be eliminated because they refer to the borrower, and (A) and (C) can be eliminated because they do not properly contrast.

20. **E** No, you aren't really expected to place the passage, which is from Hemingway's short story "Now I Lay Me." You are simply expected to know enough about Hemingway to recognize his characteristic style and his obsession with fishing.

Questions 21–23

The correct answers are as follows: **21 is (B), 22 is (C), 23 is (E)**.

You should aid your process of elimination by starting with the question you find easiest. Let's suppose you don't recognize any of the three forms right off the bat. Okay, look over the answer choices. Does anything stand out? Do you recognize any of the rhyme schemes or structural elements of the given selections? Perhaps you recognize that choice (D) is a ballad stanza *abcb*. Eliminate it. A good thing, too; otherwise you might easily have guessed (D) to be in heroic couplets because of its content. Heroic couplets do not refer to content but simply an *aabbcc* rhyme scheme (a series of rhymed pairs, called couplets) in iambic pentameter. Of the choices left, (A), (B), (C), and (E), only (E) is written in the same pattern throughout, and

therefore only (E) could be entirely written in heroic couplets, and indeed, that selection is. It comes from Alexander Pope's *An Essay on Criticism*. Pope perfected use of the heroic couplet at the beginning of the eighteenth century.

Two questions and only three answer choices remain. Choices (A) and (B) are structurally very similar. Ask yourself: Is it likely that one could contain tercets but not the other? The answer is no. That leaves choice (C), which does indeed differ markedly from (A) and (B). (C) is the first stanza of Keats's "Ode to a Nightingale." Its final six lines end in the scheme *cde cde*. A group of three lines is called a tercet. The six lines together form, naturally enough, a sestet. By the way, when a sonnet ends in a sestet, it will usually be an Italian (also called Petrarchan) sonnet.

This leaves just question 21, "Which is written in rhyme royal?" Here's a hint: The one that isn't in rhyme royal is in *ottava rima*. Memorize these two forms together. *Ottava rima* means "eight rhyme" in Italian. (A) is an eight-line stanza (from Yeats's "Sailing to Byzantium") rhymed *abababcc*. *Ottava rima* is usually in iambic pentameter, though this selection is not (however, (E)'s lines, like those of iambic pentameter, are ten syllables long). Choice (B), from Wordsworth's "Resolution and Independence" is in rhyme royal, iambic pentameter lines rhyming *ababbcc*. How do you keep rhyme royal and *ottava rima* straight? *Ottava rima* has an eight-line stanza; rhyme royal (and only rhyme royal) has a regularly rhymed seven-line stanza.

24. **E** There's one and only one clue in the selection, the name "Bigger." In essence the question is: With which author/book is the character Bigger Thomas associated? If you knew the writer was African American, you'd still be stuck because all the authors given in the answer choices are. If you knew the author was male, you'd be down to just three choices and should definitely take your best guess. The author is Richard Wright, and the book is *Native Son*.

The publication of *Native Son* in 1940 launched Wright to the forefront of African-American writers. Wright's autobiographical account of his youth, *Black Boy*, is also a work you should know.

Questions 25–28

The correct answers are as follows: **25 is (B), 26 is (C), 27 is (A), 28 is (E).**

Work from what you know best to what you know least and use the process of elimination. Again, names are your best allies on the test.

Choice (A) is from Kate Chopin's novella *The Awakening*. The names Pontellier and Lebrun should give you the answer. If you knew that *The Awakening* is set in Louisiana, the French character of the names would make this an appealing guess. Also, Kate Chopin's work often employs as a common theme the idea that women are the property of men.

Choice (B) contains the name Rochester. That name should immediately be associated with Charlotte Brontë's *Jane Eyre*.

Choice (C) is from the opening of Edith Wharton's *The House of Mirth*. The name Lily Bart and the New York City setting are clues to this answer. You might also have guessed this choice to be Wharton based on the style of its second paragraph. Wharton and Henry James (especially the later Henry James) share a famously elaborate, delicate, interior, and convoluted style.

Choice (D) is from Elizabeth Gaskell's *North and South*. Gaskell was a fashionable member of upper-crust English society. Her novels are notable for their portrayal of, and outcry against, social conditions in industrializing nineteenth-century England.

Choice (E) is from Virginia Woolf's *Mrs. Dalloway* (first name: Clarissa). You might have guessed choice (E) because its style suggests a more modern author, and Woolf is both a noted modernist and the most recent of the authors listed.

29. **D** The question asks you to interpret a few lines for meaning. As usual, the correct answer is the most straightforward choice. If you doubt yourself, it's not too hard to talk yourself into ironic interpretations, so don't do it, and don't doubt yourself.

The lines asked about in the question can be paraphrased: "and if she let herself be chastened and did not quibble or make excuses. . . ."

This selection is taken from Robert Browning's "My Last Duchess." The speaker is an Italian nobleman, the Duke of Ferrara, whose previous wife is dead, very likely at the Duke's behest. He stands before a painted portrait of his late wife addressing a person involved in arranging the Duke's next marriage. As here, many of Robert Browning's works are in the dramatic monologue form. Note also Browning's use of heroic couplets. The couplets seldom ring out in end-stopped rhymes, but are more often enjambed, which gives the rhymes an elegant internal quality. This too is characteristic of Browning.

30. **B** If you didn't recognize the passage you may have felt that more than one answer worked. But (C), (D), and (E) are all clearly wrong. He was more than mildly perturbed—scratch (C). He was increasingly disgusted, but not by his wife's adultery (and if she'd been adulterous the Duke would surely not call it a "trifle")—scratch (D). No crisis of faith is anywhere indicated—scratch (E). This leaves (A) and (B). First, it isn't clear that his wife was flirtatious. She may have been, but she may also have been simply high-spirited and fun loving. The tone of "and I choose never to stoop" should be the giveaway that this speaker's primary concern is his dignity, and that any slight to it is deeply resented. This makes (B) the better (and correct) choice.

31. **C** The passage discusses Joyce's story "The Dead." It is the final and longest story of his short story collection *Dubliners*. The "particular time and place" referred to in the passage is

Dublin at Christmas circa 1900. The name Gabriel should serve as a clue. Another clue is the line quoted at the passage's end which is from the story's last paragraph, arguably the most famous closing of any short story in English. A final very small clue is the word "exile." One of Joyce's more famous quotes is his statement that he, as an artist, needed "silence, cunning, and exile." Exile, especially that of the artist from society, is an underlying theme in much of Joyce's work.

Regarding the other answer choices, you should know:

(A) Joseph Conrad's "Youth" is a seafaring story in which the main character undergoes a terrible ordeal at sea and loves it because he is young and craves experience and having his mettle tested.

(B) Carson McCullers is an American southern gothic writer. *The Ballad of the Sad Cafe* is the story of the chaos wrought on a woman's life when her cousin Lymon Willis (a dwarf, both deformed and powerfully charismatic) enters her world.

(D) "The Odour of Chrysanthemums" is a D. H. Lawrence story set in an English coal mining town. The story's main character awaits her husband's return from work in the mines, but he has been suffocated in a cave-in. The main character, whose marriage was not happy, reflects on the gulf that separates herself and her dead husband, coming to realize that he is scarcely further away now than when alive. In this realization of inner solitude, the story resembles "The Dead."

(E) *The Aspern Papers* is James's novella about the unsuccessful attempts of the biographer of a famous and long-dead poet (Jeffrey Aspern, a fictionalized Byron) to secure some papers from the poet's aged former mistress and her homely daughter. It is set in Venice. The protagonist (at first inadvertently) encourages the daughter's growing infatuation with him in order to get to the papers.

32. **A** Virgil (C) is Dante's guide in the first two books of *The Divine Comedy*, *Inferno* and *Purgatorio*, but he cannot accompany Dante into paradise because he died before the birth of Christ (and is thus unredeemed). Beatrice was a Florentine woman of whom Dante thought highly enough to make her his guide through Heaven (*Paradiso*). Their meeting (when both were nine years old), possibly the single most famous example of love at first sight in literary history, is recorded in Dante's *Vita Nuova*.

Regarding the other answer choices:

(B) Charon is the ferryman of Greek mythology who carries dead souls across the River Styx to the underworld.

Leda (D) is a figure from Greek mythology who was raped by Zeus (who came to her in the form of a giant swan). Leda is the mother of Clytemnestra, the twins Castor and Pollux, and Helen of Troy. In most (but not all) versions of the story, Helen is conceived when Leda is raped.

Aristotle (E) is the great Greek philosopher. For the purposes of the GRE Literature in English Subject Test, you should know that his *Poetics* is a wellspring of English literary criticism and the source of the neoclassical unities.

33. **A** The meaning should be clear from the context. This is not a difficult question. If it gave you trouble, you should read up on seventeenth- and eighteenth-century poetry, paying strict attention to the vocabulary.

34. **B** Prosopopoeia is a ten-dollar word for personification (specifically when the personified object not only has human qualities but also speaks). The question isn't so much asking you to know what prosopopoeia is (because only a half-mad Scrabble™ professional might ever need to) as it is testing your ability to eliminate the other four choices, which are legitimately useful literary terms. Hyperbole (A) is a synonym for exaggeration. Symbolism (C), metaphor (D), and synecdoche (E)—along with simile, metonymy, allegory, and analogy—are

all allied concepts that are discussed in the literary terms section of this book (Chapter 8).

35. **D** This is a comprehension question. As with all comprehension questions, read carefully and use the Process of Elimination to look for wrong answers. In this case, the key to the poem's theme is in the last two lines, which characterize love as without place or time (but note: not timeless). Don't talk yourself into an answer choice by stretching to see how you can make it fit. On comprehension questions, students frequently find the right answer, identify the wrong answers, and then waste a few precious minutes agonizing because by some weird stretch of the imagination another answer choice could kind of, maybe, sort of, work. Don't do this.

36. **A** The passage is from Donne's "The Sun Rising." The poem is a famous one, but if you didn't recognize it, look over Donne's poetry, as his work will surely be on the test (probably more than once). You should notice that Donne's work falls into two distinct periods. His early poetry, like "The Sun Rising," is lighthearted and saucy, the poetry of the ambitious sixteenth-century playboy and soldier/adventurer he most certainly was. But his career took a nose-dive when he eloped with the daughter of an influential nobleman. Some years later, Donne entered the church and after considerable travail became Dean of St. Paul's in London. The poetry of Donne's later career is searchingly religious. Donne manages to evince at once a passionate sense of the Divine, a hard-nosed intelligence, and a pointed wit. The tone of these poems is unmistakable and difficult to describe. Look at the Holy Sonnets for good examples of Donne's later style.

Questions 37–39

The correct answers are as follows: **37 is (C), 38 is (A), 39 is (B).**

If these gave you trouble, read the passage through for sense and try to restate it in more natural prose. In essence the sentence says: "He has pursued Nature's most secret steps like her shadow [in the following places:] where the red volcano overcanopies fields with burning smoke, where bitumen lakes beat on islets with sluggish surge, and where secret caves expand their domes above halls."

40. **B** The passage is drawn from P. B. Shelley's "Alastor; or, The Spirit of Solitude." And yes, the whole thing's like that. You should have been able to eliminate choices (C), (D), and (E) by knowing that neither Spenser, Browning, nor Blake ever wrote in a style like that of the passage.

Questions 41–42

The correct answers are as follows: **41 is (D), 42 is (C).**

You should recognize the falling, broken-winged bird as an allusion to Icarus, who falls to his death after having flown to close to the sun. As an allegory, Icarus's fate cautions against disobedience (Icarus's father warned him about flying near the sun), fatal curiosity, and excessive ambition.

Other significant figures mentioned in the answer choices are Medusa, the monstrous snake-haired woman that Perseus killed by reflecting her image back upon herself, and Penelope, wife of Ulysses, who through a variety of ruses kept her many suitors at bay until Ulysses returned from Troy (whereupon he promptly killed the lot of them).

The passage is drawn from Kate Chopin's *The Awakening* (see question 27), but you don't need to know this in order to answer the questions.

43. **A** The key to this question lies in recognizing Shakespeare's characters Iago and Imogen. Iago is the great villain of *Othello*. Imogen, a character from *Cymbeline*, is the embodiment of goodness. Even if only Iago were familiar to you, the answer that makes the best sense in the context of the passage is (A), and it should have been your guess. Why would a poet delight in a poorly rendered character—(B), or in the product of a mediocre imagination—(D), or

in a weak personality—(E)? To guess between (C) and (A) (assuming you couldn't place Imogen), ask which answer choice describes Iago better, and which is more in keeping with the last sentence of the passage—(A).

44. **C** This question shouldn't pose too many difficulties so long as you remember to focus on what the author (John Keats, in a letter to Richard Woodhouse) is trying to do: define the type of poet he feels himself to be. Only (C) reflects this intent.

45. **C** The passage describes *Lysistrata* (the title character's name means "she breaks up armies") by Aristophanes. *Clouds* and *Frogs* are other comedies by Aristophanes. The first ridicules the philosopher Socrates, and the second pokes fun at the great Greek tragedians Sophocles, Euripides, and Aeschylus. *Knights* is a play little studied at the undergraduate level; you needn't concern yourself with it for the Literature in English Subject Test.

Medea refers to the tragedy by Euripides about a woman who, outraged at being ungratefully abandoned by her lover, Jason, kills his bride-to-be, the bride's father, Creon, and her own children (by Jason). She gets away with it, too.

46. **D** The passage alludes to "She lived amongst th' untrodden ways" by William Wordsworth. If you didn't spot the allusion to that line, you might also have received a clue from "Rydal Lake." Wordsworth and his friend Coleridge are often called the Lake Poets, because they lived in the "Lake district" of England. Because Coleridge is also in the answer choices, you would have a fifty-fifty guess. Take your chances; be aggressive about answering questions.

"She lived amongst th' untrodden ways" is a Lucy Poem. Lucy, when you see it in verse, is a name you should associate with Wordsworth although in this particular instance Lucy isn't mentioned in the question. Similarly, in (B), Robert Herrick's Julia Poems are widely celebrated. You should associate the name Julia with Robert Herrick.

47. **C** Your task was to associate the name Andromache with either Euripides or Racine. If you had to guess, a good way to proceed would be to examine the more modern playwrights that make up the second half of each answer choice. Neither Beckett in (A), Strindberg in (B), nor Sartre in (D) are notable for drawing upon classical sources. This would leave O'Neill in (E), and the correct answer (C). Although O'Neill has drawn on classical sources, most notably in *Mourning Becomes Electra*, you should know that Racine, the author of *Phaedra*, was the master of French neoclassical theater (and the better guess). Finally, if you were trying to eliminate O'Neill, you might have reasoned that the author he is paired with, Aristophanes, is not a tragic dramatist but a comic one.

48. **A** You definitely do not need to learn Old or Middle English in order to take the GRE Literature in English Subject Test. The few questions you are given that involve archaic English will rely on your ability to sound out the line without being sent into a tailspin by the inevitable presence of unfamiliar words. In the line quoted in the question, the character "7" represents "and" in the same way that we presently use "&." The words *swa swa* mean "as." The ð character is pronounced as a *th*. For more information on Old English, review Chapter 5, page 60.

49. **D** The question asks you to recognize that the poem is in honor of the "High priest of Homer." A name you should have associated with Homer is that of George Chapman, an early English translator of the Greeks. He and his translation of Homer are also the subject of one of Keats's first mature poems, "On First Looking into Chapman's Homer" (this explains the answer to question 51). The author of the passage is the Victorian poet Algernon Charles Swinburne. Swinburne was known for his rebellious attitude toward Victorian morality and excellent sense of rhyme and meter (as this passage makes evident).

50. **A** The question itself contains a clue: It asks about the "octave" of the poem above. The octave refers to the first eight lines of a sonnet, and almost always (for the purposes of the test go ahead and think *always*) refers to the first eight lines of an Italian sonnet. You should know that the Italian sonnet is also called the Petrarchan sonnet, and that the English sonnet is also called the Shakespearean sonnet. Sonnets have fourteen lines. The Italian sonnet, as mentioned above, can be divided into an octave and a sestet. The English sonnet and the Spenserian sonnet both have three quatrains and end in a couplet (rhymed pair). The sestet of the example above is not that of a classic Italian sonnet, but overall, the poem is more an Italian sonnet than any other type. By the way, do not make the mistake of thinking that the sonnet died with the nineteenth century. Several notable modern poets have used the sonnet form.

51. **E** For an explanation of this question see the notes to question 49.

52. **D** This is a tricky question. If you didn't recognize "houyhnhnms" as the allusion, you might well have tried to guess based on the hanuman reference and become lost, since none of the answer choices refer to hanuman, the Hindu monkey god. If indeed you reasoned that way and got the question wrong as a result, don't let that shake your confidence. Guessing isn't going to get you a perfect score. But it *will* improve your score. The houyhnhnms are a horse-like race that Jonathan Swift's Gulliver encounters on his travels. (The passage itself is taken from Wyndham Lewis's *The Childermass*—not a work you need to know.)

53. **B** This question addresses your knowledge of the European context of English literature. You should know that Voltaire and Rousseau (as well as Denis Diderot) were indeed prominent figures of the Enlightenment and that this period was characterized by a belief in the powers of reason. The poem is by Blake. You should also know that Blake is often considered an early Romantic, and he certainly had a profound effect upon that movement.

54. **B** This is a straightforward comprehension question that hopefully didn't pose too many difficulties. Blake was displeased by enlightenment thinking, believing that the Enlightenment's overreliance on rationality left no place for the visionary. For Blake, true wisdom could embrace contradiction and the seemingly illogical. These considerations put Blake at odds with thinkers like Voltaire and Newton. He held these people in contempt. You should recognize choice (B) as a line from Hamlet. It paraphrases Blake's position that his spiritual view of reality encompasses a broader and more meaningful understanding than does the analytical and deliberately anti-mystical perspective of Enlightenment scientists and philosophers.

55. **E** Answering this question is a matter of recognizing that the poem's author is Blake and that answer choice (E) is also by Blake. If you didn't know who wrote the poem in the question, but you did know the authors of the works in the answer choices, you might still have arrived at a good guess. Reason that (B) *Absalom and Achitophel* is by Dryden, and (D) *Volpone* is by Jonson. Both authors are earlier figures than Voltaire and Rousseau and therefore could not have written about them; eliminate (B) and (D). (C) *An Essay on Criticism* is by Pope, who is (slightly) too early. More important, Pope was a master of witty mockery and so not a poet one would expect to find chastising others so earnestly. A critique from Pope, even a scathing one, would come in droll heroic couplets. This would leave only (A) "Intimations of Immortality" by Wordsworth and (E), the correct answer. Guess.

56. **C** A careful reading of the passage should suffice to lead you to the correct answer. "The equality of words to things is very often neglected" translated to (C). This relationship is called "decorum," is a term related to the correct answer, and one you should know. In literature,

"decorum" is the specific relation of style and content in the speech of dramatic characters. For example, a low-born or rustic character should speak in a distinctly lower-class manner. In this sense, "decorum" is one of the neo-classical precepts of drama.

57. **A** Euphuism is a term you should know, as is skeltonics (in answer choice (B)). It might be easiest to remember them together as in a sense they are opposites. Euphuism is associated with the poetry of John Lyly, specifically his *Euphues* (1580). It has come to refer to language characterized by an extreme and elaborate artifice in the construction of its lines—swelling grandiose metaphors, rhetorical questions, a preponderance of mythological reference, and a general sense of the writer laying it on about as thick as he can manage. Despite seeming quite silly to modern tastes, euphuism enjoyed a considerable vogue in the late sixteenth century and probably furthered the development of rhetorical technique.

Skeltonics refers to the peculiar form of verse practiced by John Skelton in the late fifteenth and early sixteenth century. It is characterized by short lines, a choppy pronounced rhythm, and stomping end rhymes hammering away at the same sound for five, six, or more lines. It is a suitable form only for comedy and satire. The only real distinction between skeltonics and doggerel is the intelligence with which the verse is written.

58. **C** The passage is taken from Canto IV, v.180 of Byron's *Childe Harold's Pilgrimage*. Not a difficult question if you use the answer choices and the Process of Elimination. Simply reading the passage and expecting to have a clear sense that it refers to the ocean is not a good technique. Instead, look over the answer choices and wonder, "does this make sense if 'thee' refers to the reader? to humanity? etc." When you hit upon (C) the ocean, the answer should become clear. Of course time is a factor, and this might have been a good question to leave for a second pass. Take a look at the poem

for more hints. "Spray" and "dashest" should help you out.

59. **E** It isn't difficult to identify a Spenserian stanza. The easiest ways to distinguish this type of stanza are to note the number of lines in the stanza and to note the final line, which is called an alexandrine (know that term, too). The Spenserian stanza is the only major nine-line form. It always ends with an alexandrine, which is simply an iambic hexameter (six-footed) line. The rest of the stanza is pentameter. When the last line sticks out an extra foot, it's a Spenserian stanza. Of course, the Spenserian stanza has its own special rhyme scheme (which the example follows: *ababbcbcc*), but you'll only drive yourself buggy if you try to remember complex rhyme schemes like that one.

Answers (A) and (B) are relatively obscure verse forms you simply don't need to know about for the purposes of this test. In answer (C), terza rima means "three rhyme" in Italian. It is the three-line stanza form used by Dante in his *Commedia*. The stanzas link in rhyme: *aba bcb cdc ded*, etc. Again, don't bother memorizing rhyme schemes. Learn the simple distinguishing feature of the form. If it's not in three-line stanzas, it's not terza rima.

A heroic stanza (D) is a four-line stanza, usually iambic pentameter, rhyming *abab*. But don't confuse the heroic stanza with its cousin the ballad stanza, discussed in Chapter 5. The ballad stanza in its purest form rhymes *abcb*, but there are many exceptions to this rule, and some ballads do rhyme *abcb*.

60. **E** Even Byron (or especially Byron) screws up occasionally. In line 9 "lay" is used incorrectly. As a verb "lay" is transitive and must take an object. Or so says the dour schoolmaster (who writes abysmal but exquisitely correct poetry). "Lie" is the word grammarians would prefer there, but it doesn't rhyme. In terms of the Literature in English Subject Test, (E) was the best guess as confusion between "lie" and "lay" is proverbial.

61. **A** The clue here is "On the Pulse of Morning," the poem Angelou read at the inauguration of President Clinton. If you did not recognize that, you might have reasoned that, of the authors in the answer choices, Angelou is the one best known for her autobiographies (the first and most famous being *I Know Why the Caged Bird Sings*). Gwendolyn Brooks and Nikki Giovanni are above all poets, and Lorraine Hansberry is a dramatist.

62. **E** The Literature in English Subject Test will require a small amount of historical knowledge. You might have eliminated incorrect responses by reasoning that the passage mentions the author is a Puritan. Mary Queen of Scots and Queen Isabella (of Ferdinand and Isabella) were both Catholic and so unlikely to have been praised by a Puritan poet. Queen Victoria died in 1901 and so post-dates the writing of a Puritan poem. This leaves Queens Anne and Elizabeth. Here, common sense should lead you to choose Queen Elizabeth, as she has long been regarded as one of the most intelligent monarchs to sit upon a European throne, and the defeat of the Spanish Armada during her long reign made her seem a living divinity to many of her subjects. Queen Anne, daughter of Charles II, was not a particularly memorable personality.

63. **C** Anne Bradstreet is the only poet given in the answer choices. As usual, eliminate what you can. Margery Kempe (A) is a medieval figure who, at forty years of age, after a long marriage and having borne several children, devoted her life to Christ, wandering through Europe proselytizing for the Church. She later dictated her autobiography, a work we now call *The Book of Margery Kempe*. Mary Rowlandson (B) is a Puritan woman who vividly recorded her abduction by Native Americans. Sarah Orne Jewett (D) is a nineteenth-century New England writer. Her best known work, *The Country of the Pointed Firs*, is quiet and lyrical. Mary Wollstonecraft (E), an English literary figure, is noted as the author of *A Vindication of the Rights of Woman*. She also happened to be the mother of the future Mary Shelley, author of *Frankenstein* and wife of P. B. Shelley.

64. **B** A fairly straightforward comprehension question, as long as you don't get freaked out by the spelling. Just read it and you'll be fine. If (C) seems tempting, take another look; the author does not go quite that far.

65. **D** The passage is essentially *modern* English spelled strangely. Because it is modern English, editors typically modernize the spelling for contemporary readers. As a result, you aren't used to seeing sixteenth-century writing (or seventeenth, for that matter) spelled as its authors wrote it. When, as in the passage, the spelling hasn't been modernized, it is easy to think the writing is earlier than it is.

The second best answer was probably (C). You should know that in the thirteenth century English was in transition between Late Old English and Middle English. Even Chaucer's Middle English syntax and vocabulary is much less familiar than that of the passage. If you picked any of the early choices, you need to look over some Old English texts in the original and note the dates and readability (or lack thereof).

The passage is taken from Hugh Latimer's (1548) *Sermon on the Ploughers*. It is not an important work for you to know in terms of the test.

66. **D** The passage is from Marlowe's *Tamburlaine*. One way to arrive at the correct answer is to notice the martial character of the speech and the mention of Scythians, which in combination should lead you to Tamburlaine. Failing that, you might have eliminated those choices you did recognize.

Gilgamesh is the main character of an ancient Assyrian work which we call *The Gilgamesh Epic*. It's at least 1500 years older than *The Iliad*. Like *Beowulf*, *The Gilgamesh Epic* concerns a questing hero who must battle supernatural monsters.

Volpone is the main character of Ben Jonson's comedy, *Volpone, or the Fox*. Set in Venice, the play concerns the efforts of Volpone and his confederate Mosca to bilk everyone who comes across their path, in particular Volpone's heirs. Volpone and Mosca manage to outwit everyone but each other, which ultimately proves their downfall. Mosca tries to blackmail Volpone, who is too proud to be victimized and so reveals his and Mosca's scheming ways to the authorities, bringing ruin upon them both. The characters are named according to the personalities animals are given by folklore. Important names are Volpone (the fox), Mosca (the fly), and Corvino (the raven). Volpone is a favorite of ETS, and you are sure to see it in the answer choices to questions if not as the subject of a question itself.

Mercutio is Romeo's hot-headed friend in Shakespeare's *Romeo and Juliet*, the story of the bitter feud between the Veronese families the Montagues and the Capulets. Mercutio's death (in a fight with Tybalt), is avenged by Romeo.

Siegfried is the main character of the thirteenth-century epic poem *The Niebelungenlied*. The story concerns the romances, marriages, wars, betrayals, and murders that occur over time as an enormous treasure called the Niebelung hoard changes hands and places. An earlier version of the same legend was used by William Morris as the source for his *Sigurd the Volsung*.

67. **B** This question requires that you recognize Flannery O'Connor from her subject matter, which is well-described in the passage. The only close guess was (A) Eudora Welty, who you might have known was alive in 1969 (she died in 2001). She too is a Southern gothic writer whose works often comment on the religious preoccupation typical of the South, but she is simply not as extreme as O'Connor. Willa Cather (C) and her novels are more heavily associated with the West and Midwest than the South, and, furthermore, she died in 1947, and so is too early an author to be consistent

with the passage. Nadine Gordimer (D) (also quite alive as of this writing) is a South African novelist. May Sarton (E) is known as a New England poet, novelist, and diarist.

68. **E** The key here is to recognize author Henry Fielding's tone of comic irony and pick up the damning (and not terribly subtle) innuendo couched in his high-sounding phrases. The incorrect choices present overly literal misreadings of the passage or are simply wrong.

69. **C** The clearest path to the right answer is to recognize Goody Brown and Molly as characters from Fielding's *Tom Jones*. Another perfectly valid means of finding the right answer is to say: "Which of the works in the answer choices was written by an author capable of such farcical comedy?" *Tess of the D'Urbervilles* (A) is of course by Hardy, who was not much on comedy. Austen's *Emma* (B) is certainly funny (in Austen's wry, biting way), but nothing she wrote is so farcically comic. Likewise, George Eliot's *Daniel Deronda* (E) is not a guffaw kind of novel, nor was she that kind of writer. This would leave (D), Dickens's *David Copperfield*, and (C), the correct answer. Here we hope you are familiar enough with Dickens and *David Copperfield* to recognize that the passage is not drawn from that source. Between the two choices, you might also wonder whether the passage seems to be typical Dickens or typical Fielding. It is indeed typical Fielding.

70. **A** If you had missed the pseudo-epic content of the passage, the answer choices here actually point to it. (D) and (E) shouldn't have been difficult to eliminate if you recognized the comic intent of the passage. Fielding did parody Samuel Richardson, author of the huge epistolary novels-cum-doorstops *Pamela* and *Clarissa*, in a work called *Shamela*. However, it was not Richardson's classicist tendencies Fielding parodied, it was Richardson's tiresome habit of lecturing people on how to live. This eliminates (B), leaving (A), the correct answer, and (C), which refers to the epic simile. The sim-

plest approach is to look for a simile—there is none.

But *epic simile* is a term you absolutely should know. It refers to a simile (a comparison using "like" or "as") that goes absolutely off the deep end, running on for several lines and elaborating the comparison so thoroughly that the narrative flow is effectively halted and the reader or auditor is suspended in a realm of pure rhetoric. Think of it as a really *long* simile.

71. **A** This one can be pieced together with some difficulty from context, but it is more likely a question you either know or you don't. It's basically a vocabulary question.

72. **D** Ares is the Greek god of war, called Mars by the Romans. Aphrodite is the Greek goddess of love and beauty; her Roman equivalent is Venus. The Romans essentially absorbed the Greek pantheon with some variations. Here are the Greek figures that appear in the answer choices with their Roman equivalents, or near equivalents:

(A) Zeus is the big daddy of the gods up on Mount Olympus; his Roman equivalent is Jupiter (or Jove). Zeus's troublemaking wife is Hera (whom Zeus cheated on every chance he got); her Roman equivalent is Juno.

(B) Apollo, god of music and the sun to the Greeks, is also called Apollo by the Romans. Athena, Goddess of wisdom, is called Minerva by the Romans.

(C) Hermes is the Greek "messenger god" but fulfilled a variety of roles; his Roman equivalent is Mercury. Artemis is the Goddess of the hunt (and virginity); her Roman equivalent is Diana.

(D) Cupid and Psyche are from the Roman mythos, so this answer would be disqualified based on that alone. Cupid is the Roman god of love; his Greek equivalent is Eros, Aphrodite's son.

For a refresher on the Greek gods, refer back to pages 94–96.

73. **A** Pope's *The Rape of the Lock* uses the conventions of epic form for satiric effects, as does the passage. The other choices do not.

74. **B** The passage itself is fairly difficult, but this question is a gimme if you just read around the citation in context. This is a great passage on which to practice our techniques. Don't look at the answer choices. Instead, pick your own word for "earth-creeping." Maybe you chose something like "unpoetic" (it doesn't have to be a good word). Then (B) leaps out as the answer.

Also, you can do a lot of this passage without reading the entire thing. Only question 77 asks anything that has to do with the poem as a whole. If you decide to do the passage, do question 77 after you do the others; by the time you get to it, you should know a little more about the passage.

75. **A** The phrase the question asked you to restate might be "translated" as follows: [I send you this curse—] that while you are alive you are always in love with someone, but cannot get that someone's attentions because you lack the ability to write a decent sonnet.

There shouldn't have been too much trouble with (B), (C), and (D) if you read carefully. Choice (E) might have been appealing at first, but if you compare (A) and (E) further, it should become apparent that while (A) correctly paraphrases the passage, (E) does not.

76. **C** This is a process of elimination question pure and simple. The test writers do not expect you to know the tale of the musical contest between Marsyas (the piper) and Apollo (the lyrist) that Midas judged. They do expect you to be able to eliminate the four other choices. (A) refers to the Prometheus myth. (B) refers to the myth of Sisyphus. (D) refers to the story of Pandora. (E) refers to the story of Oedipus.

77. **E** You must be a very confident and competent reader if you felt certain of the right answer here. If you were less than certain, realize that after the time spent reading this long passage

and answering the other questions, it is foolish not to take your best shot, and equally foolish to waste precious minutes fretting. The passage is taken from the end of Sir Philip Sidney's *An Apology for Poetry*, probably the most important statement of literary criticism of the sixteenth century. The correct answer accurately describes the tone of the passage, but the essay as a whole is somewhat more straightforward.

78. **B** This question calls on your knowledge of the Ptolemaic model of the universe, a geocentric model in which the stars and other heavenly bodies are fixed upon nested spheres that rotate about the earth. It was believed that this motion produced a divine music. The Ptolemaic model is frequently referred to in English literature and is a concept you need to know. The Ptolemaic model was eventually supplanted by the heliocentric models of Copernicus, Kepler, and Galileo.

79. **D** Did this passage by any chance remind you of the Edith Wharton in question 26? The passage is from the opening of Henry James's *The Golden Bowl*. Wharton and Henry James have similar styles, but here, in this work from his late period, James's style is more Jamesian than ever. It is a style that shouldn't be too hard to spot, and be sure you can because it is often tested. Look for baroque sentence construction, hesitations, considerations, and possibilities envisioned and discarded. James's writing leaves the impression of a man who takes all the time he needs to explore his delicate genius.

Eliot (A) was primarily a poet; this voice is too antique (and ornate) for him. Hemingway's (B) style is completely opposite—sparse and terse. Dos Passos is known for his *U.S.A.* trilogy, an experimental work, and his antiwar stories and essays. Forster's novels examine the intricacies of human relationships (E).

80. **A** This is one of Hughes's more famous short poems. Lorraine Hansberry drew the title of her play, *A Raisin in the Sun*, from this poem.

The figures in the incorrect answer choices are all important African-American writers. Countee Cullen was a poet of the Harlem Renaissance and a peer of Hughes. Where Hughes experiments with African-American vernacular and blues and jazz rhythms, Cullen was more traditional and academic in his verse.

The Harvard-educated W.E.B. Du Bois is the author of *The Souls of Black Folk* (1903) and was instrumental in the formation of the NAACP. He was strongly critical of Booker T. Washington's accommodationist politics.

Paul Laurence Dunbar is an African-American poet of the late nineteenth century who, like Hughes, used the idioms of black speech in his verse.

Amiri Baraka (born LeRoi Jones) is an African-American poet, playwright, novelist, and belles-lettrist. His first collection of poetry is entitled *Preface to a Twenty Volume Suicide Note*. Other important works are his play *The Dutchman* and his study of jazz in America *Blues People*.

81. **D** Looking over the answer choices you should notice that they are all twentieth-century poets. Of the five choices, you need concern yourself most with (B), (C), and (D): Williams, Pound, and Thomas.

Dylan Thomas, the correct answer, is known for his extravagantly musical verse, of which this passage is a good example. His prose is similarly gorgeous. A small sampling of his work should be enough to let you identify him easily. By the way, his "Do Not Go Gentle into That Good Night" is an oft cited example of the comparatively rare (and difficult) verse form, the villanelle.

Ezra Pound is one of the towering figures of literary modernism. An American who spent the bulk of his career in Europe, he is best known for his rhyming satiric poem "Hugh Selwyn Mauberley" and his long, difficult, possibly fascist, life's work "The Cantos." Pound's influences include Asian poetry and contemporary economics; he is fond of juxtapositions of images and th e importation of quotes and illusions into his work (none of which characterize the passage given). He was a fan of Yeats and also edited T. S. Eliot's *The Wasteland*.

William Carlos Williams (B) is another American modernist. His spare but warm verse is associated with the imagist school of poetry and with his famous dictum: "no ideas but in things." His poems are characterized by easily accessible language and quotidian imagery, in contrast to the passage, which uses unusual words (such as "dingle") and is lofty ("I lordly had the trees..."). Although many of his shorter poems are standard anthology fare, his masterpiece is the book-length poem *Paterson*, which concerns life in his hometown of Paterson, New Jersey, where he practiced medicine for the better part of his life.

Ted Hughes (A) was the poet laureate of Great Britain before his death in 1998. He is perhaps best known in this country for his collection *Crow*. Hughes's poetry, characterized by its unflinching investigation of the darker side of human nature (people are frequently portrayed as beasts), is unmistakably contemporary.

Sylvia Plath (E) is an American poet known for the haunting, violent, bitter, and pitiless poems of her collection *Ariel*, and her autobiography, *The Bell Jar*, which recounts the events surrounding her nervous breakdown. She was married to Ted Hughes for several years before she committed suicide in 1963. Her poems are often about her stormy relationship with her father.

82. **A**   The test writers at ETS may actually expect you to know something about William Dean Howells, but a better approach to this question would be to know that neither Herman Melville, Mark Twain, Henry James, nor Jack London could ever have espoused critical opinions quite as joyless and leaden as those of the passage. Howells, for someone who held literature as potentially injurious, certainly

took his chances, authoring a score of novels and twice as many plays (all the while editing leading magazines like *Harper's* and *Atlantic Monthly*). He died in 1927 but can be justly considered a nineteenth-century novelist, best known for his avowal of "realist" technique in fiction, his socialist politics, and his criticism's crusty moralizing. His best-known novel is probably *The Rise of Silas Lapham*, in which a nouveau riche Bostonite loses his wealth but learns about the things that really matter.

83. **B**   The best approach to this question is to connect the mention of "Lighthouse" in line 6 with Virginia Woolf's *To the Lighthouse*. From the passage excerpted, you should note the delicate touch Woolf has with her stream-of-consciousness technique, which is less obtrusively virtuosic than James Joyce's and less bluntly idiosyncratic than William Faulkner's.

Djuna Barnes is the author of *Nightwood*, a highly regarded modernist novel but not a work you should concern yourself with for the Literature in English Subject Test.

William Faulkner, another noted practitioner of the stream-of-consciousness approach, is the author of a number of novels and short stories, many of which (and the most important of them) are set in Yoknapatawpha county, a fictionalized version of Lafayette county in Mississippi. Faulkner was a native of Oxford, Mississippi, the capital of Lafayette county.

F. Scott Fitzgerald is the author of the novels *This Side of Paradise*, *Tender Is the Night*, *The Great Gatsby*, and many short stories. Of these works, by far the most important is *The Great Gatsby*. Set in Long Island and Manhattan, it concerns Nick Carraway, the narrator; Tom and Daisy Buchanan, a husband and wife, each of whom takes an extramarital lover; and Jay Gatsby, a wealthy gangster known for throwing outlandish parties financed by his criminal activities. Gatsby, in love with Daisy since his youth, is reintroduced to her via Carraway, and she and Gatsby have an affair. When Tom's affair with a woman named Myrtle gets out of control and Daisy is implicated in Myrtle's death, the precarious situation unravels quickly. Gatsby is ultimately murdered by Myrtle's legitimate husband. This soap opera-like plot sketch does no justice to the exquisite delicacy with which Fitzgerald handles language and the subtleties of character, particularly Nick Carraway's maturing sensibility. The scene in which Gatsby (the great party-giver) is buried in a ceremony attended by only Carraway and one other man is one of celebrated poignancy.

Gertrude Stein (mama bear of expatriate-American modernism to Ezra Pound's papa bear) can be distinguished easily enough by looking for what might be called her "anti-literature." Whether Stein's writing is relatively accessible, as in her early novellas *Three Lives*, or is obscure, as in the seeming gibberish of *Tender Buttons*, her approach is distinctly unconventional. She heightens the reader's awareness of language and narrative by writing "badly" (with inane repetitions, sing-song rhythms, or in pure nonsense), but does so with such evident control that the writing cannot be dismissed offhand, despite some short-sighted critics' attempts to do just that.

84. **A** This question asks that you identify Samuel Pepys (pronounced 'peeps'). The best way to do this is to know that if there's a seventeenth-century diary question, the answer will be Pepys. He is the most famous diarist in English letters, notable for his easy style and his very frank portrayal of the private life of a London man during the restoration. The diary was written in a private code that wasn't deciphered until the early nineteenth century.

You might have eliminated several incorrect answers on the basis of the date given in the passage. More and Mallory were both dead by 1666, and Mary Wollstonecraft had not yet been born. Although John Bunyan was active in 1666, you should know that you are unlikely to need to recognize Bunyan except as the author of *The Pilgrim's Progress* and *Grace*

Abounding for the Chief of Sinners. The Pilgrim's Progress is by far the more important of the two to recognize.

85. **C** In this question, it is less important that you can identify the work than it is you know something about the authors in the answer choices. Historically, Carlyle is the only one of the writers given in the answer choices born early enough to have any personal knowledge of Lamb, but if you are that familiar with the birth and death dates of Victorians, you probably recognized Carlyle straight out. The best way to get the right answer here is to look over the answer choices and ask, "Which of these writers is funny?" Critics Ruskin, Arnold (also a prominent poet), and Pater seemed to take pains not to be funny. This would leave Wilde and Carlyle. Wilde was simply not a contemporary of Lamb's.

Carlyle's style is famously idiosyncratic. The passage excerpted is by no means Carlyle at his oddest; it comes from his sketches of his contemporaries, which are sort of Carlyle-lite. Rancorous, philosophical, funny (if you can get the jokes, which aren't always obvious), and linguistically playful—all apply to the typical Carlyle piece. His most famous work of fiction is *Sartor Resartus* (translation: the tailor reclothed), in which bombast, self-satire, and German metaphysics do battle in the speculations of the imaginary Professor Teufelsdröckh and his beleaguered editor.

86. **A** The clause has a compound subject but is otherwise straightforward. Subject—Verb—Direct object, as follows: Her form/innocence/air—overawed—his malice.

When you approached this question, we hope you did only as much work as necessary and no more. It would be a waste of time to analyze the whole passage in order to answer a question that asks only about the construction of the main clause. This advice holds as well for question 87, which concerns itself with the same lines as question 86.

The passage is from Milton's *Paradise Lost*. ETS likes to use Milton passages for grammar questions because of his often convoluted syntax.

On an entirely different tack, practicing for the GRE Literature in English Subject Test does sometimes involve understanding passages like this. If you skimmed the passage when taking the test, great, but *now* go back and read it carefully, trying to understand every word. Doing this, not just with Milton but with every challenging passage on the test, is excellent practice for comprehension questions as well as the best way to cement your knowledge of an author's style.

87. **E** This is essentially an interpretation question. In context, the answer should be clear. Again, choose your own word for "abstracted" and match it with the answer choice.

88. **A** Even if you didn't recognize the passage as from *Paradise Lost*, the stylistic incongruity between the incorrect answer choices and the passage should have led you to the right answer without too much trouble. For example, choices (C) and (E) are rhymed and therefore incorrect; this alone would have left you with reasonable odds for a guess. Additionally, (D) is obviously not in Miltonic blank verse. Here are the other choices:

(B) is from Wordsworth's *Prelude*.

(C) is from Yeats's "A Prayer for my Daughter."

(D) is from D. H. Lawrence's "Andraitx— Pomegranate Flowers."

(E) is from Pope's *The Rape of the Lock*.

89. **E** According to the principles of neo-classical dramatic form (which was derived—with considerable elaboration—from the writings of Aristotle), an ideal play takes place within the span of a single day (unity of time), within the confines of a single place (unity of place), and with an undeviating focus upon the main plot of the drama (unity of action). An ironic subplot is therefore a violation of the unity of action and so could not be a characteristic trait of neo-classical drama. Decorum, in (A), is a neoclassical trait. The rule of decorum is that a character's speech be in keeping with his or her social station.

90. **D** This is a straightforward interpretation question. Read the passage and the answer choices carefully. Not a bad question to leave for your second pass if Shakespeare isn't your cup of tea.

Questions 91–94

The correct answers are as follows: **91 is (D), 92 is (B), 93 is (E), 94 is (C)**. These four questions are in the category ETS calls "World Literature." When it comes to "World" literature, the GRE Literature in English Subject Test has tended to stick to Europe; Asian writers, Middle Eastern writers, and African writers are all but nonexistent (as are "minor" European literatures such as Polish or modern Greek). Here are the titles matched with their authors:

91. **D** *Notes from the Underground*, by Fyodor Dostoyevsky, is the memoir of a bitter, sensitive, hypochondriacal, anonymous narrator alienated from society: This theme is clearly reflected in the opening passage, so even if you didn't recognize it but knew the subject, you should be able to guess that this could be the opening of the work.

92. **B** *Remembrance of Things Past* is the epic masterpiece of French author Marcel Proust, which deals with his memories of his rather ordinary childhood. Although this opening statement doesn't give an indication of when the author is writing, the first person voice gives you a clue that it could be autobiographical; it also reads like memory; and the description is of an ordinary event, which matches the author's theme.

93. **E** *The Notebooks of Malte Laurids Brigge* is by Rainer Maria Rilke. It is arguably Rilke's most important prose work, a series of almost autobiographical spiritual musings. (Notice that it is the most "poetry-like" selection, and Rilke is the only poet among the answer choices.) Rilke is best known for his lyric "object poems"—

attempts to describe physical objects so that there is no separation between the observer and the object being observed.

94. **C** *The Stranger*, by Albert Camus, begins with the death of the narrator's mother. The plot centers around the seemingly motiveless killing of a stranger on a beach and the subsequent trial. The disaffected, matter-of-fact narrator (reflected in "which means nothing") is characteristic of this work.

Answer (A) is from Balzac's *Pere Goriot*. Balzac is known for his examinations of bourgeois life in nineteenth-century Paris, reflected in this opening passage by the French names and the straightforward reference to Paris.

95. **D** This question calls on your knowledge of major characters in American fiction. Captain Ahab is from Melville's *Moby-Dick*, of course, and he is Huck Finn's (from Mark Twain's novel *The Adventures of Huckleberry Finn*) polar opposite. Ahab is definitely a raging and tragic fool in his quest for the whale, and Huck Finn's antics belie a wisdom beyond his years.

(A) Natty Bumppo is the woodsman hero of J. F. Cooper's *Leatherstocking Tales*. Cooper (best known for *The Last of the Mohicans*) writes frontier tales of men who live freely, communing with nature. Obviously, this is a poor choice for the Protestant we're looking for in this question. Holden Caulfield is the jaded, teenage narrator from Salinger's *The Catcher in the Rye*, neither foolish nor simple.

(B) Faulkner's Yoknapatawpha novels focus on the successive generations of a few families: the Snopes, the Compsons, and the Sartorises. The name Quentin is given to a Compson each generation. As a result there are two Quentin Compsons to be found in Faulkner's novels. The most important of these are the two Quentins that appear in *The Sound and the Fury*. When critics speak of Quentin Compson, they are generally referring to the first Quentin of that novel, a young Mississippi man who harbors a deeply felt (and guilt-provoking)

incestuous passion for his sister Caddy, and who ultimately kills himself while at Harvard college. The other Quentin Compson is the first Quentin's niece, his sister Caddy's bastard daughter. Resourceful and morally ambiguous, the second Quentin steals her detestable Uncle Jason's savings and flees. She is not heard from again. Benjy Compson (brother of Quentin, Caddy, and Jason) is the "idiot man-child" who narrates the first section of *The Sound and the Fury*. Quentin is not "God obsessed" and Benjy, though simple, is not rebellious or an atheist. The first Quentin Compson also appears in Faulkner's *Absalom, Absalom* and two short stories unlikely to show up on the exam.

(C) Arthur Dimmesdale is the Puritan Reverend who fathers Hester Prynne's daughter, Pearl, in *The Scarlet Letter*. Although Dimmesdale fits the first category of a "strict New England Protestant" beautifully, Prynne is not the "sardonic atheist" we're looking for.

(E) Jake Barnes is the mysteriously injured (sexually dysfunctional, though in exactly what way is not clear) World War I veteran who narrates Hemingway's *The Sun Also Rises*, which is set in 1920s France and Spain.

Daisy Miller is the title character of Henry James's novella about a young, flirtatious, *nouveau riche* American girl in Europe. Her candid, yet ambiguously unwitting sexuality shakes the Old World sensibilities that surround her and ultimately prove to be her undoing, but, as always in James, one is deliciously unsure of any final interpretation. To help you eliminate this answer, remember that Daisy Miller is an irredeemable flirt and that Jake Barnes is hardly God obsessed.

96. **D** Samuel Butler (1613–1680) is the author of *Hudibras*. He is not to be confused with Samuel Butler (1835–1902), the author of *Erewhon* and *The Way of All Flesh*. The passage in question 96 describes "Hudibras" well enough for our purposes. Hudibras is the name of the knight

referred to, and his squire's name is Sir Ralpho. The term "hudibrastic" is used to describe verse written in the deliberately clubfoot form employed by Butler (see page 55).

The other answer choices all refer to longish works of comic verse.

(A) Pope's *The Rape of the Lock* is further discussed on pages 118–119.

(B) Dryden's *Absalom and Achitophel*, though quite witty, is ultimately a serious work that allegorizes the political situation in Restoration England, using biblical figures in order to argue an essentially pro-Charles position.

(C) Pope's *Dunciad* is a fantastical and withering satire in which Pope lambastes bad poets. It is set in the kingdom of Dulness. The chief object of Pope's scorn is the poet (and comic dramatist) Colley Cibber, who had the dire misfortune of being appointed Poet Laureate in an era that sported several vastly better poets.

(D) Dryden's *Mac Flecknoe* is also set in the land of boring poets, and like the *Dunciad*, takes a Restoration playwright (Thomas Shadwell) to task.

97. **A** Again, European literature is the issue here. Eliminate what you can.

(A) is a good summary of *The Red and the Black*.

(B) Mann's *Buddenbrooks* is one of the author's early novels. It tells of the decay of the Buddenbrooks family.

(C) Balzac's *Lost Illusions* is the story of a young, handsome, talented man, Lucian de Rubempre, who travels to Paris with a married woman to make his literary name. He loses the woman, betrays his talent, and sells out not only himself but his family, mistresses, etc. He dies in the end after making an unlikely comeback orchestrated by Balzac's criminal mastermind, Vautrin (who also figures prominently in *Père Goriot*).

(D) Flaubert's *Sentimental Education* is an extended reworking of the first part of *Lost Illusions*, material Flaubert ultimately made his own. The main character, Frederic Moreau, is struck with an obsessive love for a married bourgeois which comes to naught. As ever, Flaubert pitilessly exposes everyone and everything as petty, vain, despicably commercial, and utterly unable to live up to his or their own ideals.

(E) Knut Hamsun's *Growth of the Soil* is the story of a rustic Norwegian's stoic, self-reliant determination to persevere in a hard land.

98. **A** Marvell's "To His Coy Mistress" is a poem you should know for the GRE Literature in English Subject Test. In exquisite verse, Marvell tries to coax his lady into the sack, but the gist of his argument can be summed up in the following question, which crudely put is: "What are you saving your virginity for—the grave?"

"The Emperor of Ice-Cream" is a Wallace Stevens poem, also about death, but ambiguously; which is characteristic of Stevens, as is the use of odd and vivid imagery to convey a Zen-like vision of the cosmos.

"In Memoriam A.H.H." is Tennyson's verse tribute to a friend and fellow poet who died young. The form employed in this poem is referred to by the term "In Memoriam stanza," an *abba* iambic tetrameter stanza.

Gray's "Elegy Written in a Country Church-Yard" is one of the most famous lyrics in English and, like Marvell's "To His Coy Mistress," a work you should know for the GRE Literature in English Subject Test. The poem is a meditation on death and worldly fame. The line "Some mute inglorious Milton here may rest" is often alluded to by later writers, and the ETS people expect you to recognize it. The poem is written in heroic stanzas.

"To an Athlete Dying Young" is an A. E. Housman poem. It is in four-line stanzas of heroic couplets.

99. **E** This is an excellent example of using the answer choices to come up with an answer. If the names didn't tell you immediately that the answer was Kyd's *The Spanish Tragedy*, you might have looked over the choices and known that all but (D) and (E) are comedies and by writers best known for comedy. In choosing between (D) and (E), you might ask yourself which of the two, Dryden or Kyd, would be likely to write an exceedingly violent play. Finally, you might consider the timing. Dryden is a figure of the middle and late seventeenth century; Webster is a Jacobean playwright who wrote *The Duchess of Malfi* in 1612. In other words, Dryden could not have affected the composition of Webster's play, as the passage implies the work in the correct answer did.

100. **E** Seeing as this is a five-question passage we hope you didn't skip it for the second pass. Question 100 should be a given. The passage refers to the siege of Troy. The woman must be Helen.

101. **D** This one isn't a given. You might have easily chosen (B) Paris, but that isn't correct. Grammatically, the first five lines boil down to: The most famous worthy of the world was called Paris. "Worthy" is the subject.

102. **C** Helen was a celebrated beauty, not even-handed, albino, or fidelious, as the other answer choices suggest. If only the whole test were this easy.

103. **B** You need to be able to recognize Spenser's *The Faerie Queene*, and if you know what to look for, it isn't a difficult task. Of course, some of us have struggled long and hard to avoid reading *The Faerie Queene*, and if this describes you, there's no need to give in now just because of this silly test. Simply do the following: First, look for a poem written in Spenserian stanzas, nine-line stanzas in pentameter except for the last line, which contains an extra foot. (This last hexameter line is called an alexandrine, which we've now mentioned at least three times in this book, so you should really know it.) Finally, once you've decided the passage is a Spenserian stanza, look at the language. Spenser thought it added gravity and a certain mystique to write with an archaic style. "Warre," "whilome," "renowmd," and "hardinesse," are all Spenserisms. By the way, when ETS selects a passage from Spenser, it will often include a question asking what year the passage was written, hoping that you'll be misled by his deliberate use of anachronistic language and spelling, and think the passage earlier than it actually is. Forewarned is forearmed. *The Faerie Queene* was published between 1590 and 1596.

104. **C** See the notes to question 103 for an explanation of this answer. (And that's at least four times. You should really know this by now!)

105. **A** The key to this question is the remark, "All her characters are round, or capable of rotundity." English novelist E. M. Forster also wrote criticism. The passage is taken from his *Aspects of the Novel*. The most famous formulation of that book is the concept of "flat" and "round" characters. A flat character is one in which a single quality or desire dominates the individual utterly. A round character is more complex, more ambiguous, capable of self-contradiction and change. Forster felt that while the round character is typically the more artistically significant of the two, both types have a place in the novel. Forster cites Dickens as a writer who makes excellent use of flat characters as well as round.

106. **C** There are at least three ways to determine the answer to this question. The names Lady Bertram and Fanny might have led you to Jane Austen's *Mansfield Park*. The line that begins, "Ought not her ladyship to remain on the sofa saying, 'This is dreadful. . . .'" reads like a light parody of Austen's ironic tone. The mention of painting on a square of ivory alludes to an often cited remark Austen made about herself: ". . . the little bit (two inches wide) of ivory on which I work with so fine a brush, as produces little effect after much labor. . . ." Finally, none of the other authors in the an-

swer choices could be considered miniaturists. Iris Murdoch's novels often feature twisted, wealthy men and bizarre plot twists (A).

107. **A** Cerberus is the three-headed dog that guards the entrances to the underworld.

Charon is the ferryman who pilots dead souls across the river Styx to the underworld.

The Hydra is a mythical seven-headed dragon. When one of the heads is severed, two more grow back in its place.

Hades is the lord of the underworld. The name is also used sometimes to mean the underworld itself.

The Chimera is another mythical beast. It is made of parts of a goat, a lion, and a serpent (or dragon), with various ancient sources disagreeing as to just what parts come from what animal. It is from this creature we derive the word "chimerical," which means wildly fantastical, improbable, etc.

108. **D** The passage gives an abbreviated but adequate description of Argentinean Jorge Luis Borges. Borges is also known for his poetry, but, unlike his fiction, it is not widely studied outside of Spanish-speaking countries. His best-known work is *Ficciones*.

The writers in the incorrect answer choices are all twentieth-century writers of some importance.

George Orwell is the author of the novels *Animal Farm* and *1984* (he wrote other novels but these two are the only ones likely to be asked about on the GRE Literature in English Subject Test), as well as several autobiographical/journalistic accounts of his remarkable life, which included jobs as a colonial policeman in Burma and a hotel dishwasher in Paris, experiences in war, and a passionate but undogmatic commitment to social justice.

Vladimir Nabokov is best known for his novels *Lolita* and *Pale Fire*. An émigré from Russia, Nabokov wrote his later novels (such as *Lolita*)

in English. Nabokov's writing is characterized by an erudite, self-conscious style put to humorous effect and by a proclivity for experimentation with form. (*Pale Fire* is a novel told through the annotations to a mediocre poem, "Pale Fire." The annotator is an insane academic named Charles Kinbote.)

Bernard Malamud is an American writer descended from Russian-Jewish immigrants. He is best known for his novel *The Fixer*. Malamud is not especially important for the GRE Literature in English Subject Test.

André Gide is a French author known for his novels and diaries.

109. **E** The passage is from Shakespeare, the first act of *Richard III*. Richard is misshapen, ambitious, evil, and brilliant. The part is an actor's dream, though not one of Shakespeare's deeper psychological portraits. POE should have quickly narrowed the field to (A) and (E) if you asked yourself which of these characters is notoriously evil. In the scene from which the passage is taken, Richard glories in his own preposterous evil after having seduced Anne. Hamlet (B) and Julius Caesar (D) worry less about women than they do about politics. Mercutio (C) is the joker from "Romeo and Juliet."

110. **A** Questions on the Bible are not worth studying for, because the ratio of the material covered to the number of questions is so unfavorable. There *will* be a question or two on the Bible, but one at least will be easy enough that even if you have never taken a Bible-as-literature class and were not raised within a Bible-based faith, you've probably assimilated the information you need just by having lived in the largely Judeo-Christian United States. Also, one or two questions will not make or break your score. However, if you're the thorough type (and insist on ignoring our good advice) an excellent book to study would be G. B. Harrison's *The Bible for Students of Literature and Art*.

111. **C** "Slant of light" is the correct antecedent of "it" in line 15.

112. **B** If you recognized the author of the poem as Emily Dickinson, you shouldn't have had any problem with this one. If you didn't recognize Dickinson as the author of the passage, you might have reasoned that the choices (A), (C), (D), and (E) are not consistent with the tone and style of the poem. By the way, em dashes (—) at the end of several short lines are a give-away that the author is Emily Dickinson.

   Here are the sources of the other answer choices:

   (A) is from Robert Frost's "The Road Not Taken."

   (C) is from Tennyson's "Tithonus," a poem about a man granted eternal life but not eternal youth.

   (D) is the opening line of Allen Ginsburg's "Howl." Like his hero Walt Whitman, Ginsburg often uses long lines and emphatic repetition.

   (E) is the opening line, and title, of Walt Whitman's eulogy for Abraham Lincoln.

113. **A** The poem itself is not of course in Old or Middle English, but note that each line is broken as though for a strong caesura (pause) and that each line is organized internally by alliteration. The selection is from the poem "Junk," by Richard Wilbur.

114. **E** Not a particularly easy Shakespeare question. The lines are from *Henry IV, Part I*. Henry has just fought and killed his rival Hotspur. Despite their enmity, each respected the other. The scene is famous as the one in which Falstaff survives by playing dead, and then goes to Hotspur's corpse, stabs it (to get his knife bloody), and carries the body off in order to take credit for the victory. If you recognized the lines as Shakespeare's, you should have eliminated both (A) and (B) immediately. You might have eliminated (C) by knowing that Lear was not undone by ambition. In (D), you might know that the eulogy spoken for Lady

Macbeth is the famous speech: "Tomorrow and tomorrow and tomorrow/Creeps in this petty pace from day to day. . . ." This would leave only the correct answer.

115. **D** The passage is vulgar enough so that we can eliminate (B) immediately. The passage, from George Etherege's *The Man of Mode*, is pure Restoration comedy; it insults itself and it insults the audience, but wittily.

   Answer choice (C) refers to a Jacobean masque. The masque form is derived from the religious spectacles and plays of medieval times. By the Jacobean age, the masque had evolved into a lavish production involving spectacular sets, costumes, and even machinery. Many of the players were drawn from the court. Although dramatic, masques called for much dancing and music as well. The names you need to associate with the masque are Ben Jonson, who wrote numerous masques for which Inigo Jones designed elaborate sets, and, believe it or not, John Milton, who wrote the one masque considered to have substantial literary merit, *Comus*.

116. **C** Both 116 and 117 are little more than vocabulary questions. Look back at the context.

117. **A** Assuming you don't know seventeenth-century slang, you can still come up with the correct answer in context. We're looking for an "old mistress" whose "charms" were once impressive. Lately, the person being addressed has consorted with "dirty drabs," and his muse (i.e., a woman) has forsaken him.

   (B) is incorrect, because there is nothing in the passage that says the person being addressed is of a higher class than his consorts.

   (C) is incorrect, because we are looking for something lacking outward beauty, and dullards may be beautiful, if dull.

   (D) is incorrect, because it is taking the term "drab" too literally and applying our twenty-first-century definition for it.

(E) is incorrect, because there is no value judgment placed on the consorting, just the quality of the consorts.

118. **E** This is a straightforward comprehension question.

119. **E** The best way to answer this question is to know the poem, but if you don't, go ahead and pick the choice that sounds best. Answer choice (E) continues the thought of celebrating the splendors of the morning. None of the other answers does this.

120. **B** Aurora is the goddess of the dawn. The "god unshorn" represents Apollo the sun god.

121. **C** This is a poem you should know, as well as Herrick's poems for Julia. (They can be found in *The Norton Anthology of English Literature*.) It is a good use of time to read a few pages of a poet who is sure to show up on the GRE Literature in English Subject Test at least once. In other words, you can read the whole Bible and pick up a point or two (if you get lucky or have an extraordinary memory), or you can read five pages of Herrick and pick up a point, five pages of Marvell and pick up a point, five pages of . . . I think you catch our drift.

122. **D** The passage describes Goethe's first novel, *The Sorrows of Young Werther*. You should recognize Candide as the protagonist of the eponymous short novel by Voltaire. Axel (E) refers to the main character of a relatively obscure play of that name by Le Compte Villiers De L'isle Adam (that's just his last name). The play was brought to some prominence by *Axel's Castle*, Edmund Wilson's well-known collection of critical essays.

Lucien (C) and Frederic (B) might be the heroes of any number of novels.

123. **B** You should know that as a young man Goethe was associated with the *Sturm und Drang* ("storm and stress") movement. It had greater influence on the theater than on novels, in a large part due to the theatrical successes of Goethe's friend Schiller. In a *Sturm und Drang* work, a youthful romantic hero confronts the arbitrary or unnatural laws of society, flouts them, and ultimately pays the price.

124. **B** If you did not recognize the answer by immediately connecting Hawthorne's *The Blithedale Romance* and Brook Farm, you might have eliminated the incorrect answer choices, none of which is associated with "an actual socialist-utopian community."

(A) Twain's *Letters from Earth* is not a terribly well-known work. In *Letters*, Satan corresponds with God about the foolish notions humans have about spiritual matters.

(C) Stephen Crane's *Maggie: A Girl of the Streets* is the dystopic story of a girl who is raised in wretched poverty by a hideous, alcoholic mother. The heroine, Maggie, is driven to prostitution after having been manipulated, seduced, and cast aside by her lover Pete. She ultimately kills herself.

(D) Orwell's *Homage to Catalonia* does concern socialism (in the context of the Spanish Civil War), but the situation could hardly be called utopian.

(E) Cather's *My Ántonia* is the story of the hardscrabble Nebraska pioneer life of Jim Burden and Antonia Shimerda.

125. **A** This question relies on your knowledge of some of the few well-known details of Shakespeare's life. If you didn't immediately know that Shakespeare's wife's name was Anne Hathaway and that he left his second-best bed to her in his will, you might have asked yourself, "about which of the writers is little biographical information known?" Shakespeare.

126. **C** The question can be paraphrased: When did Shakespeare die? You should know Shakespeare's birth and death dates. His birth date is traditionally given as April 23, 1564. He died on April 23, 1616.

127. **C** The quote is taken from Ben Jonson's "To the Memory of My Beloved Master William Shakespeare." If you knew that Shakespeare was the subject of the passage but were unsure of who his friend and rival was, you might have used chronology to eliminate the wrong answers.

128. **C** These are all famous phrases. (A), (C), (D), and (E) are Latin. (B) is French, but is the motto of a British order of chivalry, The Order of the Garter.

    Here are the translations:

    (A) I came, I saw, I conquered

    (B) Shame on him who thinks this evil

    (C) Art is long, life short

    (D) I think, therefore I am

    (E) Seize the day

129. **B** This is a very difficult question, but if you knew something about the answer choices, it might have been answerable. To answer this question correctly, you should note the word "Utopia" from the passage. Thomas More wrote *Utopia*, a prose work in Latin. (A very possible source of confusion is that the excerpted passage is in verse. This is because the excerpt is not from the body of the text but from a dedicatory poem by the Poet Laureate of the island of Utopia, "Mr. Windbag, Nonsenso's sister's son.") Once you recognize that Thomas More is the author of the passage, you still need to figure out which of the answer choices refers to More. You should know that More was beheaded (for treason) after his refusal to take a position of unequivocal support for Henry VIII in the king's conflict with the Pope.

    (A) Dean of St. Paul's Cathedral is a position once held by John Donne. Donne's sermons, many of them delivered from the pulpit in St. Paul's, are the source of many of Donne's most often quoted lines. See question 36.

(C) The metaphysical poets were a seventeenth-century school led by John Donne and George Herbert.

(D) "An adventurer, poet, and confidante to Queen Elizabeth" could refer to Sir Walter Raleigh.

(E) "Able to write only between recurring bouts of suicidal madness" might refer to any number of poets (seriously), but it would refer perhaps most famously to William Cowper.

130. **A** To answer this question, you should refer to the passage; you should not rely solely on your knowledge of the word Utopia. The passage states clearly that Utopia is a place where no one goes. Although we now use utopia to mean an ideal place or community, strictly and etymologically speaking an ideal place is *eutopia*. More's coinage of utopia is as "no place."

131. **D** Again, Process of Elimination is the simplest means of proceeding if you aren't immediately certain of the answer. None of the other answers concerns either utopias or dystopias.

    Note that Erewhon is an anagram for nowhere. Note also that Samuel Butler, the author of *Erewhon*, is also notably the author of *The Way of All Flesh*, a semi-autobiographical work. There is another, much earlier Samuel Butler who wrote the mock epic poem *Hudibras*, as you should remember from question 96.

132. **D** This question calls for a straightforward reading of a passage of late Middle English. Sound out the words as well as possible. (A little bit of practice at this goes a long way.) The 'Þ' represents a 'th' sound. Note that the passage is organized by alliterative lines, as is characteristic of much Middle English verse.

133. **E** Here, you needed to recognize that the passage was Middle English. None of the other choices refer to works written in Middle English. Froissart's *Chronicle* was written in the right period, but in French. It wasn't translated into English until the sixteenth century.

134. **E** Either recognizing the passage as Middle English or noting the alliteration could have gotten you the right answer here. Remember, if you can read it, it isn't Old English.

135. **D** The passage is from *Piers Ploughman* by William Langland. It was written between 1350 and 1380, which is when Chaucer was writing. Be careful of Bunyan (B), author of *Grace Abounding for the Chief of Sinners* and *The Pilgrim's Progress*, and Edmund Spenser (C), author of *The Faerie Queene* (among other works). Students frequently think these authors wrote in an earlier age than they in fact did. Spenser deliberately used an idiosyncratic archaic English, but he was actually a close contemporary of Shakespeare. Bunyan wrote *The Pilgrim's Progress* in the seventeenth century and is a contemporary of Dryden, Pepys, Milton, etc. Caedmon (E) is the author of *Caedmon's Hymn*, written in the late seventh century. He is the first English poet known by name to history. *Beowulf* was probably written down at this time after having been sung for a number of centuries by Anglo-Saxon scops.

136. **A** The clues here are the term *Comédie Humaine*, which refers to Balzac's enormous series of interrelated novels, and Rastignac, the name of one of Balzac's most famous characters. Rastignac, as a naive young man, is the main character of *Père Goriot*. In later novels, he shows up as an increasingly cynical and successful man-about-town.

137. **D** The were two clues here. First, "Count No 'count'" is the derogatory nickname Faulkner bore during his days as a mail-clerk at the University of Mississippi. More importantly, you should know that Yoknapatawpha County is the fictional Mississippi county in which Faulkner's most important works are set.

138. **B** This is a straightforward comprehension question.

139. **D** This one is a little tougher than question 138. The key is to read the passage, think about the use of the word "sensible" in context, and perhaps think of related words such as sensitive and sensory. The speaker is not using "sensible" to mean reasonable. The eighteenth century use of the word meant "aware," with a strong suggestion of "sensitive to."

140. **C** It shouldn't have taken much to see that (A) and (B) could be eliminated, because both refer to modernist authors and the passage is recognizably pre-twentieth century. If you knew that the passage was not from Shakespeare or recognized that it was from a Restoration comedy, you would have been down to (C) and (D). Without being intimately familiar with both plays, there is nothing to do but guess, because you aren't even given names to work with. Guess! You win a few, you lose a few, but in the end, your score goes up. The passage is from Congreve's *The Way of the World*.

141. **E** This is a comprehension question. The characters are discussing ways in which to persecute men—in particular, the first character's hypothetical husband. In line 22, "it" refers to the possibility of cuckolding that husband.

142. **A** As mentioned earlier, some of John Donne's best-known lines come not from his poetry but from his sermons, and the excerpt is an excellent example of this.

143. **C** Donne, notoriously obsessed with death, is referring to the bell traditionally tolled to announce the death of a congregation member (or prominent citizen). His point is that death will ultimately call us all.

144. **D** Don't be put off by the somewhat ridiculous prose of the answer choice; it nevertheless states what Donne essentially means.

145. **C** The passage does not contain an epic simile, but it does contain a metaphor—that of "translation"—which is extended over several lines to embrace a number of further metaphors. This is closest to the device of the epic simile, which you'll remember is a simile in which the comparison is given such lengthy treatment

that it becomes a kind of poetic digression. The incorrect answer choices are all other conventions of the classical epic. Their definitions can be found in Chapter 7.

146. **B** Note that the correct answer is the most thematically and stylistically consistent with the passage, making it a good guess if you didn't have more precise knowledge.

Here are the sources for the other answer choices:

(A) is from "God's Grandeur" by Gerard Manley Hopkins.

(C) is from "Ozymandias" by P. B. Shelley.

(D) is by Emily Dickinson.

(E) is from "The Bridge" by Hart Crane.

Questions 147–151

The correct answers are as follows: **147 is (D), 148 is (C), 149 is (B), 150 is (E), 151 is (A)**.

You should know *The Canterbury Tales*. They will, in some form or another, be on the GRE Literature in English Subject Test. You should also be familiar enough with Chaucer's English to make sense of the answer choices to questions 147–151 without an undue amount of strain. If you've only read Chaucer in a modern English translation, by all means take the time to read some of the *Tales* in his own Middle English. This will not only make for a few more right answers but will speed you up considerably. The Middle English questions are like speed bumps for many students. There you are, cruising along, till you hit Chaucer (or Langland's *Piers Ploughman*) and slow to a crawl. To avoid that happening, remember that without being an expert, it isn't possible to get every word, so don't try. Get the gist of what is being said. Most of Chaucer is intelligible enough for your purposes on this test. Just think of it as misspelled English with a lot of unfamiliar slang.

Finally, there are five questions with only five answer choices; this is truly a super-POE ques-

tion. You might have used some logic to increase your odds and your speed. For example, you might have reasoned that two characters must be men. Glancing over the answer choices, you would find that (B), (D), and (E) all refer to females. Since questions 148 and 151 must be males, those questions each have only two possible answer choices, (A) and (C). For 147, 149, and 150, consequently, you can eliminate (A) and (C). At this point, you are well on your way to picking up five points.

For more on *The Canterbury Tales*, see Chapter 8.

152. **A** The passage is drawn from one of King Lear's "mad" monologues. As has been mentioned, when it comes to Shakespeare, there's a bit too much to study to begin now, but if you held guns to our heads and asked which one play of Shakespeare's you should know for the GRE Literature in English Subject Test, it would be *King Lear*. By the way, this is an extremely difficult question. Based on content alone, you might easily have picked (B) because of the passage's reference to soldiers and adultery. The tone of the passage is also consistent with Othello's speeches. As a result, to answer this question correctly, you needed to recognize the passage as being from *King Lear*. Realize that for most questions, this degree of specificity is unnecessary.

153. **D** This is another straightforward comprehension question. The word "But" in line 16 means "only" in the context of this passage.

154. **A** You should recognize the first line of the passage as the famous first line of *Pride and Prejudice*, by Jane Austen. You should then be able to recognize the title of another Austen novel, *Northanger Abbey*. On the subject of *Northanger Abbey*, that book is in large part a parody of the very popular "Gothic" novels of the time, specifically those of Anne Radcliffe.

155. **C** This question in part depends on your ability to answer the previous question correctly. That is, if you know the author is Austen, you should know that answer (C) describes one

of Austen's celebrated qualities as a stylist. If you had been unable to identify the author as Austen, or did not know Jane Austen is noted for her subtle satiric sense (as Chaucer is noted for his irony), you might have still been able to proceed by eliminating the other choices. In other words, out of context, it is difficult to typify the passage as anything very specific, but it should be easy to say that the passage is *not* farcical, *not* candid, unflinching realism, etc.

156. **B**   The phrase "in want" is adjectival. It modifies the noun "man."

157. **C**   The passage is drawn from Virginia Woolf's long essay *A Room of One's Own*. Published in 1929, the essay asserts that for a woman to fulfill her artistic (particularly literary) talent, she needs a room of her own and a source of income, and that the lack of these things has historically been a profound constraint on women writers. Virginia Woolf was concerned with the roles and rights of women in modern society, so this pro-feminist tract should point to her.

ETS seems to like *A Room of One's Own*. It's a work you should know.

(A) Aphra Behn is considered the first professional female prose writer and dramatist who lived in the seventeenth century. Her style characteristically makes the narrator part of the action and draws the reader close. This passage is obviously closer to present-day speech.

(B) Eudora Welty is a southern writer who focuses more on human relationships than on feminism.

(D) George Eliot is the pen name of a female author (Marian Evans), who discarded traditional female interests to write about common people, as she does in *Adam Bede, Middlemarch*, and *Silas Marner*. She is not the author of a feminist text.

(E) Clifford Odets is a playwright and left-wing political figure. He is the only male in the answer choices, and although this odd-man-out choice may make this answer attractive, resist.

158. **E**   "Elegy Written in a Country Church Yard" is a must. The line that Woolf alludes to—"Some mute, inglorious Milton here may rest"—is from Gray's poem. This line worms its way into a remarkable number of authors' works. For more on the works that most frequently appear on the GRE Literature in English Subject Test, see Chapter 8.

159. **B**   Ellis Bell is the pen name Emily Brontë used. Anne Brontë used the pen name Acton Bell and Charlotte Brontë used Currer Bell.

(A) George Sand is the pen name used by French novelist Amandine Aurore Lucie Dupin. Speaking of pseudonymous Georges, don't confuse George Sand with George Eliot, the English novelist, whose real name was Marian Evans.

(C) Shamela Andrews is the main character of a book Fielding wrote (pseudonymously) in parody of Richardson's *Pamela*.

(D) Elia is the name Charles Lamb adopted in his charming, witty, sophisticated *Essays of Elia* and *Last Essays of Elia*.

(E) Thomas Rowley is the author whom literary juvenile-delinquent/forger/genius Thomas Chatterton invented.

160. **C**   This is a straightforward comprehension question. We hope you weren't tripped up by (A). Yes, the passage cites Austen and Burns as examples of, respectively, a great female writer and a great working-class writer. But the passage is not an argument for their existence (A), nor is the passage about the women behind great writers (B), or a protest/plea (D), (E).

Questions 161–164

The correct answers are as follows: **161 is (A), 162 is (C), 163 is (B), 164 is (D).**

If it was a tough series of questions, it's because of the almost inevitable misdirection involved in questions 162 and 163. Upon seeing the name Odysseus, you might have immediately thought to look for Homer. Upon seeing the name Caliban, you may well have thought—aha! Shakespeare's *The Tempest*—whereas the correct answers are not from *The Tempest,* or from Homer. Very well-known or striking characters are of course sometimes "borrowed" by other authors. It may not seem fair, but ETS seems to like questions that involve this kind of sharing.

Here are the specifics of the individual answer choices:

(A) is Jaques from Shakespeare's *As You Like It.* The excerpt is from what is probably the single most famous passage of that play, sometimes referred to as "the seven ages of man speech." Its opening lines are "All the world's a stage/ And all the men and women merely players."

(B) is Caliban from Robert Browning's "Caliban upon Setebos." The name Setebos is the major clue that the speaker is Caliban. Setebos is the deity Caliban and his mother Sycorax worship. Another clue is the mention of "this isle." You should know that Caliban lives upon Prospero's island, where the action of *The Tempest* is set.

(C) is Odysseus from the opening of Ezra Pound's *Cantos.* Unless you are familiar with these lines, the best clue here is the seafaring subject matter. Also, note the rhythm's suggestion of Old English caesura (a heavy pause midway through a line) and the heavy alliteration within many of the lines. Pound, by alluding to early Anglo-Saxon epic form, mimics the antiquity of Homer's ancient Greek. (Pound was a proficient translator of Old English, as well as classical Chinese, Latin, and heaven knows how many modern languages. He consumed whole literatures the way some of us eat potato chips. A caveat to future scholar/ geniuses: Pound, despite his stunning erudition, couldn't hack all the academic rigmarole and was booted from his first college teaching position.)

(D) is Satan from Milton's *Paradise Lost.*

(E) is from Cowper's long poem *The Task.* The title refers to the task suggested by Cowper's friend Lady Austen (not to be confused with Jane), who proposed that Cowper write a poem about a sofa. *The Task* is indeed about a sofa, but from there (the sofa, both literally and metaphorically), Cowper goes on to address the small pleasures of his country-mouse life, and to a lesser extent, the discomforts of the city. Cowper's poetry is reflective, graceful, and subdued, despite the fact that Cowper himself was hounded throughout his adult life by periodic fits of suicidal depression and feelings of persecution.

Questions 165–168

The correct answers are as follows: **165 is (A), 166 is (B), 167 is (C), 168 is (D).**

The passage is Shakespeare's Sonnet 1. Remember that the paraphrases needn't be good ones (for example, the correct answer for question 165 is not a good paraphrase, but simply the best of the five). Don't quibble: Pick the one that best captures the sense of the line. The contract mentioned in line 5 is a wedding contract.

Questions 169–172

The correct answers are as follows: **169 is (B), 170 is (C), 171 is (E), 172 is (A).**

If you are at all familiar with the plays in question, this series should not have caused much difficulty. Even if you didn't know the specific works mentioned, some knowledge of the authors and their typical subject matter would provide enough information to get by. These are super-POE questions.

169. **B** Samuel Beckett was an Irish-born playwright (and novelist and poet who wrote all but his earliest work in French) whose work shouldn't be too hard to spot. His plays are Spartan in decor and the cast is rarely larger than four. The characters are always in some way disabled: physically, mentally, economically, or spiritually. They inhabit a bleakly absurd world of futility, alienation, and discomfort, in which things typically go from awful to perfectly hideous, though the gloom is enlivened (or perhaps underscored) by moments of humor, violence, and even (though very rarely) lyricism. You should know that his plays are associated with the term "Theater of the Absurd." It would also be a good idea to look over his best-known work, *Waiting for Godot*, the whole of which concerns a pair of bums, Vladimir and Estragon (a.k.a. Didi and Gogo), who await the arrival of the mysterious Godot, who fails to appear. Another pair of bums, Lucky and Pozzo, also briefly but disturbingly take the stage.

170. **C** Sartre is a French author best known for formalizing the philosophy known as "existentialism" in a work called *Being and Nothingness*. He tried his hand, more or less successfully, at nearly every type of literary production, including the well-known short plays *No Exit* and *The Flies*. Both plays are considered to be "Theater of the Absurd" works. Although an unexpected author will inevitably show up on the GRE Literature in English Subject Test, there is no use obsessing about it. Sartre, especially as a playwright, is not someone you should concern yourself with in terms of the test.

(D) is a description of American playwright Eugene O'Neill's *Long Day's Journey into Night*. At O'Neill's request, the play, which is autobiographical, was not produced until after his death. O'Neill plays have been labeled with nearly every possible dramatic fault. They can seem at times sentimental, windy, tedious, sloppy, ill-constructed, implausible, and even incomprehensible, but no other playwright since Shakespeare has worked successfully and repeatedly on so large a scale, or created characters of such epic weight. With O'Neill there is no one work on which to focus, but you can expect an ETS discussion of O'Neill to mention something of the following: his Irish-American origin, his troubled family life, the profound melancholy at the heart of much of his work, the parallels between much of his work and Greek tragedy, and the overall sense of enormous and powerful emotion that characterizes his plays.

171. **E** Genet is a French author of novels and plays, also often associated with the "Theater of the Absurd." He is one of the great antisocial authors of world literature, and spent much of his life in jail (for burglary, buggery, and just bad attitude). In his writing, he turns the moral universe on its head, relentlessly aestheticizing and eroticizing vice, crime, and cruelty in a gorgeously fevered, baroque prose. Although not an exceptionally prolific writer, nearly everything he wrote is considered masterful.

172. **A** Chekov's plays are typically set in upper-middle-class Russian homes. Although Chekov wrote intricately plotted and dramaturgically innovative plays, perhaps the most noteworthy aspect of his work is its unparalleled ability, through dialogue simultaneously natural and poetic, to convey the inner life of his characters. Be aware that Chekov was a doctor of medicine as well as a writer, and that he was not only a great playwright, but a master of the short story form as well.

173. **A** The keys here are the names Bounderby, Gradgrind, and Coketown. You should be familiar enough with Dickens to spot Dickensian names when you see them, even if you can't immediately place the novel from which they come. The industrial theme present in the passage might also lead you to guess either Dickens or Sinclair. Because the style is unmistakably nineteenth-century British, you would then guess Victorian Londoner Dickens over twentieth-century American Sinclair.

(By the way, the next time you're looking for something to read, check the complete works of Upton Sinclair out of the library. Just remember to bring a moving van. When did he sleep? It would be hard to *read* that much in one lifetime.)

174. **E** Chances are you aren't particularly familiar with Dana, Jr.'s book, which is fine. *Two Years Before the Mast* is a Harvard man's account of shipping out on a merchant vessel as a common seaman. This was a difficult question. Remember, it is impossible to study for every question on the subject test. You can miss a lot of questions and still score in the 99th percentile. On this question, you should have eliminated what you could, taken your best guess, and moved on. For example, you might have eliminated *Pierre* (B) if you knew that it takes place on dry land.

175. **C** This is an obnoxiously hard question. Not only is the passage obscure, but the incorrect answers are none too familiar either. Expect to see only a very few questions this far off the beaten track. The author of the passage, T. E. Lawrence, is more familiarly known as Lawrence of Arabia. *The Seven Pillars of Wisdom* is an account of his involvement in the Arab revolt against the Turks at the time of World War I. There are no really obvious clues to this in the passage, only the suggestion of homosexual practice in the British army ranks, a suggestion (Lawrence later becomes quite candid) which scandalized England when the book first appeared. Both cummings's (D) and Graves's (E) books are memoirs of World War I. None of the works in the answer choices have any great probability of showing up on the GRE Literature in English Subject Test.

176. **E** This question relies on your knowledge of the author's style. First eliminate (C) because Wallace Stevens is a poet, not a novelist, and eliminate (B) because you should know enough about Henry James to know his style couldn't be further from that of the passage. Eliminate (A) if you know enough about John

Dos Passos to know that a hard-headed realist and sometime socialist is probably not given to waxing about "book-tremulations." This leaves Kerouac and D. H. Lawrence, both of whom are mystically inclined (some might say flaky) enough to have written the passage, but since the passage lacks mention of dharma, night, no sleep, trains, jazz, tea, or Neal Cassady (a.k.a. Dean Moriarty), D. H. Lawrence is the better guess.

177. **A** This is another tough question. The passage is from George Eliot's *Adam Bede*. The only real clue is "This Rector of Broxton." If that doesn't ring any bells, you might eliminate Edith Wharton (C), because the passage doesn't have the Wharton polish, and Willa Cather (E) and Sarah Orne Jewett (B), because the tone is wrong. Both Cather and Jewett have a distinctly American flavor to their writing, and the passage reads as British. (The sentiment expressed in the passage fits Jewett perfectly, however.) This would leave Austen and Eliot. Alas, either makes a legitimate guess, but if you got that far, *guess*.

178. **C** The passage is stream of consciousness. Noting that would narrow the field to (A), (C), and (E). The vocabulary is pure Joyce. The passage is drawn from the Proteus episode of *Ulysses*.

179. **E** Knowing the setting is your best bet. If you knew *Under the Volcano* is set in Mexico, you'd have no problem. The novel concerns a day (the last) in the life of an alcoholic and desperately unhappy former British consul.

180. **B** The clue here is the name Henry. In modern poetry, when you see the name Henry or the name Mr. Bones, the author is John Berryman. The passage, which is a complete poem from *77 Dreamsongs*, should give you a good indication of Berryman's mordant style, although his poems are frequently not as easily accessible as this one is.

181. **E** This question is exactly the kind of question we want you to get right on the GRE Literature in English Subject Test. It is not an easy

question, but it is an answerable question. The dates should allow you to eliminate Wilde (B) easily. The test writers have included Wordsworth (A) here as a trap, hoping you'll blindly associate the two poets, but you should know enough to reason that Wordsworth, as Coleridge's close friend, was probably among the first three or four people to be acquainted with Coleridge's *Dejection* and would certainly have known it by 1826. You could eliminate Carlyle (D) by reasoning that the style is not offbeat enough to be his. This leaves Mill (E) and Newman (C). If you knew no more, guess. However, you should know just enough about Mill and Newman to make the correct distinction. Both were in some sense reformers, but of the two, only Mill would say that the object of his life was to be the reformer of the world.

John Stuart Mill was one of the leading thinkers of the Victorian Age right from his youth. His major works (for the test) are "What Is Poetry?," *On Liberty*, *The Subjection of Women*, and *Autobiography*. Key terms and names are utilitarianism (Mill's father, James, was a prominent utilitarian), Jeremy Bentham, and individualism. Much of Mill's writing concerns the importance of an individual's rights in relation to the demands of the State. Finally, you should know that Mill suffered from an extreme depression as a young man. In struggling with that depression, he revised many of his philosophical views. The passage is drawn from the chapter in *Autobiography* in which he discusses that depression.

John Henry Newman is often referred to as Cardinal Newman; he became a Roman Catholic Cardinal in 1879. Another important Victorian thinker, he wrote an influential book called *Apologia Pro Vita Sua* and also *The Idea of a University*. In both works, the style is one of clear, dispassionately logical reasoning. *The Idea of a University* champions the virtues of a liberal arts education. *Apologia* is a reasoned account of his life and the social and spiritual reflections that led to his conversion to the Roman Catholic faith. For much of his life, Newman had been a highly regarded Anglican clergyman.

A question concerning either Newman or Mill is not unlikely at all. Knowing just a little about them should be worth a point.

182. **B** This is straight reading comprehension. The passage is a poem by the Elizabethan George Gascoigne called "For That He Looked Not Upon Her." You should recognize the form as a Shakespearean (or English) sonnet. Gascoigne is not a poet you need concern yourself with for the GRE Literature in English Subject Test.

183. **E** This question shouldn't be too difficult because the paired names in the answer choices are distinct enough that you only need to recognize one of the two in the correct pair, Chatterton and Rimbaud, in order to come up with the correct response. You should know that in the 1760s, Thomas Chatterton fabricated the poems of fictional poets of earlier times, the best of the poems being "by" a fictional fifteenth-century monk, Thomas Rowley. Chatterton went so far as to forge supporting documents, such as correspondence and titles. Not until the late nineteenth century was this hoax conclusively settled, and Chatterton revealed as the author of the poems and documents. Chatterton killed himself at 18, apparently in despair at his poverty, although adolescent geniuses who fabricate the entire lives of fifteenth-century monastic poets no doubt have much to contend with already. The youngster's genius, hubris, and, one suspects, poverty made Chatterton a favorite of the Romantics.

Arthur Rimbaud was not merely a prodigy but also by any standards a great poet and important literary innovator. His colorful and profoundly rebellious life included telling (while still in his teens) eminent poets to their faces that their work was *merde*. Rimbaud does show up from time to time on the GRE Literature in English Subject Test. Know that as a theorist, his mounting disgust with the poetry of his contemporaries led him to formulate a program for becoming more than a poet. He decided to become a visionary, a seer. To that end, he practiced a "derangement of the senses," through alcohol, drugs, and debauchery. He abandoned poetry at some point in his twenties (or perhaps as early as 19) and, after a series of adventures and misadventures, became an unsuccessful and semi-legitimate trader in North Africa. Gravely ill, he returned to France, where he died at 37 in 1891.

(A) Some of the names in the incorrect answer choices may be unfamiliar. François Villon is known as the poet of the seedy, seamy side of life in medieval Paris. Though educated, he enjoyed thieving, drinking, prostitutes, and living against the grain. He popped in and out of jail, some of his best poetry being witty excoriations of jailers he detested. There is no record of his death, but we can be sure it wasn't of old age. Villon can be thought of as a real-life Sir John Falstaff without the beer gut and with a wicked pen.

(B) John Clare is a minor Romantic poet who came from a rural lower-class background, a fact which made him an instant hit with the fashionable London literati, who typically extolled the intrinsically poetic nature of just such rustics. After a brief period of literary success, Clare went mad, though he continued to write good poetry from the mental institution.

Radiguet refers to Raymond Radiguet, that rarest of creatures—the teenage novelist of genius. Radiguet, a Frenchman, died in the influenza epidemic that swept Europe (and to a lesser degree, the United States) following World War I. He is not of great importance to the GRE Literature in English Subject Test.

184. **A** Names are the only key here. All the names listed are ones with which you should very definitely be familiar for the GRE Literature in English Subject Test.

Tom and Daisy should immediately call up two of the main characters from F. Scott Fitzgerald's *The Great Gatsby*. Knowing that,

you would then look for another character created by Fitzgerald. Amory Blaine should sound like a Fitzgerald character even if you didn't recognize him from *This Side of Paradise*. Fitzgerald's characters are almost always upper class East-Coasters with names to match. His names are evocative, much like Dickens's.

(B) Jake Barnes is one of the main characters from Hemingway's *The Sun Also Rises*.

(C) Flem Snopes (and anyone with the last name of Snopes or Compson) is a character from Faulkner's Yoknapatawpha County novels and stories.

(D) Tom Joad is a significant character from John Steinbeck's *The Grapes of Wrath*.

(E) Sally Bowles is one of the main characters in Christopher Isherwood's *Berlin Stories*.

185. **C** The passage is discussed in the explanation to question 186.

186. **B** This is the first stanza of an untitled poem by W. H. Auden. It is one of his more famous compositions. Auden is remarkable for his ability to take the somewhat too-pat (to contemporary ears) rhythms and rhymes of earlier poetic forms, and rehabilitate them—through delicate modulations, half-rhymes, near rhymes, eye-rhymes, and enjambments—producing formal poetry of astonishing grace. The poem from which the stanza is excerpted is just such a *tour de force*. Its seemingly natural lines hold to an exacting scheme. The poem is a triumph of artifice over intuition and an excellent example of how structure can empower rather than limit a poet.

You might have eliminated Hopkins (D), because the poem lacks Hopkins's sprung rhythm and the energetic cadences typical of his approach. Similarly, you might have eliminated Stevens (E), because the poem lacks the modernist weirdness of Stevens's work. Unsettling ambiguities, arresting images, and peculiar syntax are the hallmarks of Stevens's style. Because this brief description might apply to any number of poets, we recommend you look over some of Stevens's poetry. He is important for your purposes on the GRE Literature in English Subject Test, and very little studying will suitably acquaint you with his style.

You might have eliminated both Swinburne (C) and Housman (A), because of the verse forms each employed. Swinburne and Housman typically use the very regular meter and rhyme schemes that modernists like Auden are in reaction against.

187. **D** The passage gives a reasonable portrait of James Baldwin's political and artistic convictions. You should know that Baldwin and Richard Wright (the author of *Native Son*) had a rancorous dispute (the rancor coming primarily from Baldwin in his collection of essays *Notes of a Native Son*) about the role a prominent black artist should most properly take amidst the racial divisions of the United States.

188. **B** All of the authors in the answer choices are twentieth-century writers known for their individually innovative, unconventional narrative approaches. You should be able to spot Gertrude Stein here by the name Melanctha, the title of one of the stories in *Three Lives*, and by her deliberate sing-song hypnotic anti-literary repetitions. Stein's writing nearly always calls attention to itself as writing, foregrounding the words until conventional meaning and narrative threaten to fly away, or, in her most radical works, such as *Tender Buttons*, meaning seems beside the point. Whatever you think of Stein's writing, it matters for the GRE Literature in English Subject Test.

189. **C** The passage is of course from Shakespeare, which would rule out (E), Marlowe's *Tamburlaine*. Placing the excerpt as a historical drama would rule out the *Two Gentlemen of Verona* and *Much Ado About Nothing*. This leaves *Henry V* and *Richard II*.

Henry V centers around the battle of Agincourt, which the English, led by Henry, won despite the heavy odds against them. Note the men-

tion of "this wooden O." The speaker is referring to the Globe theater itself. This is just the sort of thing ETS loves to ask about. The passage is from the prologue of *Henry V*.

190. **D** The question is fairly straightforward and shouldn't have posed too much difficulty if you have any familiarity with Shakespeare. If not, remember: A little practice goes a long way on this test.

The speaker directly refers to the play's violation of the unities of space and time. Elizabethans didn't give a fig about the unities, and the prologue is at least partly an excuse to get the groundlings pumped up about the truly heroic battle of Agincourt they're about to see staged. It's a little like the trailer for a movie, or the teaser on the back of a cheesy paperback, except in deathless verse.

191. **D** The passage is from Thomas Carew's "An Elegy upon the Death of the Dean of Paul's, Dr. John Donne." To answer this question, you need to get from the passage that the poet eulogized had a laudably direct, unpretentious style, and abstained from classical references. Of the choices given, this description would sensibly apply only to Donne.

192. **A** Ovid is the author of *Metamorphoses*.

193. **B** The violence expressed in the passage is characteristic of Peter Shaffer's "Equus," a play about a teenager who sadistically and inexplicably blinds horses. Arthur Miller (A) is best known, of course, for "Death of a Salesman" and "The Crucible." John Guare's plays (C) erode the boundaries of traditional realistic drama. Romulus Linney's plays (D) are characterized by an almost impenetrable southern regional dialect. Tom Stoppard's plays (E) are almost equally impenetrable for their intellectual explorations of advanced physics, ancient poetry, and the nature of love.

Questions 194–197
The correct answers are as follows: **194 is (E), 195 is (A), 196 is (B), 197 is (C).**

The passages provide mighty slim pickings, but all the same there is just enough to answer the questions. Telemachus is the son of Ulysses; only (E) mentions a son. George Etherege is a Restoration playwright; you should recognize Dorimant and Loveit (A) as characters from Restoration comedy (even if not from the specific play from which they are drawn, Etherege's *The Man of Mode*). (B) discusses Persia; that makes it the choice for Alexander. Orpheus is known for his miraculous lyre—this makes choice (C) clearly the correct match.

Here are the answer choices' sources:

(A) is from Dryden's *Mac Flecknoe*.

(B) is from Dryden's *Alexander's Feast*.

(C) is from Dryden's "A Song for St. Cecilia's Day."

(D) is from Matthew Arnold's "Shakespeare."

(E) is from Tennyson's "Ulysses."

198. **B** This question calls on your knowledge of the biographical details of Oscar Wilde's life (Wilde is the author of the passage). You should know that his scandalous relationship with the feckless Lord Alfred Douglas (a.k.a. "Bosie") led to Wilde's imprisonment.

199. **E** The passage gives not merely an example of the pathetic fallacy but is in fact excerpted from the passage by Ruskin wherein that critic first defines the concept. The pathetic fallacy is the attribution of emotional states to inanimate objects based on the feelings of the observer of those objects.

200. **A** See notes to question 199.

201. **B** The passage is from a letter by Charles Lamb. Even if you didn't know that, you should have noticed that the person to whom the letter was sent loved wandering in "groves and valleys." From this, you ought then to have guessed Wordsworth.

202. **E** If you were able to get Wordsworth in question 201, then you should use POE to arrive at

a good guess here by eliminating authors who could not have corresponded with Wordsworth. Herrick, Sterne, and Swift can be eliminated, because they are from earlier periods. Ruskin is somewhat too late a figure, and the tone is also wrong for Ruskin, especially as a much younger man addressing the poet laureate of England.

Questions 203–206

The correct answers are as follows: **203 is (B), 204 is (D), 205 is (A), 206 is (C)**. James's novella *The Turn of the Screw* is often studied and turns up fairly frequently on the GRE Literature in English Subject Test. The story is told by an English governess who attends to a pair of young children at a country estate. The children, Miles and Flora, seem to be haunted by the ghosts of two former employees, Peter Quint and Miss Jessel. A strong aura of sexual perversity and sexual hysteria pervades the story and its involvement with the children. It is never quite certain that the haunting is real, yet neither is it certain that the governess is crazy. James's achievement in producing this ambiguity and the powerful undertow of sexual anxiety are what make this work so often discussed.

(B) Melville's *Moby-Dick* is discussed in the entry on Melville in the C list, page 124.

(D) Poe's "Hop-Frog" is the story of a malicious dwarf jester named Hop-Frog. No single story or work of Poe's can be singled out for study. Although you may see a question, the points-to-pages ratio is very low. We don't recommend brushing up on Poe, except in the unlikely case that you know absolutely nothing about him.

(E) Charlotte Perkins Gilman's "The Yellow Wallpaper" (1892) is a rediscovered feminist classic. The first-person story draws on gothic conventions to narrate the mental decline of a woman taken by her physician husband to an isolated estate to undergo a "rest cure" for her neurasthenia. Gilman's feminist utopian novel *Herland*, about three male social scientists stranded in a blissful all-female society, is another work that may show up on the Literature in English Subject Test.

207. **D** The Bible questions tend to refer to the most well-known stories, as question 207 does. Note that not only is the passage a well-known one, but the incorrect answer choices refer to well-known narratives from the Old Testament. The GRE Literature in English Subject Test tends to have two Bible questions, an easy one and a medium-to-hard one. Question 207 is the easy one. You should be able to get the easy one without any study. The hard one requires more study than is worth the effort for your purposes on this test; your time could be better spent elsewhere.

208. **A** The phrase "some hideous secret" should suggest the themes of Nathaniel Hawthorne's *The Scarlet Letter*. Dimmesdale and Chillingworth are the main male characters of Hawthorne's *The Scarlet Letter*. (Hester Prynne is the female protagonist who bears the scarlet letter.) Dimmesdale is the philandering reverend who impregnates Hester. Chillingworth, incognito as the doctor, is the lawful husband of Hester Prynne.

Here are the sources for the other answer choices:

(B) Silas Marner and Eppie are the principal characters of George Eliot's *Silas Marner*. Eppie is the lovely foundling girl who (eventually) brings joy and warmth into the life of the lonely, miserly old man who takes her in, Silas Marner.

(C) Heathcliff and Lockwood are characters from Emily Brontë's *Wuthering Heights*. Heathcliff is the darkly passionate and proud foundling boy whose disastrous romance with Catherine Earnshaw, a natural daughter of Heathcliff's adoptive father, is the book's subject. Lockwood, a somewhat dopey tenant of nearby Thrushcross grange, is the narrator who provides our entry into the story, which is later taken up by other narrators through found manuscripts, diaries, recollections, etc.,

in a weave of superbly handled flashback.

(D) Frank Churchill and Mr. Woodhouse are characters from Jane Austen's *Emma*. The novel is a delicate satire of the manners of the English gentry, set around the match-making attempts and missteps of "Emma Woodhouse, handsome, clever, and rich, with a comfortable home and happy disposition. . . ." The quote just given constitutes the celebrated opening of that novel.

(E) Lydgate and Casaubon are principal characters from George Eliot's *Middlemarch*. The novel centers around Dorothea Brooke and the town of Middlemarch. Casaubon is Dorothea's first husband, a scholar of large erudition but little talent. Their marriage is a failure. Lydgate is a socially prominent doctor whose reputation is sullied by shady financial dealings.

All the works mentioned are of significance to the GRE Literature in English Subject Test.

Questions 209–212

The correct answers are as follows: **209 is (B), 210 is (D), 211 is (A), 212 is (C)**.

These should have been a snap, because knowing any two of the questions would leave you with a manageable process of elimination for the rest. Too bad there are no bonus points for knowing the source of answer choice (E), which comes from Yeats's "The Second Coming," a poem you should be familiar with in its entirety. It contains several of the best-known (and oft-cited) lines in modern poetry: "Things fall apart; the center cannot hold." "The best lack all conviction, while the worst/Are full of passionate intensity." "And what rough beast, its hour come round at last/ Slouches towards Bethlehem to be born?"

213. **E** You should know that Milton's *Paradise Lost* has been faulted for its tangled syntax (several commentators have felt that *Paradise Lost* pushes the limits of the English sentence perhaps too far), and here, as Johnson notes, it has some dull stretches as well.

214. **A** The passage describes W.E.B. Du Bois. See the explanations to question 80 for more on Du Bois. Claude McKay (B) was also an African-American radical, but he was famous for his poetry and his ardent socialism. James Baldwin (C) never went to college. His history as a preacher can be seen in the cadence of his prose. Charles Waddell Chesnutt (D) received no formal education and died in 1932; he is therefore not a contemporary of Booker T. Washington. Jean Toomer (E) is known for his novel *Cane* and is a religious philosopher and poet.

215. **B** Antigone is the daughter of Oedipus who is condemned to death for defying an order to leave her brother ("my mother's son") unburied, which should be a huge arrow in the direction of answer (B). (For more background, refer back to pages 100–101).

(A) For an explanation of Jason and Medea, refer back to the explanation for question 45. Here, we'll just say that Jason does not consider death a friend, nor does he mourn a brother.

(C) Oedipus is also discussed in detail on pages 100–101. He murders his father and marries his mother; there is plenty of angst, but none is about a brother.

(D) Clytemnestra and Agamemnon are from the House of Atreus (refer back to the family tree on page 99). She is killed out of revenge by her son, Orestes; again, there is no brother mentioned.

(E) Lampito and Lysistrata are characters from the eponymous comedy. This passage has nothing comedic about it.

216. **C** The key here is to read the passage all the way through, and thus avoid being trapped by the first line's mention of the Bishop of Canterbury. The later mention of Mordred and King Arthur are giveaways that the passage is from *Le Morte D'Arthur*.

217. **E** This is a very tricky question, and the distinctions being made are somewhat subjective. Essentially, the line in question uses synaesthesia. The color of the sky is described as "hot." When senses cross domains, as here touch and vision do, the figure of speech employed is synaesthesia. (E), in which laughter is described in purely visual terms, is a clear example of this rhetorical effect.

(A) is simply figurative language.

(B) is an example of a relatively obscure type of punning called zeugma, in which a verb is called upon for double duty. Here, "stain" is used metaphorically (with "honour") and literally (with "brocade").

(C) is a metaphor.

(D) is a weak example of synecdoche, in which a significant and closely associated part of something is made to stand for the whole. Here the face of Helen of Troy is made to stand for the whole woman, and the forces that brought about the Trojan War. A better example would be the military sense of "brass," for officers, or "hands," for sailors (e.g., "all hands on deck"). Synecdoche and its nearly synonymous sister metonymy are terms you should be familiar with for the GRE Literature in English Subject Test. Don't worry about differentiating between metonymy and synecdoche for the test.

218. **B** This passage, along with Marvell's "To His Coy Mistress," and Gray's "Elegy Written in a Country Church-Yard," is a must-know. The lines to know are, "Come live with me and be my love/And we will all the pleasures prove." They are the opening lines of Marlowe's "The Passionate Shepherd to His Love." In response to the Marlowe poem, Walter Raleigh composed "The Nymph's Reply to the Passionate Shepherd."

Questions 219–221

The correct answers are as follows: **219 is (E), 220 is (B), 221 is (C).**

You need to recognize that Calypso's cave appears in *The Odyssey*, that Agamemnon is of the House of Atreus, and that the riddling sphinx and city of Thebes are found in the Oedipus story. See Chapter 6 if you didn't catch these references. (A) is from Edna St. Vincent Millay's poem "I Dreamed I Moved Among the Elysian Field," a fantasy wherein Millay meets women of myth. (D) is Percy Shelley's "Adonais XXXVI," an elegy to John Keats.

222. **A** Here you need to recognize the name Nora, or recognize that *A Doll's House* concerns a woman who ultimately leaves her husband and children. Ibsen's drama is associated with the phrase "problem play," which refers to a drama that centers around a social problem. In *A Doll's House,* Ibsen fashions a drama from the tensions between a woman longing for some freedom from her role as parlor-wife and the repressive, selfish husband who doesn't understand.

223. **D** You need to recognize the name Hans Castorp as belonging to one of the main characters of Mann's *The Magic Mountain*. You might also have eliminated (B), (C), and (E), because the subject of the passage has little to do with the concerns of the authors mentioned in those choices. Neither Céline, Nabokov, nor Kafka wrote works that offer the promise of hope through experience.

Remarque (A) is not an author likely to appear on the test.

224. **C** This question is a simple matter of identifying a well-known quote from Emerson.

225. **A** You should recognize the source of (A), which is Walt Whitman's *Song of Myself.*

Here are the sources of the incorrect answers:

(B) is from Robert Burns's "The Cotter's Saturday Night."

(C) is the opening of Dryden's *Mac Flecknoe.*

(D) is the closing of Tennyson's "Crossing the Bar."

(E) is the couplet that closes Shakespeare's ninety-fourth sonnet.

226. **E** You need to know that Gerard Manley Hopkins is the poet who formalized the concept of sprung rhythm, which is the metrical principal of organizing lines based on the number of stressed syllables they contain; the unstressed syllables are not taken into account.

227. **D** See the note to question 226.

228. **C** This question, like question 230, tests your ability to identify the poet Walt Whitman. Many of the hallmarks of his distinctive style are present in this passage, most notably an exuberant diction and rhythm, and exceptionally long individual lines of free verse that repeat words and phrases (indeed, Whitman's characteristic repetitions are often more pronounced than in the selection given). Once Whitman, that most American of poets, is identified, it should be easy to then eliminate the incorrect answer choices—(A), (B), (D), and (E)—because they pertain to areas (Europe and the American Midwest) not associated with Whitman. His birthplace is Brooklyn, and the selection is from "Crossing Brooklyn Ferry."

You should also be aware that much of Whitman's poetry celebrates the fellowship of humanity, often in the context of the Civil War.

Even without identifying Whitman, you might have eliminated choices (A) and (E), because the Thames in London and the Mississippi in St. Louis have no noticeable "flood-tide."

229. **B** The only difficulty here is avoiding over-interpretation, which will have you searching for allusions and references that simply aren't there.

230. **A** This is a straightforward identification problem. The explanation to question 228 provides tips for identifying Whitman.

Paying for
Graduate School 101

You've been to college. You've got the degree (and the student loans) to show for it. Now that you're thinking of going to grad school, you're probably wondering if you really need to go through all the financial shenanigans again.

Yes. You do.

More Great Titles from The Princeton Review
1,014 GRE Practice Questions

Graduate School Companion

There are significant differences in the aid available for undergrads and graduate students. You're not becoming a freshman again, are you? So why assume that lenders are going to treat you like a freshman?

Unfortunately, your educational status isn't the only thing that's changed in the past year or so. When there's an elephant in the room, it's best to just admit it: The economy stinks. As 2008 came to an end, the United States' economy went into sharp decline. The economic downturn has put a serious cramp on the finances of most colleges and universities. Before the close of 2008, Harvard's endowment took an $8 billion hit. Ouch!

This would, in and of itself, be bad news. But it gets worse. Sketchy lending practices on the part of federally insured banks were a major, if not the primary, cause of this mess. Consequently, private lenders are becoming more and more stingy about who they'll lend to.

There. Now that we've gotten all the bad news out in the open, let's focus on the positive.

There are still numerous financing alternatives out there. Private lenders *are* still willing to take risks on graduate students, schools are still offering scholarships and other forms of aid, and, in recent years, the federal government has actually boosted federal aid to students. To find the aid you need, all it takes is a bit of determination.

You're Not an Undergrad Anymore.

Okay. So there was that guy you knew in school who was entering his fifth, sixth, seventh, or even eighth year as an undergrad and referring it as his "post-grad year." But, in the real world, graduate school isn't just an extension of your undergraduate experience. Not only are your studies going to be completely different, but your circumstances aren't the same either. You might be coming to grad school after a few years in the professional world. You might need to hold down a job at the same time as you pursue your degree. You may have a family now. Whatever the changes, you need to take these factors into account when figuring out how you're going to pay for school.

You aren't the only one who will notice your changed circumstance. With rare exceptions, government and private lenders are going to treat you as financially independent. When you were an undergrad, your parents' credit history was the chief factor in determining how much of a loan risk you were. Now, lenders will be looking squarely at *your* credit history. If your credit history leaves something to be desired, private lenders will most likely require a co-signer.

NON-LOAN OPTIONS

Here's the first rule of post-grad financing: Exhaust every non-loan option you can before looking for a loan. Non-loan options include employer-financed opportunities, scholarships and grants, and various fellowship or stipend programs. These may not get you all the way through school, but every bit helps and these options are as close to "free money" as you can get.

Employer-financed opportunities

If you're currently employed, check your benefits package to see if your company will help with financing any continuing education programs. Many employers recognize that an advanced degree will improve employee performance, so they're willing to kick in on the cost. Keep in mind, though, that this help often comes with certain conditions. For example, some employers will expect you to commit to staying with the company a specific number of years after you get your degree. If you're going back to school in order to change careers, this might not be the best option for you. Investigate your employer's tuition reimbursement program before signing on.

Scholarships and grants

These are the "get-out-of-jail-free cards" of financial aid. You don't have to pay them back. However, scholarships and grants often come with a slew of qualifications, such as maintaining a specified minimum GPA throughout grad school. Furthermore, in a tight economy, the competition for scholarships will intensify. Many scholarships are funded by private donors. In the current economic environment, many of these donors will be less generous with their funds. Finally, remember that some grants come with a time limit—they run out, even if you're still in school. When evaluating your payment options, keep any time limits in mind.

Caveats aside, apply for any grant or scholarship you think you might be qualified for. The worst they can do is say no, and the award of any grant or scholarship money will be a step in the right direction.

Check out the Scholarship Search Page
PrincetonReview.com/ scholarships-financial-aid .aspx

Fellowships, stipends, and assistantships

Fellowships, stipends, and assistantships are other options available to grad students. As with scholarships and grants, you will not be required to pay this money back. As with scholarships and grants, however, there are many common restrictions on this sort of aid. Usually these awards take the form of some sort of work-for-assistance deal. You will be required to earn the award by leading classes as a teaching assistant, helping faculty members with their research, or similar activities—chances are, you'll spend a lot of time grading undergraduates' papers. Also, the college or university might deduct the award directly from your tuition, meaning that you get very little say in how the money is spent. Finally, awards of this sort are rarely granted in professional degree programs such as law, business, or medicine.

Not every stipend dollar is equal.
When you're trying to figure out how far non-loan options will take you, be sure you consider the regional differences in cost of living. In a 2008 study, researchers at Harvard adjusted the size of stipends to show their value relative to the region. Adjusting for these regional differences, the researchers found that stipends from schools in relatively inexpensive areas, such as Philadelphia, Baltimore, and Houston, were nearly twice as valuable (they amounted to more buying power) as larger stipends awarded by schools in more expensive regions, such as Santa Barbara and Berkeley. Consider rents, gas prices, and other regional variations in your calculations.

Another important thing to keep in mind is that these awards rarely amount to enough money to cover your entire cost of attendance. In 2008, the single highest graduate student stipend reported was a just over $30,000 a year. Most stipends amount to considerably less. At the University of California, Santa Barbara, with cost of living adjustments figured in, the average stipend amounted to just over $19,000 a year. If that sounds skimpy, wait until tax time rolls around. Fellowships, stipends, and assistantships are considered taxable income. These awards are well worth pursuing, but you need to understand that even if you receive such an award, you will probably also need additional funding from another source.

Federal work-study

One special category of non-loan aid is a federal work-study (FWS) award. Awards through FWS programs are similar to normal assistantships, except that the money you're receiving comes from the federal government, distributed either through your school or work-study employer. FWS awards are granted on the basis of financial need. Work-study jobs can vary, though they tend to emphasize community service and should be relevant to your field of study. You may end up working for your university or the university may have a special deal with a private employer. Work-study jobs must provide compensation at least equal to the federal minimum wage ($7.25 per hour effective July 24, 2009) and can pay more depending on the type of skills and experience required. However, unlike a normal job, your work-study compensation cannot exceed the amount of your reward; that is to say, you'll have to work for the money in the award, but once you've earned that amount, both the job and the award are gone.

LOAN OPTIONS

Once you've exhausted all non-loan options, it is time to start hunting for a loan. There are two main sources of student loans: the federal government and private lenders. Traditionally, government has been the lender of choice for graduate students. Government loans are easy to qualify for and come with very generous interest rates. Private lenders, on the other hand, generally have more restrictive qualifications and offer loans at higher rates of interest. The trade off has always been that money from private lenders usually comes with fewer restrictions on spending, a degree of freedom welcomed by students with families or other important financial obligations.

Federal Loans

In the current economic climate, there are almost no circumstances under which it makes more sense to approach a private lender before going to Uncle Sam. Changes in aid laws have drastically increased the amount of money available for graduate students, and the fixed, low rates the government offers can't be beaten by private lenders. Start by applying for a Stafford loan.

Stafford Loan

Created by the Higher Education Act of 1965, the Stafford loan remains the most popular form of government loan. There are two kinds of Stafford loans: direct Stafford loans, which are administered by the Department of Education, and Federal Family Education Loans (FFEL), which are administered by a private lender bound by the terms the government sets for Stafford loans (these are sometimes called indirect Stafford loans). Both direct and FFEL Stafford loans can be subsidized or unsubsidized. Students with demonstrated financial need may qualify for subsidized loans. This means that the government pays off any interest accumulated during the time the student is in school. Students with unsubsidized Stafford loans are responsible for the interest accumulated while in school.

Direct or FFEL, subsidized or unsubsidized; the qualifications and terms of the Stafford loan are set by the government. Stafford loans are available to all full-time students and most part-time students. Though the terms of the loan are based on demonstrated financial need, lack of need is not considered grounds for rejection. No payment is expected while the student is attending school. The interest rate on Stafford loans has been set at 6.8 percent, a fixed rate for all loans granted prior to 2013.

Depending on financial need, graduate students may be eligible for up to $20,500 a year, $8,500 of which may be subsidized, up to a lifetime cumulative maximum of $138,500 to $224,000. Your field of study will determine your allowable lifetime maximum. Take note: If you took out a Stafford loan to finance your undergraduate education, the amount you borrowed then *is* going to count against your lifetime limit.

To apply for a Stafford loan, you must start by completing the Free Application for Federal Student Aid (FAFSA). This form, along with FAQ pages and other forms of assistance, can be found online at www.fafsa.ed.gov.

Check out our Financial Aid Library
PrincetonReview.com/
FinancialAidAdvice.aspx

Direct Plus Loans for Graduate and Professional Students

Sometimes called GradPLUS loans, these fixed rate loans have no fixed annual or lifetime borrowing limits. Instead, the limit for each borrower is based on the cost of attendance minus any other financial aid you may receive. GradPLUS loans have a fixed 7.9 percent interest rate. There is also a 4 percent loan fee that the Department of Education will deduct from the principle of the loan. Most borrowers will be eligible to delay payment on their GradPLUS loan until after graduation.

Eligibility is determined by your credit history, so make sure you've got your finances as tidy as you can get them. To apply for a GradPLUS loan you must complete and submit both the standard Free Application for Federal Student Aid (FAFSA) and a Federal Direct PLUS Loan Application and Master Promissory Note (PLUS MPN). Both forms can be found online at www.fafsa.ed.gov and https://dlenote.ed.gov/empn/index.jsp.

Perkins Loan

A Perkins loan is a fixed interest loan that is made through the financial aid office of your school using government funds provided to the school. Perkins loans are need-based and intended to help students in extreme financial straits. Borrowers can receive up to $8,000 per year, with a lifetime total of $60,000 (as with the Stafford loan, this will include any undergrad borrowing you may have done). Perkins loans have a fixed 5 percent interest rate. Your window for paying the loan back will be determined by the number of courses you're taking. In general, part-time students have nine months from their graduation date before beginning repayment. Because schools act as the lenders of Perkins loans, see your school's financial office for directions on how to apply.

Private Lenders

If this section had been written a few years ago, we would have started off with a discussion of common criticisms of the federal loan system. Then we would have mentioned a few private lenders who were fighting what they believed was the good fight against a government-subsidized monopoly. Whether or not this critique was valid, the sudden collapse of the housing bubble, spurred on in no small part by shoddy lending practices from major banks, has made the argument irrelevant.

We said it before, and we'll say it again: DO NOT get a private loan until you've exhausted all other options.

Before the crisis, many private lenders could offer competitive interest rates and relatively generous qualification standards. Now, for the most part, that's no longer the case. Borrowers with credit scores lower than 700 will find themselves fighting an uphill battle. Furthermore, the average interest rate for private loans hovers around 13 percent (compared to the 6.8 percent of the Stafford loan).

Still, there are some benefits to securing a private loan. First off, many students find that non-loan

Know your credit rating.

Private lenders will judge you by your credit rating. To get a credit report, contact a credit-reporting agency, such as TransUnion or Equifax. There will be four sections of your credit report: a profile of personal information; a report of public record defaults, tax liens, and legal decisions against you; a record of companies that have requested your credit report; and a credit rating. Your credit rating will be a number between 300 and 850. Most people have a credit rating between 600 and 700. To improve your credit rating:

1. Pay your bills on time—this boosts your credit rating more than anything else.
2. Pay down as much debt as you can.
3. Keep open any paid off accounts, but don't apply for credit you don't need.
4. Get credit counseling if you need it.
5. Avoid bankruptcy if at all possible— filing for bankruptcy can knock more than 200 points from your credit score.

and federal loan options do not end up covering the entire bill. If that's the case, then private lenders just might save the day. Second, loans from private sources generally offer you greater flexibility with how you can use the funds. Third, private loans can be taken out at anytime during your academic career. Unlike most non-loan and government-backed financial options, you can turn to private lenders whenever you need them.

All private lenders are not the same! As the old song says, "You better shop around." Every lender is going to offer you a different package of terms. What you need to do is find the package that best fits your needs and plans. Aside from low interest rates, which are crucially important, there are some other terms and conditions you will want to look out for.

Cosigner benefits   In the face of the credit crunch, many lenders are increasingly strict about who they will lend money to. These days, many lenders will reject outright any student loan applications that lack cosigners. On the bright side, some lenders will offer you more generous terms, including reduced rates and fees, if you can produce a cosigner.

Low origination fees   Origination fees are fees that lenders charge you for taking out a loan. Usually the fee is simply deducted automatically from your loan checks. Obviously, the lower the origination fee, the better.

Minimal guaranty fees   A guaranty fee is an amount you pay to a third-party who agrees to insure your loan. That way, if the borrower—that is you—can't pay the loan back, the guarantor steps in and pays the difference. Again, if you can minimize or eliminate this fee, all the better.

Interest rate reductions   Some lenders will reduce your interest rates if you're reliable with your payments. Some will even agree to knock a little off the interest rate if you agree to pay your loans through a direct deposit system. When shopping for the best loan, pay careful attention to factors that might help you curb your interest rates.

Flexible payment plans   One of the great things about most federal loans is the fact that you don't have to start paying them off until you leave school. In order to compete, many private lenders have been forced to adopt similarly flexible payment plans. Before saying yes to a private loan, make sure that it comes with a payment timetable you can live with.

WHERE THERE'S A WILL THERE'S A WAY

Despite the economic downturn, going to grad school still makes good financial sense. When hiring slows down, what better place to be than in the classroom, getting ready for the inevitable upswing? And, especially with federal assistance programs, you'll find that there are still plenty of excellent financing options available. Be smart, be frugal, and you'll be able to pay your way without breaking the bank.

1

YOUR NAME: _____
(Print)   Last   First   M.I.

SIGNATURE: _____   DATE: __ / __ / __

HOME ADDRESS: _____
(Print)   Number and Street

_____
City   State   Zip Code

PHONE NO.: _____
(Print)

IMPORTANT: Please fill in these boxes exactly as shown on the back cover of your test book.

2. TEST FORM

_____

3. TEST CODE   4. REGISTRATION NUMBER

⊂0⊃	⊂A⊃	⊂0⊃	⊂0⊃	⊂0⊃	⊂0⊃	⊂0⊃	⊂0⊃	⊂0⊃	⊂0⊃	⊂0⊃
⊂1⊃	⊂B⊃	⊂1⊃	⊂1⊃	⊂1⊃	⊂1⊃	⊂1⊃	⊂1⊃	⊂1⊃	⊂1⊃	⊂1⊃
⊂2⊃	⊂C⊃	⊂2⊃	⊂2⊃	⊂2⊃	⊂2⊃	⊂2⊃	⊂2⊃	⊂2⊃	⊂2⊃	⊂2⊃
⊂3⊃	⊂D⊃	⊂3⊃	⊂3⊃	⊂3⊃	⊂3⊃	⊂3⊃	⊂3⊃	⊂3⊃	⊂3⊃	⊂3⊃
⊂4⊃	⊂E⊃	⊂4⊃	⊂4⊃	⊂4⊃	⊂4⊃	⊂4⊃	⊂4⊃	⊂4⊃	⊂4⊃	⊂4⊃
⊂5⊃	⊂F⊃	⊂5⊃	⊂5⊃	⊂5⊃	⊂5⊃	⊂5⊃	⊂5⊃	⊂5⊃	⊂5⊃	⊂5⊃
⊂6⊃	⊂G⊃	⊂6⊃	⊂6⊃	⊂6⊃	⊂6⊃	⊂6⊃	⊂6⊃	⊂6⊃	⊂6⊃	⊂6⊃
⊂7⊃		⊂7⊃	⊂7⊃	⊂7⊃	⊂7⊃	⊂7⊃	⊂7⊃	⊂7⊃	⊂7⊃	⊂7⊃
⊂8⊃		⊂8⊃	⊂8⊃	⊂8⊃	⊂8⊃	⊂8⊃	⊂8⊃	⊂8⊃	⊂8⊃	⊂8⊃
⊂9⊃		⊂9⊃	⊂9⊃	⊂9⊃	⊂9⊃	⊂9⊃	⊂9⊃	⊂9⊃	⊂9⊃	⊂9⊃

6. DATE OF BIRTH

Month	Day		Year	
⊂ ⊃ JAN				
⊂ ⊃ FEB				
⊂ ⊃ MAR	⊂0⊃	⊂0⊃	⊂0⊃	⊂0⊃
⊂ ⊃ APR	⊂1⊃	⊂1⊃	⊂1⊃	⊂1⊃
⊂ ⊃ MAY	⊂2⊃	⊂2⊃	⊂2⊃	⊂2⊃
⊂ ⊃ JUN	⊂3⊃	⊂3⊃	⊂3⊃	⊂3⊃
⊂ ⊃ JUL		⊂4⊃	⊂4⊃	⊂4⊃
⊂ ⊃ AUG		⊂5⊃	⊂5⊃	⊂5⊃
⊂ ⊃ SEP		⊂6⊃	⊂6⊃	⊂6⊃
⊂ ⊃ OCT		⊂7⊃	⊂7⊃	⊂7⊃
⊂ ⊃ NOV		⊂8⊃	⊂8⊃	⊂8⊃
⊂ ⊃ DEC		⊂9⊃	⊂9⊃	⊂9⊃

7. SEX
⊂ ⊃ MALE
⊂ ⊃ FEMALE

The Princeton Review
© 1995 The Princeton Review
FORM NO. 00001-PR

5. YOUR NAME

First 4 letters of last name				FIRST INIT	MID INIT
⊂A⊃	⊂A⊃	⊂A⊃	⊂A⊃	⊂A⊃	⊂A⊃
⊂B⊃	⊂B⊃	⊂B⊃	⊂B⊃	⊂B⊃	⊂B⊃
⊂C⊃	⊂C⊃	⊂C⊃	⊂C⊃	⊂C⊃	⊂C⊃
⊂D⊃	⊂D⊃	⊂D⊃	⊂D⊃	⊂D⊃	⊂D⊃
⊂E⊃	⊂E⊃	⊂E⊃	⊂E⊃	⊂E⊃	⊂E⊃
⊂F⊃	⊂F⊃	⊂F⊃	⊂F⊃	⊂F⊃	⊂F⊃
⊂G⊃	⊂G⊃	⊂G⊃	⊂G⊃	⊂G⊃	⊂G⊃
⊂H⊃	⊂H⊃	⊂H⊃	⊂H⊃	⊂H⊃	⊂H⊃
⊂I⊃	⊂I⊃	⊂I⊃	⊂I⊃	⊂I⊃	⊂I⊃
⊂J⊃	⊂J⊃	⊂J⊃	⊂J⊃	⊂J⊃	⊂J⊃
⊂K⊃	⊂K⊃	⊂K⊃	⊂K⊃	⊂K⊃	⊂K⊃
⊂L⊃	⊂L⊃	⊂L⊃	⊂L⊃	⊂L⊃	⊂L⊃
⊂M⊃	⊂M⊃	⊂M⊃	⊂M⊃	⊂M⊃	⊂M⊃
⊂N⊃	⊂N⊃	⊂N⊃	⊂N⊃	⊂N⊃	⊂N⊃
⊂O⊃	⊂O⊃	⊂O⊃	⊂O⊃	⊂O⊃	⊂O⊃
⊂P⊃	⊂P⊃	⊂P⊃	⊂P⊃	⊂P⊃	⊂P⊃
⊂Q⊃	⊂Q⊃	⊂Q⊃	⊂Q⊃	⊂Q⊃	⊂Q⊃
⊂R⊃	⊂R⊃	⊂R⊃	⊂R⊃	⊂R⊃	⊂R⊃
⊂S⊃	⊂S⊃	⊂S⊃	⊂S⊃	⊂S⊃	⊂S⊃
⊂T⊃	⊂T⊃	⊂T⊃	⊂T⊃	⊂T⊃	⊂T⊃
⊂U⊃	⊂U⊃	⊂U⊃	⊂U⊃	⊂U⊃	⊂U⊃
⊂V⊃	⊂V⊃	⊂V⊃	⊂V⊃	⊂V⊃	⊂V⊃
⊂W⊃	⊂W⊃	⊂W⊃	⊂W⊃	⊂W⊃	⊂W⊃
⊂X⊃	⊂X⊃	⊂X⊃	⊂X⊃	⊂X⊃	⊂X⊃
⊂Y⊃	⊂Y⊃	⊂Y⊃	⊂Y⊃	⊂Y⊃	⊂Y⊃
⊂Z⊃	⊂Z⊃	⊂Z⊃	⊂Z⊃	⊂Z⊃	⊂Z⊃

Start with number 1 for each new section. If a section has fewer questions than answer spaces, leave the extra answer spaces blank.

1 ⊂A⊃ ⊂B⊃ ⊂C⊃ ⊂D⊃ ⊂E⊃   21 ⊂A⊃ ⊂B⊃ ⊂C⊃ ⊂D⊃ ⊂E⊃   41 ⊂A⊃ ⊂B⊃ ⊂C⊃ ⊂D⊃ ⊂E⊃   61 ⊂A⊃ ⊂B⊃ ⊂C⊃ ⊂D⊃ ⊂E⊃
2 ⊂A⊃ ⊂B⊃ ⊂C⊃ ⊂D⊃ ⊂E⊃   22 ⊂A⊃ ⊂B⊃ ⊂C⊃ ⊂D⊃ ⊂E⊃   42 ⊂A⊃ ⊂B⊃ ⊂C⊃ ⊂D⊃ ⊂E⊃   62 ⊂A⊃ ⊂B⊃ ⊂C⊃ ⊂D⊃ ⊂E⊃
3 ⊂A⊃ ⊂B⊃ ⊂C⊃ ⊂D⊃ ⊂E⊃   23 ⊂A⊃ ⊂B⊃ ⊂C⊃ ⊂D⊃ ⊂E⊃   43 ⊂A⊃ ⊂B⊃ ⊂C⊃ ⊂D⊃ ⊂E⊃   63 ⊂A⊃ ⊂B⊃ ⊂C⊃ ⊂D⊃ ⊂E⊃
4 ⊂A⊃ ⊂B⊃ ⊂C⊃ ⊂D⊃ ⊂E⊃   24 ⊂A⊃ ⊂B⊃ ⊂C⊃ ⊂D⊃ ⊂E⊃   44 ⊂A⊃ ⊂B⊃ ⊂C⊃ ⊂D⊃ ⊂E⊃   64 ⊂A⊃ ⊂B⊃ ⊂C⊃ ⊂D⊃ ⊂E⊃
5 ⊂A⊃ ⊂B⊃ ⊂C⊃ ⊂D⊃ ⊂E⊃   25 ⊂A⊃ ⊂B⊃ ⊂C⊃ ⊂D⊃ ⊂E⊃   45 ⊂A⊃ ⊂B⊃ ⊂C⊃ ⊂D⊃ ⊂E⊃   65 ⊂A⊃ ⊂B⊃ ⊂C⊃ ⊂D⊃ ⊂E⊃
6 ⊂A⊃ ⊂B⊃ ⊂C⊃ ⊂D⊃ ⊂E⊃   26 ⊂A⊃ ⊂B⊃ ⊂C⊃ ⊂D⊃ ⊂E⊃   46 ⊂A⊃ ⊂B⊃ ⊂C⊃ ⊂D⊃ ⊂E⊃   66 ⊂A⊃ ⊂B⊃ ⊂C⊃ ⊂D⊃ ⊂E⊃
7 ⊂A⊃ ⊂B⊃ ⊂C⊃ ⊂D⊃ ⊂E⊃   27 ⊂A⊃ ⊂B⊃ ⊂C⊃ ⊂D⊃ ⊂E⊃   47 ⊂A⊃ ⊂B⊃ ⊂C⊃ ⊂D⊃ ⊂E⊃   67 ⊂A⊃ ⊂B⊃ ⊂C⊃ ⊂D⊃ ⊂E⊃
8 ⊂A⊃ ⊂B⊃ ⊂C⊃ ⊂D⊃ ⊂E⊃   28 ⊂A⊃ ⊂B⊃ ⊂C⊃ ⊂D⊃ ⊂E⊃   48 ⊂A⊃ ⊂B⊃ ⊂C⊃ ⊂D⊃ ⊂E⊃   68 ⊂A⊃ ⊂B⊃ ⊂C⊃ ⊂D⊃ ⊂E⊃
9 ⊂A⊃ ⊂B⊃ ⊂C⊃ ⊂D⊃ ⊂E⊃   29 ⊂A⊃ ⊂B⊃ ⊂C⊃ ⊂D⊃ ⊂E⊃   49 ⊂A⊃ ⊂B⊃ ⊂C⊃ ⊂D⊃ ⊂E⊃   69 ⊂A⊃ ⊂B⊃ ⊂C⊃ ⊂D⊃ ⊂E⊃
10 ⊂A⊃ ⊂B⊃ ⊂C⊃ ⊂D⊃ ⊂E⊃   30 ⊂A⊃ ⊂B⊃ ⊂C⊃ ⊂D⊃ ⊂E⊃   50 ⊂A⊃ ⊂B⊃ ⊂C⊃ ⊂D⊃ ⊂E⊃   70 ⊂A⊃ ⊂B⊃ ⊂C⊃ ⊂D⊃ ⊂E⊃
11 ⊂A⊃ ⊂B⊃ ⊂C⊃ ⊂D⊃ ⊂E⊃   31 ⊂A⊃ ⊂B⊃ ⊂C⊃ ⊂D⊃ ⊂E⊃   51 ⊂A⊃ ⊂B⊃ ⊂C⊃ ⊂D⊃ ⊂E⊃   71 ⊂A⊃ ⊂B⊃ ⊂C⊃ ⊂D⊃ ⊂E⊃
12 ⊂A⊃ ⊂B⊃ ⊂C⊃ ⊂D⊃ ⊂E⊃   32 ⊂A⊃ ⊂B⊃ ⊂C⊃ ⊂D⊃ ⊂E⊃   52 ⊂A⊃ ⊂B⊃ ⊂C⊃ ⊂D⊃ ⊂E⊃   72 ⊂A⊃ ⊂B⊃ ⊂C⊃ ⊂D⊃ ⊂E⊃
13 ⊂A⊃ ⊂B⊃ ⊂C⊃ ⊂D⊃ ⊂E⊃   33 ⊂A⊃ ⊂B⊃ ⊂C⊃ ⊂D⊃ ⊂E⊃   53 ⊂A⊃ ⊂B⊃ ⊂C⊃ ⊂D⊃ ⊂E⊃   73 ⊂A⊃ ⊂B⊃ ⊂C⊃ ⊂D⊃ ⊂E⊃
14 ⊂A⊃ ⊂B⊃ ⊂C⊃ ⊂D⊃ ⊂E⊃   34 ⊂A⊃ ⊂B⊃ ⊂C⊃ ⊂D⊃ ⊂E⊃   54 ⊂A⊃ ⊂B⊃ ⊂C⊃ ⊂D⊃ ⊂E⊃   74 ⊂A⊃ ⊂B⊃ ⊂C⊃ ⊂D⊃ ⊂E⊃
15 ⊂A⊃ ⊂B⊃ ⊂C⊃ ⊂D⊃ ⊂E⊃   35 ⊂A⊃ ⊂B⊃ ⊂C⊃ ⊂D⊃ ⊂E⊃   55 ⊂A⊃ ⊂B⊃ ⊂C⊃ ⊂D⊃ ⊂E⊃   75 ⊂A⊃ ⊂B⊃ ⊂C⊃ ⊂D⊃ ⊂E⊃
16 ⊂A⊃ ⊂B⊃ ⊂C⊃ ⊂D⊃ ⊂E⊃   36 ⊂A⊃ ⊂B⊃ ⊂C⊃ ⊂D⊃ ⊂E⊃   56 ⊂A⊃ ⊂B⊃ ⊂C⊃ ⊂D⊃ ⊂E⊃   76 ⊂A⊃ ⊂B⊃ ⊂C⊃ ⊂D⊃ ⊂E⊃
17 ⊂A⊃ ⊂B⊃ ⊂C⊃ ⊂D⊃ ⊂E⊃   37 ⊂A⊃ ⊂B⊃ ⊂C⊃ ⊂D⊃ ⊂E⊃   57 ⊂A⊃ ⊂B⊃ ⊂C⊃ ⊂D⊃ ⊂E⊃   77 ⊂A⊃ ⊂B⊃ ⊂C⊃ ⊂D⊃ ⊂E⊃
18 ⊂A⊃ ⊂B⊃ ⊂C⊃ ⊂D⊃ ⊂E⊃   38 ⊂A⊃ ⊂B⊃ ⊂C⊃ ⊂D⊃ ⊂E⊃   58 ⊂A⊃ ⊂B⊃ ⊂C⊃ ⊂D⊃ ⊂E⊃   78 ⊂A⊃ ⊂B⊃ ⊂C⊃ ⊂D⊃ ⊂E⊃
19 ⊂A⊃ ⊂B⊃ ⊂C⊃ ⊂D⊃ ⊂E⊃   39 ⊂A⊃ ⊂B⊃ ⊂C⊃ ⊂D⊃ ⊂E⊃   59 ⊂A⊃ ⊂B⊃ ⊂C⊃ ⊂D⊃ ⊂E⊃   79 ⊂A⊃ ⊂B⊃ ⊂C⊃ ⊂D⊃ ⊂E⊃
20 ⊂A⊃ ⊂B⊃ ⊂C⊃ ⊂D⊃ ⊂E⊃   40 ⊂A⊃ ⊂B⊃ ⊂C⊃ ⊂D⊃ ⊂E⊃   60 ⊂A⊃ ⊂B⊃ ⊂C⊃ ⊂D⊃ ⊂E⊃   80 ⊂A⊃ ⊂B⊃ ⊂C⊃ ⊂D⊃ ⊂E⊃

```
 81 ⊂A⊃ ⊂B⊃ ⊂C⊃ ⊂D⊃ ⊂E⊃       101 ⊂A⊃ ⊂B⊃ ⊂C⊃ ⊂D⊃ ⊂E⊃       121 ⊂A⊃ ⊂B⊃ ⊂C⊃ ⊂D⊃ ⊂E⊃       141 ⊂A⊃ ⊂B⊃ ⊂C⊃ ⊂D⊃ ⊂E⊃
 82 ⊂A⊃ ⊂B⊃ ⊂C⊃ ⊂D⊃ ⊂E⊃       102 ⊂A⊃ ⊂B⊃ ⊂C⊃ ⊂D⊃ ⊂E⊃       122 ⊂A⊃ ⊂B⊃ ⊂C⊃ ⊂D⊃ ⊂E⊃       142 ⊂A⊃ ⊂B⊃ ⊂C⊃ ⊂D⊃ ⊂E⊃
 83 ⊂A⊃ ⊂B⊃ ⊂C⊃ ⊂D⊃ ⊂E⊃       103 ⊂A⊃ ⊂B⊃ ⊂C⊃ ⊂D⊃ ⊂E⊃       123 ⊂A⊃ ⊂B⊃ ⊂C⊃ ⊂D⊃ ⊂E⊃       143 ⊂A⊃ ⊂B⊃ ⊂C⊃ ⊂D⊃ ⊂E⊃
 84 ⊂A⊃ ⊂B⊃ ⊂C⊃ ⊂D⊃ ⊂E⊃       104 ⊂A⊃ ⊂B⊃ ⊂C⊃ ⊂D⊃ ⊂E⊃       124 ⊂A⊃ ⊂B⊃ ⊂C⊃ ⊂D⊃ ⊂E⊃       144 ⊂A⊃ ⊂B⊃ ⊂C⊃ ⊂D⊃ ⊂E⊃
 85 ⊂A⊃ ⊂B⊃ ⊂C⊃ ⊂D⊃ ⊂E⊃       105 ⊂A⊃ ⊂B⊃ ⊂C⊃ ⊂D⊃ ⊂E⊃       125 ⊂A⊃ ⊂B⊃ ⊂C⊃ ⊂D⊃ ⊂E⊃       145 ⊂A⊃ ⊂B⊃ ⊂C⊃ ⊂D⊃ ⊂E⊃
 86 ⊂A⊃ ⊂B⊃ ⊂C⊃ ⊂D⊃ ⊂E⊃       106 ⊂A⊃ ⊂B⊃ ⊂C⊃ ⊂D⊃ ⊂E⊃       126 ⊂A⊃ ⊂B⊃ ⊂C⊃ ⊂D⊃ ⊂E⊃       146 ⊂A⊃ ⊂B⊃ ⊂C⊃ ⊂D⊃ ⊂E⊃
 87 ⊂A⊃ ⊂B⊃ ⊂C⊃ ⊂D⊃ ⊂E⊃       107 ⊂A⊃ ⊂B⊃ ⊂C⊃ ⊂D⊃ ⊂E⊃       127 ⊂A⊃ ⊂B⊃ ⊂C⊃ ⊂D⊃ ⊂E⊃       147 ⊂A⊃ ⊂B⊃ ⊂C⊃ ⊂D⊃ ⊂E⊃
 88 ⊂A⊃ ⊂B⊃ ⊂C⊃ ⊂D⊃ ⊂E⊃       108 ⊂A⊃ ⊂B⊃ ⊂C⊃ ⊂D⊃ ⊂E⊃       128 ⊂A⊃ ⊂B⊃ ⊂C⊃ ⊂D⊃ ⊂E⊃       148 ⊂A⊃ ⊂B⊃ ⊂C⊃ ⊂D⊃ ⊂E⊃
 89 ⊂A⊃ ⊂B⊃ ⊂C⊃ ⊂D⊃ ⊂E⊃       109 ⊂A⊃ ⊂B⊃ ⊂C⊃ ⊂D⊃ ⊂E⊃       129 ⊂A⊃ ⊂B⊃ ⊂C⊃ ⊂D⊃ ⊂E⊃       149 ⊂A⊃ ⊂B⊃ ⊂C⊃ ⊂D⊃ ⊂E⊃
 90 ⊂A⊃ ⊂B⊃ ⊂C⊃ ⊂D⊃ ⊂E⊃       110 ⊂A⊃ ⊂B⊃ ⊂C⊃ ⊂D⊃ ⊂E⊃       130 ⊂A⊃ ⊂B⊃ ⊂C⊃ ⊂D⊃ ⊂E⊃       150 ⊂A⊃ ⊂B⊃ ⊂C⊃ ⊂D⊃ ⊂E⊃
 91 ⊂A⊃ ⊂B⊃ ⊂C⊃ ⊂D⊃ ⊂E⊃       111 ⊂A⊃ ⊂B⊃ ⊂C⊃ ⊂D⊃ ⊂E⊃       131 ⊂A⊃ ⊂B⊃ ⊂C⊃ ⊂D⊃ ⊂E⊃       151 ⊂A⊃ ⊂B⊃ ⊂C⊃ ⊂D⊃ ⊂E⊃
 92 ⊂A⊃ ⊂B⊃ ⊂C⊃ ⊂D⊃ ⊂E⊃       112 ⊂A⊃ ⊂B⊃ ⊂C⊃ ⊂D⊃ ⊂E⊃       132 ⊂A⊃ ⊂B⊃ ⊂C⊃ ⊂D⊃ ⊂E⊃       152 ⊂A⊃ ⊂B⊃ ⊂C⊃ ⊂D⊃ ⊂E⊃
 93 ⊂A⊃ ⊂B⊃ ⊂C⊃ ⊂D⊃ ⊂E⊃       113 ⊂A⊃ ⊂B⊃ ⊂C⊃ ⊂D⊃ ⊂E⊃       133 ⊂A⊃ ⊂B⊃ ⊂C⊃ ⊂D⊃ ⊂E⊃       153 ⊂A⊃ ⊂B⊃ ⊂C⊃ ⊂D⊃ ⊂E⊃
 94 ⊂A⊃ ⊂B⊃ ⊂C⊃ ⊂D⊃ ⊂E⊃       114 ⊂A⊃ ⊂B⊃ ⊂C⊃ ⊂D⊃ ⊂E⊃       134 ⊂A⊃ ⊂B⊃ ⊂C⊃ ⊂D⊃ ⊂E⊃       154 ⊂A⊃ ⊂B⊃ ⊂C⊃ ⊂D⊃ ⊂E⊃
 95 ⊂A⊃ ⊂B⊃ ⊂C⊃ ⊂D⊃ ⊂E⊃       115 ⊂A⊃ ⊂B⊃ ⊂C⊃ ⊂D⊃ ⊂E⊃       135 ⊂A⊃ ⊂B⊃ ⊂C⊃ ⊂D⊃ ⊂E⊃       155 ⊂A⊃ ⊂B⊃ ⊂C⊃ ⊂D⊃ ⊂E⊃
 96 ⊂A⊃ ⊂B⊃ ⊂C⊃ ⊂D⊃ ⊂E⊃       116 ⊂A⊃ ⊂B⊃ ⊂C⊃ ⊂D⊃ ⊂E⊃       136 ⊂A⊃ ⊂B⊃ ⊂C⊃ ⊂D⊃ ⊂E⊃       156 ⊂A⊃ ⊂B⊃ ⊂C⊃ ⊂D⊃ ⊂E⊃
 97 ⊂A⊃ ⊂B⊃ ⊂C⊃ ⊂D⊃ ⊂E⊃       117 ⊂A⊃ ⊂B⊃ ⊂C⊃ ⊂D⊃ ⊂E⊃       137 ⊂A⊃ ⊂B⊃ ⊂C⊃ ⊂D⊃ ⊂E⊃       157 ⊂A⊃ ⊂B⊃ ⊂C⊃ ⊂D⊃ ⊂E⊃
 98 ⊂A⊃ ⊂B⊃ ⊂C⊃ ⊂D⊃ ⊂E⊃       118 ⊂A⊃ ⊂B⊃ ⊂C⊃ ⊂D⊃ ⊂E⊃       138 ⊂A⊃ ⊂B⊃ ⊂C⊃ ⊂D⊃ ⊂E⊃       158 ⊂A⊃ ⊂B⊃ ⊂C⊃ ⊂D⊃ ⊂E⊃
 99 ⊂A⊃ ⊂B⊃ ⊂C⊃ ⊂D⊃ ⊂E⊃       119 ⊂A⊃ ⊂B⊃ ⊂C⊃ ⊂D⊃ ⊂E⊃       139 ⊂A⊃ ⊂B⊃ ⊂C⊃ ⊂D⊃ ⊂E⊃       159 ⊂A⊃ ⊂B⊃ ⊂C⊃ ⊂D⊃ ⊂E⊃
100 ⊂A⊃ ⊂B⊃ ⊂C⊃ ⊂D⊃ ⊂E⊃       120 ⊂A⊃ ⊂B⊃ ⊂C⊃ ⊂D⊃ ⊂E⊃       140 ⊂A⊃ ⊂B⊃ ⊂C⊃ ⊂D⊃ ⊂E⊃       160 ⊂A⊃ ⊂B⊃ ⊂C⊃ ⊂D⊃ ⊂E⊃

161 ⊂A⊃ ⊂B⊃ ⊂C⊃ ⊂D⊃ ⊂E⊃       181 ⊂A⊃ ⊂B⊃ ⊂C⊃ ⊂D⊃ ⊂E⊃       201 ⊂A⊃ ⊂B⊃ ⊂C⊃ ⊂D⊃ ⊂E⊃       221 ⊂A⊃ ⊂B⊃ ⊂C⊃ ⊂D⊃ ⊂E⊃
162 ⊂A⊃ ⊂B⊃ ⊂C⊃ ⊂D⊃ ⊂E⊃       182 ⊂A⊃ ⊂B⊃ ⊂C⊃ ⊂D⊃ ⊂E⊃       202 ⊂A⊃ ⊂B⊃ ⊂C⊃ ⊂D⊃ ⊂E⊃       222 ⊂A⊃ ⊂B⊃ ⊂C⊃ ⊂D⊃ ⊂E⊃
163 ⊂A⊃ ⊂B⊃ ⊂C⊃ ⊂D⊃ ⊂E⊃       183 ⊂A⊃ ⊂B⊃ ⊂C⊃ ⊂D⊃ ⊂E⊃       203 ⊂A⊃ ⊂B⊃ ⊂C⊃ ⊂D⊃ ⊂E⊃       223 ⊂A⊃ ⊂B⊃ ⊂C⊃ ⊂D⊃ ⊂E⊃
164 ⊂A⊃ ⊂B⊃ ⊂C⊃ ⊂D⊃ ⊂E⊃       184 ⊂A⊃ ⊂B⊃ ⊂C⊃ ⊂D⊃ ⊂E⊃       204 ⊂A⊃ ⊂B⊃ ⊂C⊃ ⊂D⊃ ⊂E⊃       224 ⊂A⊃ ⊂B⊃ ⊂C⊃ ⊂D⊃ ⊂E⊃
165 ⊂A⊃ ⊂B⊃ ⊂C⊃ ⊂D⊃ ⊂E⊃       185 ⊂A⊃ ⊂B⊃ ⊂C⊃ ⊂D⊃ ⊂E⊃       205 ⊂A⊃ ⊂B⊃ ⊂C⊃ ⊂D⊃ ⊂E⊃       225 ⊂A⊃ ⊂B⊃ ⊂C⊃ ⊂D⊃ ⊂E⊃
166 ⊂A⊃ ⊂B⊃ ⊂C⊃ ⊂D⊃ ⊂E⊃       186 ⊂A⊃ ⊂B⊃ ⊂C⊃ ⊂D⊃ ⊂E⊃       206 ⊂A⊃ ⊂B⊃ ⊂C⊃ ⊂D⊃ ⊂E⊃       226 ⊂A⊃ ⊂B⊃ ⊂C⊃ ⊂D⊃ ⊂E⊃
167 ⊂A⊃ ⊂B⊃ ⊂C⊃ ⊂D⊃ ⊂E⊃       187 ⊂A⊃ ⊂B⊃ ⊂C⊃ ⊂D⊃ ⊂E⊃       207 ⊂A⊃ ⊂B⊃ ⊂C⊃ ⊂D⊃ ⊂E⊃       227 ⊂A⊃ ⊂B⊃ ⊂C⊃ ⊂D⊃ ⊂E⊃
168 ⊂A⊃ ⊂B⊃ ⊂C⊃ ⊂D⊃ ⊂E⊃       188 ⊂A⊃ ⊂B⊃ ⊂C⊃ ⊂D⊃ ⊂E⊃       208 ⊂A⊃ ⊂B⊃ ⊂C⊃ ⊂D⊃ ⊂E⊃       228 ⊂A⊃ ⊂B⊃ ⊂C⊃ ⊂D⊃ ⊂E⊃
169 ⊂A⊃ ⊂B⊃ ⊂C⊃ ⊂D⊃ ⊂E⊃       189 ⊂A⊃ ⊂B⊃ ⊂C⊃ ⊂D⊃ ⊂E⊃       209 ⊂A⊃ ⊂B⊃ ⊂C⊃ ⊂D⊃ ⊂E⊃       229 ⊂A⊃ ⊂B⊃ ⊂C⊃ ⊂D⊃ ⊂E⊃
170 ⊂A⊃ ⊂B⊃ ⊂C⊃ ⊂D⊃ ⊂E⊃       190 ⊂A⊃ ⊂B⊃ ⊂C⊃ ⊂D⊃ ⊂E⊃       210 ⊂A⊃ ⊂B⊃ ⊂C⊃ ⊂D⊃ ⊂E⊃       230 ⊂A⊃ ⊂B⊃ ⊂C⊃ ⊂D⊃ ⊂E⊃
171 ⊂A⊃ ⊂B⊃ ⊂C⊃ ⊂D⊃ ⊂E⊃       191 ⊂A⊃ ⊂B⊃ ⊂C⊃ ⊂D⊃ ⊂E⊃       211 ⊂A⊃ ⊂B⊃ ⊂C⊃ ⊂D⊃ ⊂E⊃       231 ⊂A⊃ ⊂B⊃ ⊂C⊃ ⊂D⊃ ⊂E⊃
172 ⊂A⊃ ⊂B⊃ ⊂C⊃ ⊂D⊃ ⊂E⊃       192 ⊂A⊃ ⊂B⊃ ⊂C⊃ ⊂D⊃ ⊂E⊃       212 ⊂A⊃ ⊂B⊃ ⊂C⊃ ⊂D⊃ ⊂E⊃       232 ⊂A⊃ ⊂B⊃ ⊂C⊃ ⊂D⊃ ⊂E⊃
173 ⊂A⊃ ⊂B⊃ ⊂C⊃ ⊂D⊃ ⊂E⊃       193 ⊂A⊃ ⊂B⊃ ⊂C⊃ ⊂D⊃ ⊂E⊃       213 ⊂A⊃ ⊂B⊃ ⊂C⊃ ⊂D⊃ ⊂E⊃       233 ⊂A⊃ ⊂B⊃ ⊂C⊃ ⊂D⊃ ⊂E⊃
174 ⊂A⊃ ⊂B⊃ ⊂C⊃ ⊂D⊃ ⊂E⊃       194 ⊂A⊃ ⊂B⊃ ⊂C⊃ ⊂D⊃ ⊂E⊃       214 ⊂A⊃ ⊂B⊃ ⊂C⊃ ⊂D⊃ ⊂E⊃       234 ⊂A⊃ ⊂B⊃ ⊂C⊃ ⊂D⊃ ⊂E⊃
175 ⊂A⊃ ⊂B⊃ ⊂C⊃ ⊂D⊃ ⊂E⊃       195 ⊂A⊃ ⊂B⊃ ⊂C⊃ ⊂D⊃ ⊂E⊃       215 ⊂A⊃ ⊂B⊃ ⊂C⊃ ⊂D⊃ ⊂E⊃       235 ⊂A⊃ ⊂B⊃ ⊂C⊃ ⊂D⊃ ⊂E⊃
176 ⊂A⊃ ⊂B⊃ ⊂C⊃ ⊂D⊃ ⊂E⊃       196 ⊂A⊃ ⊂B⊃ ⊂C⊃ ⊂D⊃ ⊂E⊃       216 ⊂A⊃ ⊂B⊃ ⊂C⊃ ⊂D⊃ ⊂E⊃       236 ⊂A⊃ ⊂B⊃ ⊂C⊃ ⊂D⊃ ⊂E⊃
177 ⊂A⊃ ⊂B⊃ ⊂C⊃ ⊂D⊃ ⊂E⊃       197 ⊂A⊃ ⊂B⊃ ⊂C⊃ ⊂D⊃ ⊂E⊃       217 ⊂A⊃ ⊂B⊃ ⊂C⊃ ⊂D⊃ ⊂E⊃       237 ⊂A⊃ ⊂B⊃ ⊂C⊃ ⊂D⊃ ⊂E⊃
178 ⊂A⊃ ⊂B⊃ ⊂C⊃ ⊂D⊃ ⊂E⊃       198 ⊂A⊃ ⊂B⊃ ⊂C⊃ ⊂D⊃ ⊂E⊃       218 ⊂A⊃ ⊂B⊃ ⊂C⊃ ⊂D⊃ ⊂E⊃       238 ⊂A⊃ ⊂B⊃ ⊂C⊃ ⊂D⊃ ⊂E⊃
179 ⊂A⊃ ⊂B⊃ ⊂C⊃ ⊂D⊃ ⊂E⊃       199 ⊂A⊃ ⊂B⊃ ⊂C⊃ ⊂D⊃ ⊂E⊃       219 ⊂A⊃ ⊂B⊃ ⊂C⊃ ⊂D⊃ ⊂E⊃       239 ⊂A⊃ ⊂B⊃ ⊂C⊃ ⊂D⊃ ⊂E⊃
180 ⊂A⊃ ⊂B⊃ ⊂C⊃ ⊂D⊃ ⊂E⊃       200 ⊂A⊃ ⊂B⊃ ⊂C⊃ ⊂D⊃ ⊂E⊃       220 ⊂A⊃ ⊂B⊃ ⊂C⊃ ⊂D⊃ ⊂E⊃       240 ⊂A⊃ ⊂B⊃ ⊂C⊃ ⊂D⊃ ⊂E⊃
```

NOTES

NOTES

NOTES

NOTES

NOTES